Revolution to Secession
Constitution Making in the Old Dominion

Virginia Constitutional Convention, 1829–30, by George Catlin.
Courtesy of the Virginia Historical Society

REVOLUTION TO SECESSION

Constitution Making
in the Old Dominion

Robert P. Sutton

UNIVERSITY PRESS OF VIRGINIA

CHARLOTTESVILLE

THE UNIVERSITY PRESS OF VIRGINIA
Copyright © 1989 by the Rector and Visitors
of the University of Virginia

First published 1989

Library of Congress Cataloging-in-Publication Data
Sutton, Robert P.
    Revolution to secession : constitution making in the Old Dominion
/ Robert P. Sutton.
    p. cm.
    Bibliography: p.
    Includes index.
    ISBN 0-8139-1215-6
    1. Virginia—Constitutional history. 2. Constitutional
conventions—Virginia—History. 3. Virginia—Constitutional
history—Social aspects. I. Title.
KFV2801.5.S87   1989
342.755'029—dc19
[347.550229]   89-30947
                                                                CIP

Contents

Maps

Preface

PHILOSOPHERS AND SCHOLARS have been trying to define the meaning and purpose of constitutional law since the time of the ancient Greeks. Over two thousand years ago, Aristotle observed in *The Politics* that a constitution was not just an arrangement of offices or the organization of a polis. It fixed the identity of the state in providing the common object to which all citizens served in association. By drawing each person together in mutual interest, the constitution made possible the good life, the "chief end, both for the community as a whole and for each of us individually." Thomas M. Cooley, in his *General Principles of Constitutional Law,* published in 1880, adopted a modern, much narrower, view. He wrote that the "term Constitution may be defined as the body of rules and maxims in accordance with which the powers of sovereignty are habitually exercised." In the 1940s Charles H. McIlwain likewise looked upon a constitution as the means to limit the power of government within established laws. And in the 1970s Professors Kelly and Harbison in *The American Constitution* thought along the same line, that a constitution was "the supreme law by which a state is organized and governed." By whatever means a constitution is defined, it is the most important public law a society can produce, and constitution making is the most vital activity in which a people can engage. The fundamental law and the process creating it establish the character of government and the society it governs.[1]

In the English colonies of North America, after they declared independence from George III, constitution making was the most important civilian event. How, the Americans asked, were governments formed and how and when could they be changed? In answering these questions, as Americans moved from colony to commonwealth, they quickly embraced sweeping assumptions about what their constitutions would be: they would be written down and based upon the will of the people. These ideas combined to create the truly revolutionary aspect of the American Revolution because, in putting them into practice, we invented a workable republic, first at the state level and then for the nation as a whole.

Virginia's constitution making in 1776 was in the vanguard of America's crafting of fundamental law. In writing their constitution Virginians were able in spite of wartime exigencies to draft a document that included such untried principles as separation of powers and checks and balances. The logic of these premises of government led to a constitution with an executive branch, a bicameral legislature, and a system of state courts. There were errors of commission and omission, however. The governor, for instance, was too weak and in effect was dependent upon the lower house of the legislature. Also, Virginians in 1776 little appreciated the distinction, which Jefferson soon made, between a legislature and a constitutional convention as the proper body to write fundamental law. The delegates at the 1776 "convention" in Williamsburg did not feel compelled to submit their work to the people for approval. Lastly, the document allowed for no process of amendment.

Yet there was more to this creation of a republic than theory and logic. By accepting the requirements of a written constitution based on popular sovereignty, Virginians had to condense on paper their entire experience in government, their legacy of statutory and judge-made law, and their social customs and values. And so, alongside the revolutionary innovations in the structure of government, Virginians retained the heart of the British Commonwealthman tradition and its insistence upon strict guarantees of individual liberty. In fact, they were so concerned with liberty that they adopted a bill of rights before they dealt with the constitution itself. In this way they hoped to protect their way of life forever from the tyranny of the abuse of power. To assure this goal they invoked the prevailing doctrine of natural rights, perhaps the most sacred concept of Enlightenment thought, and thereby enshrined in their first constitution legal guarantees of the ordered world of Virginia's eighteenth-century plantation society.

Within a generation, however, the plantation life-style that seemed guaranteed by natural rights was challenged outright by this very same principle. In the four decades after independence Virginians moved steadily and in rapidly increasing numbers across the Blue Ridge Mountains into the western half of the commonwealth. These Virginians, small, nonslaveholding farmers for the most part, demanded a new constitution based upon the natural right, as they saw it, of unobstructed majority rule. But to the sons of the Virginia gentry who had written the first constitution this version of natural rights was a grave danger to liberty, an idea by then inseparable in the gentry mind from the security of slave property. So it was, ironically, that one part of the 1776 constitution, natural rights and popular sovereignty, became a threat to another part of it, liberty that meant protection of rights in human property. Consequently, in the Age of Jackson, at a time of vast expansion of democratic opportunity in American politics, the scions of the colonial Virginia gentry were the foremost defenders of property against democracy.

In the long run constitution making in the Old Dominion before the Civil War did not work. It was impossible for Virginians to agree for any length of time on a fundamental law that was acceptable permanently to most of the people of the state. As a consequence the documents produced by the conventions of 1829–30 and 1850–51 soon lost their legitimacy and became for the white majority instruments of minority rule. Ironically, by the mid-nineteenth century the rhetoric of constitution making had come full circle. Virginians in the majority, in the Valley and Mountain counties, advanced the same arguments of natural rights against the abuse of power by the eastern minority that the gentry patriots had used against the tyranny of the king and his ministers across the Atlantic. To many voters in Virginia by the 1850s the earlier victims of oppression had become the oppressors.

Virginia's constitution making did not take place in a vacuum. Other states, notably New York, Massachusetts, Maryland, and South Carolina went through similar steps of calling conventions to write and rewrite their governmental structure during the eighty-five-odd years after independence. Merrill D. Peterson, in his edition of the debates of state constitutional conventions of the 1820s, showed how the two northern states, like Virginia, wrestled with the task of reconciling the ideas of democracy, liberty, and property. And Fletcher M. Green sketched as the central issue of constitutionalism in the slaveholding states the presence or absence of the advance of democracy. Both historians dealt with Virginia's role in this story.[2]

Nevertheless, Virginia's constitutional history is unique and deserves special treatment. In the first place, the people involved in the conventions of 1776 and 1829–30 were illustrious Americans who elevated the debates, both conceptually and forensically, to a classical level of quality. Furthermore, unlike the constitutional conventions in some other states, those in Virginia were barely touched by strong loyalty to national political parties, except obliquely in the decade before the Convention of 1850–51. Rather, loyalties were drawn internally between traditionalists and progressives in terms of the ideology of majority rule versus aristocracy, social backgrounds and identities, and economic issues such as banking and internal improvements. Virginia's struggle to rewrite its constitution, more than in any other state, resulted in a dichotomy of two groups irreconcilably divided on the question of whether to change their fundamental law. Because there was no way merely to amend the existing constitution, the sectional cleavage was forced into an all-or-nothing conflict—creating a new constitution or keeping the old one—that exacerbated, indeed dramatized, the divisions in the Old Dominion. It was an irrepressible conflict.

This monograph has two purposes. One task is to provide a detailed narrative of the proceedings of the conventions themselves, of the personalities, ideas, and tactical infighting that led to new constitutions and to the temporary acceptance of them by the people in 1830 and 1851. To supplement the story of the conventions and the ratification fights, I have culled data from the census records, tax lists, and other sources to compile biographical sketches of the delegates, and this prosopography appears as an appendix.

The other purpose is to demonstrate how Virginia's constitutional history was shaped by its social matrix. This matrix determined the course of the proceedings, debates, and results of the three conventions. It accounted for the high degree of continuity, if not resiliency, of the East's conservative values and attitudes in the face of increasingly hostile and often shrill attacks by western Virginians on the state's constitution and the way it was written. It perpetuated a continuous sectional conflict of East and West over such issues as representation, suffrage, and taxation which was unresolvable because of the differences between the two ways of life that evolved in the Old Dominion during the eighty-five years after independence. This connection, this linkage, between Virginia's constitutional law and its social environment contributed to the scission of the commonwealth into two states, one slave and one free, in 1860–61. Perhaps Oliver Wendell Holmes was correct when he wrote in *The Common Law*, published in 1881, that "the life of the law has not been logic: it has been experience." "The felt necessities of the time," he reflected, "the prevalent moral and political theories, intuitions of public policy, avowed or unconscious, . . . have a good deal more to do than the syllogism in determining the rule by which men should be governed."[3]

A few years ago, Harry N. Scheiber, Professor of Law at Columbia University, asked whether constitutional history was dead. He noted that its core had become eclipsed by too much emphasis on the "new legal history" and by an overall lack of attention to what he called "public-sector themes." Scheiber found that the older school of writing had lost ground because its practitioners wrote "as if law were divorced from life" and were overconcerned with institutional history, particularly of the courts. By the same token, he blamed the "new legal history" scholars for being too absorbed in "behavioral theory, quantification, and self-proclaimed 'value free' analysis."[4] With these criticisms in mind, I have tried to integrate the customary focus of constitutional history on public law and institutions (the constitutional conventions) with the social milieu in which this history developed. The result, I hope, is a broader dimension to the study and understanding of our fundamental law.

There are many individuals to whom I am grateful for their aid and advice in a project I have been crafting, on and off, for twenty years. Merrill D. Peterson, Thomas Jefferson Memorial Foundation Professor Emeritus of History at the University of Virginia, first started me on the road of constitutional history in 1964 when he directed my dissertation on the Convention of 1829–30. Later he offered invaluable suggestions and comments on the revised manuscript. Thad W. Tate, Director of the Institute of Early American History and Culture at Williamsburg, took time out from his crammed agenda to read the manuscript and to offer detailed comments, especially on the first three chapters. Charles W. McCurdy, Associate Professor of History and Law at the University of Virginia, found essential matters for revision in the scope and focus of the study as I had originally prepared it. Grants from the National Endowment for the Humanities and the Research Council of Western Illinois University allowed me to return to the Old Dominion to peruse the manuscripts and records at Charlottesville and Richmond. The staffs of the University of Virginia Library, the Virginia State Library and Archives, and the Virginia Historical Society all were patient and helpful with my innumerable requests. And Allene Jones has worked dependably and diligently during the many hours of typing and editing of the manuscript from handwritten draft to final copy.

Revolution to Secession
Constitution Making in the Old Dominion

I

Continuity amid Crisis

THE OLD DOMINION by the second half of the eighteenth century was still run by the same plantation gentry who had controlled it for over one hundred years. More than in any other colony except perhaps South Carolina, the gentry monopolized Virginia's wealth by regulating its system of tobacco production and determining its land sales. They set standards of polite social behavior and were the leaders of Virginia's intellectual and cultural life. In political matters they occupied all important offices from the county court to the governor's council. Most importantly, this colony's gentry was a homogeneous group of adult white men of closely related families, a small, self-conscious minority of probably not more than 5 percent of the population. Yet, despite the power, they maintained an extraordinarily high sense of stewardship and responsibility.

James Reid of King William County observed at the time that they were men with "money, negroes, and land enough" who nevertheless were committed by training to a special kind of public service.[1] These planters assumed without question that they should rule, but to them the object of power was to create and perpetuate harmony, order, and enlightenment. They worked hard at their jobs. Their duties included attention to the minutia of local government and demanding stays away from their families for long stretches in Williamsburg as members of the House of Burgesses. Fortunately, they had the same impressive energy that their forebears had shown when they carved a new society out of a raw wilderness. Above all, the gentry of the mid-eighteenth century was eminently successful as a ruling class, and this

simple fact determined the course of events in Virginia between 1764 and 1776 that led to independence and shaped
the contours of its first fundamental law.

The happy combination in the gentry of energy, devotion
to duty, and self-confidence produced salutary results. The
multitude of men born outside the class willingly accepted its
benevolent leadership. In simple terms, about 95 percent of
the adult white males were content to follow directions from
above. Who were these other Virginians? Just below the
planter gentry walked the so-called halfbreeds, younger sons
of the gentry whose modest share of their father's partible
estate did not enable them to achieve the landholdings requisite of the aristocracy. Next in line were the "middling
sort," modestly wealthy men of ability but with meager lands
and slaves, people like Patrick Henry, James Southall, James
Taylor, and Peter Jones.[2] Then there was a relatively large
nonslaveowning yeomanry whom Thomas Jefferson described as "looking askance at those above, yet not venturing
to jostle them."[3] At the very bottom of Virginia's white society
were the "meaner sort"—traders, farm workers, tenants,
overseers, and indentured servants. Somewhat apart from
these agrarian classes stood the prosperous merchants and
artisans of the two incorporated towns, Williamsburg and
Norfolk, who were roughly equivalent in social standing to
the halfbreeds and middling sort.[4]

The gentry probably looked down upon this vast majority
of Virginians with a certain disdain, an attitude shared by all
colonial elite in America; they frequently labeled the meaner
sort as the "vulgar herd," "ignorant vulgar," or "idiots." Yet,
except for Jefferson's remark, there is no record of class re-
sentment or antagonism. Instead, the Virginia middling and
meaner sorts displayed an abject respect and deference toward the wealthy planters, no doubt in appreciation of the
ordered society they saw everywhere around them. Jack P.
Greene has pointed out that no commentator on Virginia
saw any of the class rivalries, religious antagonisms, and political factionalism that disturbed its sister colonies in North
America. In a word, the gentry and the "people" of the Old
Dominion, by the time of the crisis of independence and con-

stitution making, were historically glued to each other by ties of habit, expectations, and obligations.

Virginia's "constitution," as it existed on the eve of independence, mirrored this exceptionally tranquil society. All branches of government were attuned to, and responded to, the needs and wishes of the gentry leadership. The royal governor and his lieutenant more often than not went along with the demands of the House of Burgesses. Lieutenant Governor Alexander Spotswood's attempts to cut back on the power of the council met the immediate, firm resistance of the burgesses; and when he became governor, his tenure (1710–22) was a model of accord with the gentry. His successors, Hugh Drysdale (1722–26) and William Gooch (1727–49), likewise believed in conciliation with the gentry and their spokesmen in the lower house. Gooch, because of his accommodation, was admired by Virginians with a devotion akin to their love for the good King George II. Gooch was no patsy, however. In return for his acceptance of the gentry's domination, he asked them to allow him a personal role in colonial legislation. Accordingly, on the governor's insistence, the burgesses passed a much-needed tobacco inspection law against the wishes of most of the nongentry planters.

Gooch's rule of "pragmatic compromise and institutional cooperation" was only briefly set off track by one of his successors, Robert Dinwiddie (1752–58), in an unsuccessful attempt to persuade the burgesses to let him collect a tax, or pistole, for signing land patents.[5] The next two governors, Francis Fauquier (1758–68) and Norborne Berkeley, baron de Botetourt (1768–70), fell back in line with Gooch's habit of cooperation. Botetourt was able and ingratiating but could not surmount the growing opposition to parliamentary taxation, which had first flared up in the mid-1760s during Fauquier's term in response to the stamp tax. Virginians also would not accept the external tax of the Townshend duties levied in the first year of Botetourt's administration. In 1770, when the House of Burgesses defiantly asserted, as it had more generally five years earlier in the Stamp Act Resolves, that the Virginia legislature and not Parliament had the sole right to tax, the governor dismissed the assembly. This event, in turn, led to a rapid deterioration of royal authority under Botetourt's successor, John Murray, earl of Dunmore.

Before the burgesses' crisis of power with Governor Dunmore, however, the Old Dominion's legislature had reduced the office of royal governor to that of administrator. By Botetourt's time he could, with the approval of council or House of Burgesses, make appointments only to the local offices of justice of the peace and sheriff. He was still commander of Virginia's militia and of British regular troops of the line stationed in the colony, but the governor needed money from the burgesses to conduct any military operations. The twelve-man council, always appointed from the inner gentry as a branch of the colony's executive agency, was only a part-time advisory body to the governor, for members of this body also sat as the Virginia court of appeals. In practice the council also had the responsibility to amend or veto laws sent to it by the burgesses, a power largely defunct by mid-eighteenth century. The executive power of Virginia, then, by 1770 was subordinated to that of the gentry organ, the House of Burgesses.

Another part of Virginia's colonial government, the county court, was even more the prisoner of the gentry. By the 1770s the courts had taken over responsibility for all legal functions that were not exercised by the house. It was a court of law and equity and a probate court. When not sitting at the courthouse, county justices sometimes took turns serving as sheriff, constable, and coroner. More often, though, they recommended friends and relatives to be named by the governor as permanent officers in these functions. The justices assessed the taxes levied by the house in Williamsburg, regulated mills, built and maintained roads and bridges, licensed inns and taverns, sat as a trial court for slaves, and heard morals cases brought from the vestries. The towns of Norfolk and Williamsburg had the equivalent of a county court in their hustings courts made up of mayor, recorder, and aldermen. These local tribunals—either county courts or hustings courts—were manned by the gentry and appointed for life, with vacancies filled only by the recommendations of the sitting justices or mayor. The Virginia local system of government and law, according to A. E. Dick Howard, was in practice "a hodgepodge of jurisdictions, with a blissful ignorance of the concept of separation of powers," all under the thumb of the gentry class. There was, therefore, no possibility for separation of powers in colonial Virginia since there was only one real power, the House of Burgesses. It introduced all legislation and, with only a theoretical threat of a veto, passed all statutes. It controlled all appropriations and levied all taxes.[6]

The burgesses, two from each county, were overwhelmingly large planters. All were slaveholders. Over 50 percent of them were sons of the first families; very few were self-made men. Most were Anglicans. Jackson Turner Main has written of the delegates that "in general they seem much of a piece culturally; the exceptions exerted little political influence."[7] Every spring the burgesses were chosen by the voice vote of the freeholders. Candidates for office—usually there were five names from which the voters could pick—were well known to the freeholders and were aware of and sensitive to their problems and wishes. The winners were of two kinds. Some were disinterested gentlemen who prided themselves on their virtue and integrity and were unwilling to court their constituents. Others were more realistic politicians who were willing to accommodate their behavior to suit the lower intellectual tone of the voters. The voters who selected the gentlemen burgesses were in a majority mainly in the counties above the James River that extended westward toward the foothills of the Blue Ridge Mountains. In the 1760s parts of this region, especially in the Northern Neck, were still largely underdeveloped, and huge tracts of land were entitled to a few families. It was conducive to large-scale plantation agriculture because almost every plantation had access to one of the rivers. The other type of burgess, the realist, was seen most often coming from a cluster of counties south of the James River extending to the North Carolina border and westward to, and spilling over and beyond, the first line of the Blue Ridge Mountains into the Valley.[8]

The tax records of two northern Tidewater counties, Richmond and Lancaster, reveal a great deal about this region's constituency. These counties were first settled by wealthy planters who purchased vast acreage for speculation, leasing to tenants, and personal estates.[9] Vertical mobility below the gentry class was slight. Only one-third of the Richmond County landless adult males tabulated in 1773 had acquired land by 1782. Horizontal mobility likewise was negligible. The tax lists show that only 3 percent of the landless males left Lancaster County in the decade of the Revolution. The quitrent rolls and tax lists for Richmond County also show that most of the 200 landowners living there in 1765 were still there in 1782. There were also few new people coming in: the increase in the number of recent landowners during the same seventeen-year period was only about 25 percent.

The records for counties south and west of the James River, on the other hand, reveal a more fluid society. Main has analyzed Lunenburg County, located in about the center of this region. By 1764 this county was inhabited by small planters, owning between 100 and 500 acres, who made up over half the names on the tax lists. There were, compared to the northern Tidewater, fewer wealthy planters; only 6 percent of the adult males owned plantations of 1,000 or more acres. Yet this 6 percent had title to 40 percent of the county's land. White farm laborers constituted 30 percent of Lunenburg's society, and adult male slaves numbered just over 15 percent of the total population. Main found that many residents of Lunenburg were recent arrivals and some were still on the move. About one-third of the adult males had emigrated to another area by 1782. Significantly, more landowners moved into the county between 1764 and 1782 than moved out: there was a 50 percent increase in recent arrivals. Lunenburg had a high degree of upward vertical mobility. Of 150 men without land in 1764, three-fourths had bought a farm by 1782. It also exhibited substantial downward vertical movement. Over one-half of the gentry (planters with 500 to 1,000 acres) had lost land.[10]

The voters of colonial Virginia, despite regional peculiarities, stood together in the series of rapidly moving events after 1770 that led to independence. When Governor Dunmore came to Williamsburg in the spring of 1771 after Botetourt's death the previous year, he found his government in shambles. The burgesses, when disolved by Botetourt for their defiance of the Townshend duties, had reassembled illegally down the Duke of Gloucester Street at the Raleigh Tavern. There, under the able leadership of Peyton Randolph, they had adopted resolutions boycotting the enumerated items—lead, paper, paint, glass, and tea—on the Townshend duty list. They also had agreed not to buy any other items that were taxed for revenue.

Even though the nonimportation measures adopted by the burgesses went largely unenforced, the legislators and the new governor were at a standoff from the start. On a motion by Dabney Carr, the burgesses created a Committee of Correspondence to keep in touch with disturbing events in New England such as the sinking of the British patrol sloop *Gaspee* off Rhode Island in the summer of 1772. Soon more distressing news arrived from the north. In 1773 Parliament, in a desperate effort to save the East India Company from bankruptcy, passed the Tea Act. By this statute the company in effect was given a monopoly on all tea shipped to the American colonies and the privilege of selling tea directly through its own agents and not American import merchants. On the night of December 16, 1773, radicals in Boston, the largest port in America, dumped 342 chests of East India tea into the bay. Parliament, under Lord North, reacted immediately with the Coercive Acts. By these punitive measures Parliament intended to leave no doubt as to who was in charge. Boston was closed to all traffic, Massachusetts was placed under martial law, and troops were billeted in private homes. One of the Coercive Acts was the Quebec Act, a statute which gave all of Virginia north of the Ohio River to Canada.

The burgesses, by then legitimately meeting again in the east side of the Capitol, reacted immediately, partly out of a fear that what had happened to Massachusetts under the whip of Parliament (whereby a self-governing colony had been virtually legislated out of existence) could happen in Virginia and partly out of outrage at the lopping off of about one-half of Virginia's western lands. They condemned the Coercive Acts as a hostile invasion and fixed a day of prayer as a gesture of public support for the beleaguered Bostonians. Dunmore imitated Botetourt and dissolved the burgesses. The burgesses, as before, walked about a half mile west on the Duke of Gloucester Street to the Raleigh Tavern where, again, they set up shop under Peyton Randolph. This time the mood of the gentry was grim. They agreed that a meeting of delegates from all the colonies should be called because "an attack made on one of our sister colonies . . . is an attack made on all British America." They directed their Committee of Correspondence to contact the other colonies. On September 5, 1774, the First Continental Congress, with seven Virginia delegates present, convened at Philadelphia. There, as a first order of business, the Congress elected Peyton Randolph as its presiding officer.[11]

In Williamsburg, Dunmore flip-flopped. He wanted to summon the house to gain some control over events, but at the same time he fretted about what might happen if the burgesses were called together legitimately. By the time he finally got around to fixing a firm date, in May 1775, they were already meeting extralegally sixty miles west of the capital, at St. John's Church in Richmond. There Patrick Henry's peroration against tyranny and for liberty was only one of several calls for placing Virginia on a war footing after news of the battles of Lexington and Concord. George Washington and Edmund Pendleton cautioned restraint. Richard Henry Lee and Thomas Jefferson supported Henry's stand. Henry's resolution passed, and Henry, with Lee as associate chair, was placed in charge of a committee to get the colony ready for war.

Dunmore ordered the seizure of all powder and military supplies stored in the magazine across the street from the courthouse in Williamsburg. A contingent of the town's militia marched on the palace to arrest the governor. Dunmore, flabbergasted by the presence of armed men at his door, promised to return the powder, and the militia disbanded. At about the same time Henry, now viewing himself as an acting commanding general of the militia, led a band of Hanover County men toward the capital. Dunmore heard rumors of a "Fredericksburg militia" on the march and de-

clared Henry an outlaw. Dunmore tried one last time to get
control of events. He called the burgesses for their regularly
scheduled spring session.[12]

The burgesses promptly returned to Williamsburg. They
and the governor were at loggerheads. No sooner had the
burgesses arrived at the Capitol than they learned that Dunmore had left town and was sitting on the British warship
Fowey anchored in the York River. They invited Dunmore to
return. He invited the burgesses to meet with him instead on
the *Fowey.* Armed militiamen from the outlying settlements
drifted into town, and Richard Bland's plan, advanced in the
legislature, to hang the governor gathered a momentum of
popular support. Dunmore, aboard the *Fowey,* opted for dis-
cretion instead of valor and drifted down river to tie up at
Norfolk harbor where he felt far less likely to have his neck
stretched. In the harbor he organized his military forces for
an assault on Williamsburg. He embarked his troops at Norfolk, seized a printing press, and then moved westward into
Princess Anne County where the British regulars took control of the county seat at Kempsville. Dunmore next issued
an edict freeing all slaves and indentured servants who
would support the crown. Pendleton, sitting in the chair of
the assembly, ordered out a militia regiment under William
Woodford against Dunmore's army. At the battle of Great
Bridge, near Norfolk, the regulars were decimated by the
Virginians and fell back to the port town in chaos. Dunmore
quickly pulled out of Norfolk and with his flotilla anchored
in the harbor opened up the ships' batteries on the town.
Finally, in the summer of 1776, he left the Old Dominion
forever. With Dunmore's exodus royal government in Virginia collapsed entirely. At Williamsburg, the last House of
Burgesses, in June 1775, found itself unable to do anything
except watch the unfolding military events. So, on June 21 it
officially adjourned. Before the burgesses disbanded sine
die, Peyton Randolph formally issued a call for a convention
"appointed by the towns and corporation of the colony" to
meet in Richmond within two weeks to establish a new, permanent government.[13]

The July Convention, as it was called, was preoccupied

with the problems of how to keep the peace, support the militia, and operate the government after the collapse of royal authority. As a first item, in August, the Convention created a Committee of Safety. It was made up of eleven men, including Edmund Pendleton (chair), George Mason, Richard Bland, Thomas Ludwell Lee, and Carter Braxton, whose main job was "to execute the several ordinances and resolutions of this convention." This committee was the commonwealth's first executive branch of government. Its war-making powers were spelled out during the third week of August. It had the authority to commission officers, purchase military supplies, conscript and dispatch troops, and conduct military operations.[14]

In other matters the Convention hurriedly voted to keep the existing suffrage requirement of a fifty-acre freehold. Anyone eligible to vote could serve in the Convention and in all other local offices. Elections were scheduled for the following April with two delegates allotted to each county. A second Convention would then convene on the first Monday of May 1776 with "power to adjourn from time to time" subject to recall by the chosen president of that body. Local government would be in the hands of Committees of Twenty-one "of the most discreet, fit, and able men," to be elected in November. These juntas were authorized to enforce any measures adopted by either the Convention or the Continental Congress. In addition, they were to serve as intelligence-gathering bodies to provide the Convention with all information on loyalist activities at the county level. They were to function when necessary as county courts and were allowed to hear complaints "where any person shall think himself aggrieved." Lastly, the Convention adopted strictly legislative prerogatives, as opposed to executive orders or local government measures. It voted to raise and appropriate taxes to cover all militia expenses and to pay the expenses of delegates to the next session of the Continental Congress. In November, when the military events around Norfolk intensified, the Convention authorized the manufacturing of arms and the purchase of additional military supplies from other colonies, if necessary. It cracked down on suspected loyalists by directing the creation in each county of a Committee of Five specifically to pinpoint tory sympathizers, to conduct a jury trial, and if the accused was found guilty of siding with the crown, to confiscate their property.[15]

By the winter of 1775–76, with Dunmore hiding out in his boat in Norfolk harbor, with militia skirmishes in and around the town, with the Convention in effect enforcing martial law, the Virginia gentry had reached a point where they had to come to grips with the obvious. Yet the obvious, independence, that winter was accepted most reluctantly. The Convention persisted in denying what had happened. Its members insisted that resistance would bring a change of policy from London. One such planter, William Reynolds, echoed the sentiments of many of his colleagues when he said the previous August that the colonies wanted only an honorable conciliation. Even Edmund Pendleton, who as much as anyone else in the Old Dominion was fully aware of what was going on, wrote that he was hopeful "that our petition may yet produce peace."[16]

In the early spring of 1776, however, the gentry at Williamsburg realized that they had to acknowledge their predicament: royal government had vanished, war had broken out in the Tidewater, and the choice was either acquiescense to Parliament or independence. The decision for independence, therefore, came late in Virginia, as it did in the other colonies, but when it came, it was fast and overwhelming. A series of events helps to account for this change of heart. Copies of Thomas Paine's *Common Sense* were circulating among the delegates, and the logic of Paine's argument, given the alarming episodes of the past year and a half, was irrefutable. Added to the weight of Paine's simple reasoning—that common sense demanded either submission to despotism or resistance and overthrow of a government which had become tyrannical (and monarchy to Paine sooner or later was always tyrannical)—was the failure of any alternative to independence. The economic boycotts of the Continental Congress had done nothing to change the British policy of punitive repression as seen in the application of the Coercive Acts in Massachusetts.

Sensing this frustration, Virginia's representative to the Congress, Benjamin Harrison, in March condemned what he called a "fatal attachment" to Great Britain. An anonymous writer, a member of the July Convention, pointed out at about the same time that the colony was already independent of its mother country. Applying Paine's thinking to the situation in the Old Dominion, he asked: "Have we not made laws, created courts of judicature, established magistrates, made money, levied war, and regulated commerce, not only without his Majesty's interventions, but absolutely against his will?"[17] In April, John Page said that every man at the Convention except Robert Carter Nicholas was willing to push for independence. Richard Henry Lee wrote to Patrick Henry that "we cannot be rebels excluded from the King's protection, and magistrates acting under his authority at the same time."[18] George Wythe, by the end of the month, likewise had concluded that the time had come to declare independence and to write a constitution. Only Henry, surprisingly, dragged his feet. He had two problems with independence. One was a question on procedure. Could the Continental Congress declare it, or must each colony, one by one, come to its own decision first? Second, he wanted to find out what France and Spain planned to do if the colonies and Great Britain went to war. Paine's arguments prevailed. As Lee had pointed out, the Virginia gentry could not continue to have it both ways; they could not be loyal subjects of George III and rebels, guilty of high treason, at the same time.

Outside the Convention, throughout Virginia, public pressure for independence had been building for some time. As early as January 1775 the voters of Fincastle County, in the Valley, had adopted a resolution asserting their determination not to give up their rights of government "to any power upon earth but at the expense of our lives."[19] On April 4, 1776, Cumberland County, located on the Southside, selected a four-man committee to draft instructions to its representatives at Williamsburg to vote in favor of separation from England. The May 10 issue of Alexander Purdie's *Virginia Gazette* printed two extraordinary documents. One was an April 23 instruction from Charlotte County, another Southside county, to support independence. The other item was an outline for a new constitution, written by Richard Henry Lee, entitled "A Government Scheme." This second document, a brief summation of the ideas exchanged between Lee and John Adams earlier that year in Philadelphia, was pivotal in persuading the delegates that there was a better government than royal authority. Lee's message was clear: independence "was conceivable without undue dislocation in Virginia."[20]

While this change of attitude took place in the spring of 1776, new elections, in accordance with the instructions of the July Convention, were held in April for what turned out to be Virginia's first constitutional convention. When the voters selected their delegates that April, they had no idea they were choosing anything other than a legislative body. There was no distinction in the minds of either the voters or the delegates between a body selected to draft a constitution and an ordinary assembly elected to write statutes. Lee, for example, in the first item of his *Government Scheme,* published as a handbill that month, merely suggested that the voters or "the people" "choose as usual (where there is no good objection) a Representative body." This body would elect an upper house, a governor, and judges for the "colony." Lee's handbill was the only publicly circulated proposal for a procedure to create a new constitution. Unlike the Massachusetts creators of the Concord Town Meeting Demands of October 21, 1776, who asked for a special convention for the sole purpose of framing a constitution, Virginians had no sensitivity to the point made by Concord voters that "the same body that forms a constitution have of consequence the power to alter it" and "a Constitution alterable by the . . . legislature is no security at all."[21]

The April elections went without a hitch despite forebodings by some members of the July Convention that their constituents might choose other less experienced representatives. Josiah Parker, an Isle of Wight County planter and a friend of Landon Carter, was one such pessimist. He predicted that men like Pendleton, Harrison, and Braxton might be rejected by "our mad freeholders." These were "strange times indeed," Parker brooded. But Parker was unnecessarily gloomy. By and large the voters throughout the colony stayed with the same class, the experienced gentry, but not always the same names. Extant data for counties in the northern Tidewater show the strong continuity of gentry leadership. In King William County, for example, where just 20 percent of the eligible voters turned out that spring, the two incumbents were returned to Williamsburg. In Richmond County two gentlemen planters and vestrymen, Hudson Muse and Charles McCarty, replaced Robert Wormeley Carter and Francis Lightfoot Lee, who was away in Philadelphia serving in the Second Continental Congress. The Carters claimed that Muse had won by demagoguery: Landon Carter said that Muse promised voters a new government in Virginia where "every man would then be able to do as he pleased." Muse also got some support for a harebrained idea, according to the Carters, of not requiring residents to turn out on slave patrols. In Stafford County the voters replaced another Carter, Charles, with William Brent, a planter and county justice. In King William County, Carter Braxton lost to William Aylett, a planter, in a contest so close that the results had to be decided later by the Convention. There were two other tight races that April. In Prince William County, Henry Lee (father of Light-Horse Harry Lee, then just twenty years of age and soon a cavalry leader in the war) was narrowly reelected, and, in adjacent Fairfax County, George Mason barely squeezed through over his opponent. By April 26 the *Virginia Gazette* published the final list of delegates and commented that all but a handful of counties had chosen their incumbent representatives.[22]

The results of the election demonstrate a remarkable pattern of continuity amid crisis. The membership of the Convention of 1776 was not quite the same as that of the July Convention, but two-thirds of the delegates had sat in Williamsburg since 1774. Most of the 128 members of the 1776 Convention, therefore, had some experience in colonial government. Ninety-two of them, about 72 percent, had served in the House of Burgesses. Of those without such experience, nine men were from families that claimed burgesses as relatives and four others had been active in county offices. Three of the latter had been sheriffs of Lunenburg, Henrico, and Amherst counties, and the fourth, young Edmund Randolph, then twenty-three years old, was the nephew of Speaker Peyton Randolph.

By nine o'clock in the morning of Monday, May 6, 1776, a crowd had already gathered on the portico between the two halves of the colonial Capitol. Within an hour the delegates moved into the east wing and squeezed into the old House of Burgesses chamber. When everyone had taken a seat, John Tazewell, clerk of the July Convention, was unanimously chosen to continue in that function. After Tazewell took his seat at the table in front of the Speaker's chair, about in the middle of the circle of delegates, the aged Richard Bland took the floor. This gray-haired, slightly bent-over scholar who wore tinted glasses to shield his sensitive blue eyes, proposed Edmund Pendleton, then serving as head of the Committee of Safety for Caroline County, as the presiding officer. Archibald Cary, a fifty-five-year-old planter of Chesterfield County, seconded the motion. Thomas Johnson, of Louisa County, a close friend of Patrick Henry, nominated instead Thomas Ludwell Lee, a Stafford County lawyer. His motion was seconded by Bartholomew Dandridge of New Kent County. Pendleton won. A man with twenty-five years' experience as a burgess and one of its most impressive orators, the fifty-five-year-old, six-foot-tall, handsome parliamentarian acknowledged the honor bestowed upon him and called the Convention to order. After appointing a chaplain, the Reverend Thomas Price of Bruton Parish Church, Pendleton adjourned the session until the following morning. The next day, Tuesday, May 7, promptly at seven o'clock, the Convention was opened by a prayer read by Chaplain Price. Then it set about to establish the all-important standing committees that would decide the question of the colony's independence and draft its first fundamental law.[23]

Pendleton, standing erect and imposing before a crippling accident the next year left him permanently lame, spoke first. He opened with a statement about the gravity of the matters before them and predicted that "subjects of the most important and interesting nature" would be decided. Then, after this rather polite reference to independence and war, he got down to specifics. He said that in his opinion there had been no royal government in Virginia for over two years. Things had gone on, obviously, for too long. Independence was already a fact, and the delegates had to focus on the question of what to do after independence. How would the Convention deal with the immediate and pressing problems of law and order in wartime? For instance, he pointed out, what about the problem of appropriating enough money to keep the militia in the field? What about treatment of loyalists? How would they acquire new sources of salt for the curing of food supplies?[24]

For three days the delegates milled about after the morning prayer deciding on nothing, just talking informally among themselves about what to do next. At last on Friday, May 10, decisions began to jell. That morning the myopic, bespectacled Thomas Lewis, an Irish immigrant of Augusta County in the Shenandoah Valley, was given the floor by Pendleton. Lewis, in his Irish brogue, said that after a week of talk about the matter it was now time to act to create an independent and lasting confederacy. Pendleton then appointed a committee to consider the question, called the Committee on the State of the Colony. Its chair was Archibald Cary.

Cary's committee on Monday, May 13, got down to work. Meanwhile, on the floor of the Convention it was apparent that there were divergent views about how to deal with independence. Only a few delegates from the region north of the James River, led by Robert Carter Nicholas of James City County, former treasurer of the colony, wanted to delay independence entirely out of fear that the colonies could never win a war against the mother country.[25] Favoring independence, but reluctantly, were some delegates led by Henry. Henry, along with his friend Thomas Ludwell Lee, felt strongly that Virginia's decision on separation should be held back until a "uniform plan of government" could be agreed upon by all the colonies. Henry, too, was deeply afraid that events were moving too fast for Virginia to act by itself; he felt that the Congress in Philadelphia, responding to the momentum of events, should adopt a colonywide resolution of independence.[26] Henry's group also thought that delaying a decision on independence in Williamsburg, and consequently the writing of a constitution, would enable the Convention to have time to consider changes in the existing structure of government rather than, in the necessity of haste, merely duplicate what had been done in the colony. Henry, too, had a personal interest in delay. He was reluctant to be blamed, because of his well-known rhetorical flourishes against the king and Parliament, for pushing independence upon the people of Virginia. Henry was concerned in early May that his fellow citizens might backtrack on independence "after the present stimulus should cease to operate." Henry just could not make up his mind whether to move or stay put. His resolution, introduced by Thomas Nelson, Jr., of Yorktown, to have Congress declare independence nevertheless was sent to the Cary committee.[27]

Two other resolutions were given to Cary, one by Meriwether ("Fiddlehead") Smith and the other by Pendleton. Smith, a planter of Bathurst in Essex County, wanted to focus the blame for forcing independence on Parliament rather than on King George III. It was Parliament, Smith noted, that had actually declared the colonies to be in a state of rebellion. In fact, Smith's supporters, all from the northern Tidewater, avoided the issue of actually declaring independence and asked instead that the colony formally "dissolve" the existing colonial government (which it had done already in actual fact) and write a new constitution. Pendleton focused on the king and independence. He agreed with Smith that Parliament had usurped unlimited authority in passing its recent acts against America but said that the crown was the real culprit in the present "barbarous war," which had violated the natural and common-law rights of the colonists.[28]

The wording of the proposals reflected the different approaches of the options placed before the Cary committee. Henry's resolution read: "Resolved, that our delegates in

Congress be enjoined . . . to exert their ability in procuring an immediate, clear, and full Declaration of Independency." The Smith resolution advised: "That the government of this colony be dissolved, and that a committee be appointed to prepare a Declaration of Rights, and . . . a plan of government." Smith's position skirted the knotty issue of who should declare independence (Congress or the colonies) and when. Pendleton was, as usual, the most forthright. He wanted the Convention to agree: "That the Union . . . between Great Britain and the American Colonies is hereby totally dissolved, and that the inhabitants of this colony are discharged from any allegiance to the Crown of Great Britain." To Pendleton it was a matter of first things first. Virginians were committing high treason under English law, and they might as well say so.[29]

The resolution that was drafted by the Cary committee and discussed by the Convention sitting as a committee of the whole on Wednesday, May 15, was a compromise of the Smith and Pendleton wordings. It was written out by the Speaker himself and was surprisingly wordy and badly phrased. The committee report was presented in three parts, a lengthy preamble, a resolution instructing the Virginia delegation in Philadelphia to move that Congress declare independence, and a resolution appointing a committee to write a declaration of rights and a constitution. The preamble, Pendleton's own handiwork, was a rambling list of the recent actions of "an imperious and vindictive administration" whereby the king and Parliament together had tried to achieve the "total destruction" of Virginia. Property was confiscated. Virginians were forced to join Dunmore in "the murder and plunder of their relations and countrymen" and the "rapine and oppression" of Americans along the Atlantic seaboard. Armies and navies and "foreign troops" were deployed in the colony, and a "piratical" governor had urged race war by the slaves on their Virginia masters. The preamble did contain, toward the end, the simple and effective logic of the Convention's position. "We have no alternative left," Pendleton wrote, "but an abject submission to the will of those overbearing tyrants, or a total separation from the crown and government of Great Britain." Pendleton ended the preamble by appealing not to natural rights or English common law but to the "external laws of self-preservation."[30]

The second part of the report failed to accomplish what Pendleton wanted, that is, Virginia's independence declared on its own. Instead, the resolution, as Henry had hoped, instructed the "delegates appointed to represent this Colony in the General Congress" to move the "United Colonies" independent of the crown and Parliament. It required, naturally, that the Virginia delegation both move for independence and vote in favor of their resolution. The delegation was further directed to go along with whatever measures Congress wished to take to form a new "confederation" of the colonies with the all-important, as it turned out for the new national constitution, restriction that the states would have the sole power over their "internal concerns." The "general confederation," in turn, was to be given the power to form "foreign alliances."[31]

The third part of the Cary committee report created an ad hoc committee to write a new government. The sequence of events to follow, or the procedure, was clear. First the new committee was to write a declaration of rights. After that essential matter had been dealt with, and only then, was the committee, and the Convention itself, to go on to prepare "such a plan of government as will be most likely to maintain peace and order in this Colony, and secure substantial and equal liberty to the people." The language of constitution making was exclusively functional. The new government should keep the peace in wartime and not bother with major reforms or revisions of constitutional law. In the second part of the instruction, to secure equal liberty to the people, the blessings of such liberty were meant to apply to "the people" as the Convention conceived them to be, namely the adult white male freeholders of Virginia. In sum, the instructions of the resolutions were clear: assert Virginia's rights so egregiously threatened and keep the peace.[32]

The Cary resolutions that passed unanimously by the 112 delegates on May 15 were very much a compromise. Pendleton compromised because he was finally persuaded by Henry that Virginians, by going through the Continental Congress rather than declaring independence on their own, would reduce the risk of being cut off from their Massachusetts comrades in arms. Pendleton knew that Virginia needed a lot of support, financial and military, from Congress for the fight going on within its own borders in the eastern Tidewater. When the result was announced, Williamsburg went wild "with every demonstration of joy." [33]

The *Virginia Gazette* described how the resolutions were read aloud the following day to the militia then organizing in town for an assault on Dunmore's troops near Norfolk. A "feast" was spread out for the men that night in Waller's Grove. That same balmy spring evening inside the former House of Burgesses chamber the silver mace, "once the superb and princely symbol of imperial power," lay dormant on the clerk's table, now a trophy of the newly independent state.

II

From Colony to Commonwealth: The Constitution of 1776

LATE THAT WEDNESDAY AFTERNOON, May 15, Edmund Pendleton solemnly declared the Cary resolution as having unanimously passed the Convention. Then as a final order of business, he focused his attention on its instruction: write a declaration of rights and a constitution. Historical reasons dictated the delegates' desire to adopt a bill of rights before they formed a structure of government. Most of the men were raised on Lockean notions of the social contract and consequently saw themselves now thrown into "a state of nature upon dissolution of the bond with Great Britain," so they believed it absolutely necessary to declare on paper man's inherent rights, untouchable by any government, as a basis for their constitution.[1]

However universal the principles upon which the first pillars of the state's fundamental law might rest, Pendleton, always the sensitive parliamentarian, was careful to see that the particular interests of his northern Tidewater friends and their ideas would prevail. As a first step he created a committee to draft the declaration of rights large enough to include men from south of the James River, or Southsiders, but one that would nevertheless remain comfortably in the hands of the conservative gentry, or Tuckahoes as they were called. As appointed by Pendleton, there were thirty-six members, and Archibald Cary, old reliable, was named as its chair.[2] Twenty-two delegates were Pendleton men who had stood with him on the preliminary measures against Henry and Smith. Twelve delegates were from counties south and west of the James River, supported by both Henry and maverick Northern Neck lawyer Thomas Ludwell Lee. Two other committeemen defied classification, James Madison and George Mason. So, by the end of the afternoon of May 15, Pendleton had made it a certainty that his supporters were in control.[3]

The differences between the two groups within this committee were not just ideological or over matters of procedure. There were contrasts in the backgrounds of the Tuckahoes and Southsiders. Age was one factor. The Tuckahoes were mature men. The average age of this group was about forty-seven, or just a little above the prime of life for the time. Southside committeemen were younger, in their thirties. Tuckahoes were also men of substantial wealth. Sixteen men were large planters and slaveowners; some individuals in this group paid taxes on between forty to one hundred chattels (Richard Cary, Meriwether Smith, Robert Carter Nicholas, Thomas Mann Randolph, Richard Henry Lee). Thomas Read owned thirty-eight slaves. Southside committeemen were, on the other hand, a more modest and diversified bunch. There was only one wealthy planter from the Southside, William Cabell of Amherst County, and just two modest planters with about forty slaves. Most of the others were practicing lawyers (five). The Southsiders claimed a physician and a teacher. Two of the committeemen's occupations and backgrounds are unknown.[4]

Cary, realizing that the sheer size of his committee would make expeditious work on its assignment difficult, awarded the responsibility for drafting the declaration of rights to George Mason. This tall, swarthy, forty-year-old planter of Gunston Hall in Fairfax County came to Williamsburg with his chronic gout in mid-May; he also brought along a reputation for scholarship in constitutional law.[5] Although never serving as a burgess, he had gained widespread recognition throughout the colony for the ideas he put forth in the *Fairfax Resolves*, printed in 1774. Here, drawing on his close study of the early charters of the Old Dominion, especially their language guaranteeing to all colonists the "liberties, franchises, and immunities" enjoyed in England, he asserted that the foundation of all these "rights of Englishmen" in Virginia was the right to be governed, as were they at home, only by their elected representatives. English subjects, he had written, could be "governed by no laws to which they have not given their consent by Representatives freely chosen of themselves." In 1775 he published another important tract, the *Fairfax County Militia Plan*. In this pamphlet he charged that Parliament had already destroyed Virginia's "ancient Laws and Liberty" and everything else that was precious to "Freemen" of England. Then he proposed to do something other than write about it. Mason urged, demanded, military resistance. He wanted to raise a company of militiamen ready to fight and die to preserve and regain the "principles of the English Constitution."[6]

By the time Mason gathered together his ideas for the bill of rights, it was evident that he was drawing upon sources other than the colonial charters. He turned to English libertarian writers, such as Milton, Sidney, and Locke, who had grounded their arguments in defense of liberty not so much on English law and English history as on the universal rights of natural law. This addition was absolutely necessary to what Mason had in mind. There was no legal or historical precedent in their English heritage to justify the new and sweeping assertion that "all power is vested in, and derived from, the people." Under the English system all power was held by Parliament; now under Mason's thinking all power was held by the people. Sovereignty, in the American system, would be transferred from the government to the governed.[7]

Mason had arrived in town on Friday, May 17, and took his seat in the Convention the next day. He began working on the draft that weekend, and members of the committee met with him Monday morning to discuss the substance of his ideas. Thomas Ludwell Lee raised the first objection. Lee said that Mason had overstated the case for natural rights in the preamble. He thought Mason had carved the rights in stone, and if it stood as it read, the declaration of rights would be fixed for all time. Lee, more specifically, felt that the wording of the clause "which rights do pertain to them and their posterity" was too rigid. Change the sentence to "recommend" such rights "to posterity as the bases and foundation of their government." This alteration, Lee believed, would allow future generations to adjust the bill of rights, that is, to add to or amend it, according to changed conditions. The committee rejected Lee's argument, and Mason's preamble stood as he presented it.[8]

Lee was undaunted. Since the committee did not wish to alter Mason's preamble to Lee's more flexible and, in his mind, more forward-looking legal philosophy, then Lee would get the same idea, or ideas, added to the list of the rights themselves. Lee's reasoning was fuzzy, but he appeared to want to make a test of the statement, in the draft document, against ex post facto laws. Lee rephrased it to allow the principle that there were exceptions to the rule. His provision read: "That all laws having a retrospect to crime and punishing offenses committed before the existence of such laws are dangerous, and ought to be avoided, except in cases of great and evident necessity where the safety of the State absolutely requires them."[9] Mason and the Tuckahoes would not budge. He objected to the change on philosophical grounds. To him, Lee's idea would permit a constitutional loophole to such laws and would allow a majority of the legislature under the excuse of "safety" to pass and enforce them. Other Tuckahoes felt that any flexibility in ex post facto laws would allow reprisals on suspected loyalists, some of whom were close friends and relatives in the shore counties of the Tidewater. So, Lee failed a second time. The article stood as it was, and ex post facto laws were condemned as "dangerous, and ought to be avoided."[10]

Mason's first article asserting natural rights as unalterable constitutional principles was criticized by conservative delegates from the northern Tidewater. Committeemen like Robert Carter Nicholas of James City County felt jittery about language that bluntly claimed: "All men are created equally free and independent, and have certain inherent natural rights, of which they cannot, by any compact, deprive or divest their posterity." Nicholas feared such words could be interpreted to apply to slaves and be "the forerunner or pretext of civil convulsion." Young Edmund Randolph recalled later that other delegates came to Mason's defense. The article, they said, could never apply to slaves. Its language referred only to those citizens who could agree by "any compact" to give away their natural rights. A "compact," in legal terminology, to these eighteenth-century men meant a contract, and no slave could enter into any contract. The whole article, therefore, had to be applicable only to members of society who were sui juris. Slaves in Virginia were not "constituted members of our society."[11]

Nicholas would not shut up. He was distressed, slaves aside, at such a sweeping advocation of equality. Liberty as an operating principle of free government, he believed, was irrefutable in principle. That was what they were in Williamsburg for, he said. But equality and liberty were something else again. "Equally free and independent," the way Mason had written it, to Nicholas sounded like a justification of democracy and a dangerous social equality of all white men. That radical goal, he said, was definitely not the way to preserve liberty. In fact, it was a sure invitation to liberty's quick destruction and could never be conceived of as the basis for, or the object of, a new government in the Old Dominion. Mason, this time backed by Thomas Ludwell Lee and some Southsiders, had enough support to keep his first article intact.[12]

In the second draft article Mason wrote that the people were the only source of power. "Magistrates"—in other words, government—"are their trustees and servants." The first part of this article was actually redundant because Mason had already claimed popular sovereignty, but the second half did add an important and logical refinement: civil officers were accountable to the electorate. As he originally wrote it, Mason, like Jefferson the next month at Philadelphia, had put in a phrase that gave the power of the people a divine sanction. It had read: "All power is by God and Nature." This reference to Providence was deleted in committee. Article three, stating that government was instituted "for the common benefit, and security of the people," was accepted by the committee, as was article four, that all offices were elective. Draft article five also met with consensus. It asserted the principle of the "separate and distinct" powers of the legislative, executive, and judicial departments of government. In his draft Mason had stressed the independence of the judiciary by stating that the legislative and executive branches both should be separate from the courts. This distinction between the assembly and the governor on one hand and the judiciary on the other hand was temporary. Mason quickly agreed to lump all three branches together as being separated from one another. In this article Mason also advanced his ideas on regular elections and rotation in office for the executive and legislative divisions with return to private life mandated for all such officials. The committee went along with his ideas.[13]

Committee consensus continued when it came to discuss Mason's sixth article, on suffrage and taxation, two issues over which grave sectional divisions developed in the subsequent constitutional history of the state. Mason, without much reflection or many reservations, wanted to keep the suffrage restricted to the existing fifty-acre freehold requirement. He believed, like almost all of the gentry at the time, in the concept of a stake in society as a prerequisite for citizen participation. Voting, to him, was a privilege and an obligation to be exercised by those adult white males who could prove they had such a stake. But Mason did not say as much in his first draft. He originally dealt only with the sanctity of this stake, or interest, and its protection against governmental appropriation in any form. Mason wrote that a man's property could not be taken from him or used for public purposes under the common law of eminent domain unless he agreed to the forfeiture or "his legal Representatives" decided to do it for "their common Good." When the committee got around to discussing what amounted to a broad statement about consent of the governed, the conservatives attached a restricted statement between this covenant and the right to vote. Thus article six was amended, with Mason's consent, to read that the suffrage was given, as a matter of natural right, only to men who "had sufficient evidence of permanent common interest with, and attachment to, the community." The amendment also added a strong statement that all such elections "ought to be free," a concern historically rooted in the delegates' recollection of the crown's interference with parliamentary elections under the Stuart monarchs. As a third modification, the Convention itself later inserted the statement that Virginia property owners could not be taxed without their consent, a curious omission by Mason and the committee given the recent imbroglio with Parliament over its revenue taxes. Thomas Ludwell Lee, the only critic of the language of article six, ignored entirely the issue of universal versus restricted suffrage. He made an effort to alter the phrase "representatives duly elected" to "legal representatives," a quibble that, understandably, the committee rejected.[14]

Following several articles concerned with legal issues of criminal law and procedure, freedom of the press, and standing armies were two other articles, numbers fifteen and sixteen, dealing with the philosophy of the new government.[15] Article fifteen in Mason's draft listed the essential qualities of all free governments. The article, in extolling justice, moderation, temperance, frugality, virtue, and "frequent recurrence to fundamental principles," was eminently of its time. It represented, as Howard has pointed out, Mason's "extensive knowledge of English legal and constitutional history" and the prevailing confidence of the Enlightenment in man's rational capacity to deal with all of society's problems. These were sentiments Mason had already clearly expressed in his *Fairfax County Resolves* and in his 1775 tract *Remarks on Annual Elections for the Fairfax Independent Company.* His ideas met with easy acceptance by the committee.[16]

Article sixteen, the last, dealt with the free exercise of religion. James Madison wanted substantial revision of Mason's language, which read: "all men should enjoy the fullest toleration in the exercise of religion, according to the dictates of conscience . . . unless . . . any man disturb the peace, the happiness, or safety of society or of individuals." This position was essentially conservative, that is, Virginians in the future as in the past should be granted toleration, within limits. But if some individuals in the exercise of that privilege were to cause trouble or become a nuisance, the toleration could be withdrawn. Religious toleration was, to Mason and to a large number of the gentry class, a benevolent grant by the state. Madison, then and during the following decade, spoke for a growing number of Virginians who wanted religious liberty to be equated with freedom of conscience and, more importantly, wanted this liberty to be the entitlement of every citizen without restriction or qualification, immune from attack by the state. His intention, according to biographer Irving Brant, was to plant the guarantee of complete freedom of conscience in constitutional law, untouchable by statute, and to extend "that same principle to all the other rights and liberties that gave dignity to human life." So, Madison's amendment read that "all men are equally entitled to the full and free exercise of religion" and "that no man or class of men ought, on account of religion, be invested with any emoluments or privileges." This bar on privileges, in one clause, disbanded the colonial practice of financial support of the Anglican church.[17]

Madison, a recent (1771) graduate of Princeton (the College of New Jersey) who was aware of his youth (he was just twenty-five), asked the popular Patrick Henry to move the amendment in committee. Henry complied but then realized that the change both grounded religious liberty on the firm basis of natural right and at the same time disestablished the Anglican church. He was willing to go along with the first idea on the philosophical grounds that the most complete liberty was the best liberty, but for political reasons—alienation of many northern Tidewater gentry who wanted to keep tax support of the church—he could not swallow the second idea. So, after preliminary discussion of these changes with the committee, Henry backed away from the amendment. Madison, recognizing that without Henry he was wasting his time going up against Mason, then drafted a substitute that deleted the part about disestablishment. His amendment now stated that because religion was directed by "reason and conviction," all men should freely and equally practice it "according to the dictates of conscience." He put in the place of the disestablishment clause a weak statement about the Christian duty to love one another. For these political considerations the idea of religious liberty was embraced, but the issue of establishment was left undecided.[18]

The failure of Madison's disestablishment amendment

marked the end of the Cary committee's discussion of the declaration of rights, and the chairman reported the draft document to the Convention on Monday morning, May 27. Standing in his place as delegate from Chesterfield County, Cary read the preamble and the articles. He then gave a copy to Tazewell, the clerk, to be officially entered into the record of the proceedings. For two weeks the document was discussed on and off in intervals along with other matters dealing with prosecuting the war. Thereupon a final draft, written out by Mason, was ordered printed and distributed to members of the Convention for their perusal.[19]

From its inception, the Virginia declaration bill of rights was considered as a separate instrument from the state's constitution. But whether it was in any way the foundation of the constitution and by position superior to the fundamental law was never discussed at Williamsburg. Howard feels that the bill of rights was generally thought of as "complementary to" the constitution. All of the delegates agreed with the wording of its preamble. The language put Virginians into a state of nature where they must renew the government by a social contract that above all had to guarantee those natural rights so violated, in their eyes, by the crown and Parliament. They understood, too, that in taking this step they were going beyond the English Bill of Rights of 1688. Now Virginians would claim and assert not just "English rights" but natural rights. Now Virginians would take sovereignty away from Parliament, or Parliament and the king, and give it to the people, thereby placing natural rights beyond infringement by any branch of government. The preamble, with all of its profound implications, was accepted by the Convention as it stood, and the rest of the text of the declaration was then adopted or amended, in the language of the preamble, by "the good people of Virginia assembled in full and free convention."[20]

Section one, on equality, created the same dissension in the Convention over the meaning of "equality" that had disturbed the conservatives in the committee. But, as in committee, Mason's position prevailed. The delegates did not feel that slaves in Virginia were relevant to the guarantees of the social compact because they were not fully human. But some members of the Convention felt gravely concerned, as Robert Carter Nicholas was, about the dangerously democratic implications of the language. Other members had more faith in the conservative instincts of the Virginia freeholder and his continued willingness to acquiesce to gentry leadership than did this sixty-one-year-old James City planter-lawyer and former treasurer of the colony. To allay the lingering uneasiness of some conservative northern Tidewater slaveholders, Pendleton suggested a refinement of the wording of the draft. Instead of allowing Mason's already changed sentence (from all men are "born equally free" to "are by nature equally free") to stand, Pendleton added the further qualification "when they enter into a state of society." Thus amended, the wording of section one was accepted by the Convention.[21]

What did the gentry delegates believe they were guaranteeing in these "certain inherent rights"? In the 1770s the rights of man were a potpourri concept that embraced a sweep of ideas from the right to brew beer to the right to life itself. Narrowed down to constitutional or judicial application, there were three concepts accepted by the Convention delegates when they finally assented to the language of section one. The first right they were claiming was the right to resist oppression, an essentially Lockean concept contained in the *Two Treatises of Government:* that is, the right to preserve one's life from tyranny. The second idea implicit in the language of, and discussions about, section one was the natural right to acquire and possess property. Here, beyond doubt, the Virginia gentry, collectively, meant slave property as well as real and tangible property. The only modification of the right of slave property then in the wind was the idea of limiting the number of slaves in Virginia, hence restricting the available property in slaves, by prohibiting the importation of African slaves. Mason had already suggested such a plan in number 17 of his *Fairfax Resolves.* But most of the delegates wanted to let the right to own slaves stand as inviolate, along with the other rights. The right to liberty was the third concept of natural rights already absorbed by these Virginians before they arrived at the momentous decisions of the spring of 1776. Liberty, written about more than any of the other rights, generally meant the privilege to use and enjoy all of one's faculties in a lawful way. It meant, specifically and practically, to be able to live and to work wherever one wanted and to have the chance of "pursueing and obtaining Happiness and Safety," a concept soon rephrased at the Second Continental Congress by Jefferson to read the "pursuit of Happiness."[22]

Other alterations of the draft, all relatively minor, were made during two weeks of discussion on the Convention floor. Section two was taken as it was written, with the clear understanding by the gentry delegates that the "magistrates" representing the "people" meant two representatives from each county elected by the freeholders. The Convention adopted section three with one addition. The first clause read in draft form: "That government is, or ought to be, instituted for the common benefit and security of the people." The delegates inserted the word "protection" between "benefit" and "security." The change only reinforced the focus of this part of the declaration on the firm assertion that the end of all government was the happiness and security of the majority of its citizens. Mason had written that when government failed to achieve these ends, the majority of the community had an "indubitable, inalienable, and indefeasible" right to abolish it. The printed draft read "unalienable." The committee may have made this change in order to distinguish between "inalienable," or that which could not be changed by law, a narrow definition, and "unalienable," or that which could not be altered by any means. Or, as Howard suggests, this switch might have been a compositor's accident; another printer appears to have made exactly the same change in Jefferson's Declaration of Independence. Deliberate or accidental, the wording claimed the right of the majority of Virginia voters to rewrite their constitution. It did not, however, spell out the right to amend it.[23]

Section five, on separation of powers, the judiciary, and frequent elections, was accepted by the Convention with no

substantial objections. The delegates agreed with two concepts that they assumed would be brought up soon in the
constitution itself. The first idea was frequent, meaning annual, elections of the executive and legislative branches. The
second precept, a holdover from common law and later a
whipping post for Jefferson, was that judges should hold life
tenure during good behavior. There was little debate on the
sixth section, maintaining the freehold suffrage as the evidence of "common interest with, and attachment to, the community." From a practical standpoint, the gentry felt debate
on whether this meant a restrictive franchise was meaningless. Most believed that a majority of those who should vote
could do so, and recent research has shown that almost 60
percent of the white adult males were qualified to vote in
1776.[24]

Section eight, on criminal prosecutions, was one of the
longest of the legal sections of the declaration. The discussion in the Convention was brief, despite the detailed listing
of criminal procedure, because of gentry's wide experience
on the county courts. Many fundamental rights of due process, interestingly, were not mentioned by Mason or added in
the Convention, perhaps because such rights were assumed
to be covered in "English rights" or natural rights. These un-
named rights include those of habeas corpus, freedom from
double jeopardy, grand jury, and prohibition of bills of attainder. The omission of the last right, however, was deliberate. These gentlemen were sympathetic to, and their new
constitution would provide for, legislative punishment without a court trial. They had in mind a specific problem in
Virginia, the Phillips episode, which seemed to justify bills of
attainder. Josiah Phillips, a renegade Norfolk laborer, in
1775 had used the confusion of Dunmore's military activities
in and around Princess Anne County to organize a cutthroat
band of robbers that terrorized the locality for three years.
Henry, and soon Jefferson upon his return to Williamsburg
in July, wanted the man declared an outlaw. Thus, section
eleven allowed a person to be "deprived of his liberty" not
exclusively by due process of law but "by the law of the land
or the judgment of his peers."[25]

Understandably, given the events of that spring, the delegates spent a lot of time on section thirteen, dealing with the militia. Mason in his draft had delineated the function and limited purpose of the militia, ideas he had already spelled out in his writings on the Fairfax County militia. He injected his own strong view that the militia was the only means the people had to resist the mercenary army of the crown. The July Convention likewise had condemned the use of mercenaries in Dunmore's imposition of martial law in December 1775. So, it was an unquestioned consensus at Williamsburg that asserted the evil of standing armies. The Convention did add, however, an all-important supplement to this section. It stated, in final form, "that in all cases, the military should be under strict subordination to, and governed by, the civil power." Article fourteen, on the need for uniform and sovereign state government, went through the Convention without debate. Section fifteen, a broad statement on the need to preserve free government, also was agreed upon without change. And the last section, on religious freedom, with the difficult political issue of disestablishment already handled by the committee, passed the approval of the Convention.[26]

The Virginia Declaration of Rights, in one form or another, became the model for other states writing their own bills of rights and, over a decade later, for the federal Bill of Rights. It stated, although in somewhat disorganized form, a philosophy of republican government and outlined its structure and objectives. It spelled out many of the English rights of criminal procedure. It asserted civil liberties such as freedom of the press, subordination of the military to civilian will, and religious toleration in a form mature for the day. The Declaration of Rights was not without serious weaknesses, as Leonard Levy has pointed out. It did not ban bills of attainder. There was no separation of church and state. There was nothing on freedom of speech, of assembly, or to petition. Those common-law rights, such as habeas corpus and double jeopardy, that were omitted were "as numerous and important as those included." Yet the Cary committee and the Convention, by mid-June, felt they had done a major part of their assigned job. On Wednesday, June 12, Pendleton called for the vote, and the Declaration of Rights was accepted unanimously.[27]

While the committee and then the delegates were dealing with the bill of rights and with other matters pertaining to the war effort, they began to consider the state's fundamental law. To the gentry gathered at Williamsburg the word *constitution* was one of the "most hallowed terms in their political vocabulary." A constitution, to these men, had one primary purpose, liberty: to place each person beyond the reach of arbitrary political power. Then, as a secondary consideration, they believed that a fundamental law had to secure a person's rights in property. Third, they felt that a constitution was "the ultimate repository of a people's considered judgement about basic matters of public policy." They saw a constitution as "confined to the fundamentals of government" and as separate from the details of legislative statutes.[28]

Did these gentlemen consider themselves a constitutional convention, a body qualified to write fundamental law as distinguished from statutes? And, equally important, did they think themselves qualified both to draft and to adopt such a document? The answer is yes. To them the process whereby the House of Burgesses was selected and, in turn, the two provisional governments of 1775 and 1776 were chosen was the only known (or, more accurately, conceivable) way that the people of Virginia gave their consent. The distinction between a true constitutional convention and a legislature, such as that first made in October 1776 in Massachusetts and which became a sore point later on for reformers in the Old Dominion, was not thought of at Williamsburg in May and June 1776. Viewing the finished document, there can be no doubt that its framers intended it to be constitutional law devoted to that law's perceived purposes. Indeed, it stands with unique distinction in the history of constitutional law. According to Howard, "no document of American constitutionalism, save the Federal Constitution, draws so deeply on the great themes of American constitutional and legal development as does the Virginia Constitution."[29]

Some of the most important ideas about what should go into this constitution came from young Thomas Jefferson.

That thirty-three-year-old Virginia gentleman was in Philadelphia as a member of the colony's delegation to the Second Continental Congress when he sent his first letters to Williamsburg on what was about to take place there. Unaware of the procedures adopted by the Convention on May 15, Jefferson wrote, as was his habit, with the purpose of giving advice and of telling others what to do. The two letters that survive were something of a contradiction. In a letter of May 16 to his friend Edmund Randolph, whose father John was about to depart as a loyalist, he raised for the first time the need to call a special convention for the sole purpose of writing a permanent constitution.[30] But he must have been aware that his point was moot because almost immediately, without waiting for a reply from Randolph, Jefferson set to work to write his own fundamental law for the state. A second letter, also written on the sixteenth, was sent to his fellow delegate to Congress, Thomas Nelson, Jr., then on vacation at his home in Williamsburg. He told the Cambridge-educated, thirty-eight-year-old planter from York County that the Virginia delegates at Philadelphia ought to be recalled so they could assist in drafting the state's constitution; other colonies were calling back their delegates. In his own mind Jefferson was having it both ways. On the one hand, he declared the proceedings in Williamsburg improper. On the other hand, he wanted to be there to take part in the Convention, and he submitted to that "illegal" body his own version of Virginia's constitution.[31]

At Williamsburg, Edmund Randolph presented Jefferson's procedural objections to the gentry, but they rejected them unanimously. Edmund Pendleton, Patrick Henry, and George Mason all agreed that if the Convention had power from the people to declare independence, it had the power to frame a new, permanent government. If the Convention, by dissolving the existing government, could place Virginians in a state of nature, it had the authority to remove them from this condition. St. George Tucker, as Fletcher M. Green has pointed out, soon criticized Jefferson's position. Tucker argued, in his edition of Blackstone's *Commentaries on the Constitution*, the the voters knew they were selecting a convention both to declare independence and to write a permanent government. Tucker felt that, sovereignty being indivisible, the Convention actually could do anything it wanted to do: declare independence, form a constitution, pass statutes, act as a judicial body, confiscate property, and direct the conduct of war. Finally, Tucker argued that the Convention was not an ordinary legislative body at all but an extralegal assembly of the people with prerogatives to sever ties with one government and to establish another.[32]

When Jefferson realized that the Convention had rejected his arguments against writing a constitution, he finished his own plan of government, which, after three drafts, he sent with George Wythe to Williamsburg in mid-June. At the same time, in order to get his ideas before the delegates as soon as possible, he elaborated on them in an exchange of letters with Edmund Pendleton beginning on May 24. Jefferson wanted an extension of the suffrage, apportionment in the legislature according to population, an allodial system of land tenure, and fairer treatment of the Indians. Even though his ideas and his constitution arrived late, some of the concepts they contained and some of the reforms he had communicated to Pendleton were incorporated in the state's first fundamental law, but not the most significant ones, on suffrage and apportionment, that would have affected the distribution of power in the commonwealth.[33]

The Convention was not without other suggestions as to what sort of constitution it should write. Excluding Jefferson's draft, three partial plans and four outline drafts were offered to the delegates. Of the three partial proposals, probably the earliest was suggested by Jefferson's Albemarle County neighbor and his surrogate in Williamsburg, Dr. George Gilmer. Gilmer wanted, either in the Declaration of Rights or the body of the constitution, a statement in favor of "free toleration" of all clergy, including dissenters, veto power for the governor, establishment of courts of equity, a guarantee of habeas corpus, and a tax on luxuries. He wanted to banish perquisites and sinecure offices—practices that Gilmer thought of as only "a genteel way of picking the pocket of the public." Philip Mazzei, the Italian horticulturalist who since 1774 had been experimenting with wine making at Colle not far from Monticello, offered another partial scheme. On May 16 he gave a copy of his plan to Henry through an intermediary, John Page, Jefferson's close friend. Mazzei told Henry to avoid the "weak basis and heavy errors" of the English system. Meriwether Smith, a forty-six-year-old wealthy planter from Essex County, apparently offered a third plan to the convention. He never wrote down his ideas, but it appears that he advised little change from the colonial system of government other than to have the governor elected to office, although by whom Smith did not say.[34]

While the delegates were entertaining these sketchy suggestions on what to put in or to exclude from their government, and before Wythe gave them Jefferson's extensive draft constitution, they were aware of four other separate outline proposals for a new constitution. One of these plans, the first to be taken up by the Convention, was written by Richard Henry Lee as a *Government Scheme* and appeared in the May 10 *Virginia Gazette*. A copy of a handbill of the plan, also published by Purdie, had been sent to Henry three weeks earlier. Another plan, almost the same as Lee's, was written by John Adams. Called *Thoughts on Government,* Adams's ideas had been circulated as a copy of a letter to Lee of November 15, 1775, among the Virginia members of the Continental Congress. A printed version was distributed in Williamsburg after April 20. Carter Braxton, the conservative Tuckahoe, presented a third plan, largely his reaction to the Adams and Lee proposals, as an *Address to the Convention . . . of Virginia*. It was laid before the Convention by Landon Carter on May 20. Finally, George Mason gave his ideas, the fourth outline, in writing to the Cary committee on June 8.[35]

The Lee scheme, long thought to be a mere précis of Adams's ideas, was in fact an original plan of government thought up by Lee that spring. Recent investigations prove that Lee's ideas were circulated by Henry at the very start of the Convention and were in the air at Williamsburg at the same time as the suggestions of the New Englander. Lee, attending the Congress at Philadelphia when he put the ideas together, had already received Adams's letter of November

15, 1775, wherein Adams had sketched casually some suggestions about "what form of government is more readily
and easily adopted by a colony upon a sudden emergency."[36]
Lee had not, however, had a chance to read Adams's more
extensive *Thoughts on Government.* Lee proposed a seven-
point plan. He wanted a two-house legislature with the lower
house of two delegates from each county elected annually by
the freeholders. This body would choose a twenty-four-man
upper house for terms of seven years. The two houses would
elect a governor for one year. A governor's council of state of
twelve men also would be "promiscuously chosen" from both
houses each year. It would function as a restraint upon the
governor, who would be allowed to exercise his enumerated
powers and to appoint county officers only with approval of
the council. The legislature would choose the judiciary for
life tenure on good behavior. All other officers—lieutenant
governor, secretary, treasurer, commissary, attorney, soliciter
general—were to be chosen by joint ballot of the legislature.

Adams's ideas were promoted by Thomas Ludwell Lee,
who had received a copy of his *Thoughts on Government* from
Wythe. Henry, Charles Lee, and Robert Carter Nicholas also
had in hand copies of Adams's pamphlet. The tract opened
with a heavy, Adams-style lecture on the noble ends of all
"good governments," meaning, of course, a republican government of "the most wise and good." Specifically, Adams
wanted a bicameral legislature elected by men of property in
which the lower house chose the upper and the two together
elected state judges. All state officers except judges should
stand for election annually because "where annual elections
end, there slavery begins." Adams wanted a rigid system of
rotation in office and no more than three years' consecutive
service at a time. He gave the governor a veto and had him
elected by the people.[37]

While the Lee and Adams plans are remarkably similar in
structure, there were important differences. First of all,
Adams wanted a much stronger governor than Lee did.
Adams also touched on governmental responsibilities to the
citizenry, such as providing "laws for the liberal education of
youth," that never entered Lee's mind. Lee wanted the upper

house to have a seven-year term while Adams said one year was sufficient. They differed on the role of the council of state. While both stripped it of its colonial role in the judiciary, Adams wanted it to continue both as an executive and legislative body by making the council, of between twelve to twenty-eight men, the upper house of the legislature. Lee, though, wanted "an absolute separation of the council from the upper house" or, in other words, a separation of powers. Lee was unwilling to have local officers chosen by any means other than "as usual," while Adams wanted to have at least the sheriff elected by the freeholders.[38]

At Philadelphia, Carter Braxton read *Thoughts on Government*, believed it both silly in tone and dangerous to ordered society in some of its provisions, and composed a rebuttal. He sent copies of his pamphlet to Landon Carter for distribution at Williamsburg. The unsigned plan, entitled *Address to the Convention of the Colony and Ancient Dominion of Virginia, on the Subject of Government in General, and Recommending a Particular Form to Their Consideration,* arrived about May 20. The "contemptable little tract," as Richard Henry Lee described it, praised the merits of the British constitution but was careful to emphasize that reunion with the mother country was impossible. Above all, Braxton charged the delegates, avoid "a restless spirit of innovation" and abjure the creation of a "novel government to give up our laws, our customs, and our manners." Virginia, being a vast geographic entity, could never adapt to the ideas of Adams, suited as they were for a much smaller commonwealth like Massachusetts. Virginians must keep what had proved workable: a house of representatives (elected every three years by freeholders); a council (elected for life by the assembly), which would function as the upper house; and an executive branch (also elected for life tenure "during good behavior" by the assembly) consisting of a governor and a seven-man privy council. The governor would appoint judges and military officers, but the assembly would choose all the remaining state officials. The *Address* departed from Virginia's colonial government only in providing for impeachment of the governor, specifying an upper house of the legislature modeled on the English

House of Lords, and having just the governor, not the privy council and governor, appoint judges.[39]

Braxton's main worry was that the Adams and the Lee plans would destroy the separation of powers by placing all Virginians at the mercy of a powerful assembly. Moreover, Adams was asking for the destruction of property by giving this assembly the power to tax luxuries. Under this dangerous scheme tobacco itself could be taxed and the plantation system imperiled. Another Adams-Lee mistake, Braxton believed, was the confusion of public and private virtue in their assertion that because all individuals had the latter quality to some extent, all or almost all could claim the former. Public virtue, to this Virginian, was possessed only "by a few individuals," never "the mass of people in any state." So, responsibility of government should be in the hands of those who have "a disinterested attachment" to the public good, exclusive and independent of all private and selfish interest.[40]

At the Convention, Braxton's proposal received the enthusiastic endorsement of Robert Carter Nicholas and other Tuckahoe conservatives. Henry observed right away, pessimistically, that Adams's plan encountered "many powerful enemies." He wrote to Adams that "there is among most of our opulent families a strong bias to aristocracy." Thomas Ludwell Lee entreated his younger brother Richard Henry to come to Williamsburg to help fight for his ideas. Lee left Philadelphia immediately, but before he arrived, most Tuckahoes had pulled together under Pendleton. The rallying point for the Pendleton men was a constitution proposed by George Mason.[41]

Mason, with the Lee and Adams plans in hand, began working on his constitution in late May and spent time on it intermittently for about three weeks. It is likely that he was aware of some of the suggestions Jefferson was communicating by letter to Edmund Randolph, although Jefferson's draft of a constitution was not presented to the delegates until after Mason had finished his work and his own draft was being revised by the Cary committee. By June 10 Mason gave a copy of his constitution to the select committee. There, after a couple of days' delay while the committee had its Declaration of Rights accepted by the Convention, it was discussed and revised.[42]

Mason gave the Cary committee a fifteen-section constitution, each part beginning, as had those of Adams and Lee, with the godlike imperative: "Let there be. . . ." Only three of the articles, one, two, and six, were accepted by the committee intact; they were shifted in order to stand as articles three, four, and eight. The committee agreed with Mason's bicameral structure of the legislature but changed the composition of the lower house to allow for one representative elected from nonincorporated towns when the town registered "half the number of voters in some one county." In the upper house Mason wanted a cumbersome division of the new state into twenty-four districts each with its own senator. Each county within a district would elect twelve "deputies" who had resided for at least a year there and who had property worth £500. Then the district deputies would choose the twenty-four senators for rotating terms of four years. A senator had to be twenty-eight years of age, own an estate the equivalent of 700 acres, and be a resident of his district for one year. The committee went along with Mason's senate but significantly reduced the officeholding qualifications to that of a "freeholder residing in the district" and deleted the age requirement. The suffrage was extended by Mason to seven-year leaseholders and to fathers who were "housekeepers" and had "three or more" children in the county provided the man had lived where he was voting for one year. The committee wanted none of this democratization of the franchise. It simply deleted the half of section five that dealt with the right to vote and substituted the terse statement, as a separate section, "That the right of suffrage in the election of members of both Houses shall remain as exercised at present."[43]

Mason's draft of the executive powers went well beyond Lee's brief statement on exercising "executive powers of government" but fell short of Adams's concept of a governor elected by the people and armed with a veto as a check on the power of the legislature. Mason's middle-of-the-road position had the governor elected annually by joint ballot of the legislature for a possible three-year stint in office. As governor he could, in addition to the vague right to "exercise the executive powers of government" (with the advice of a council of state), call and adjourn the General Assembly and grant pardons and reprieves. The committee cut back on the power of Mason's governor. It prohibited him, after serving for three years, from being reelected for another four years. It denied the pardoning prerogative in cases where "prosecution shall be carried on by the House of Delegates" unless that body approved. More importantly, the committee specified that the governor was to exercise "the executive powers of government according to the laws of this commonwealth." The legislature, not the governor, would define and determine what executive power meant.

Mason limited the council to an executive function by deleting all reference to its colonial role as the upper house of the legislature. Lee had wanted essentially the same thing. Adams, on the other hand, in his November 15 letter to Lee had been vague in referring to the council both as an advising group to the governor and, possibly, as a "twelve, sixteen, twenty-four, or twenty-eight"–member upper house. Mason called the body the council of state and had it composed of eight men elected by the legislature. Every three years one-fourth of the council would step down and would be ineligible for reelection for a period of three years. Mason wanted the governor to sit as president of the council. It then could function as an advisory body with the governor and three members present. The committee kept Mason's council largely intact with one important change. It pulled the governor out of the council and, instead, had the council choose the presiding officer from its own membership. The committee wanted at least one-half of the council to be present as a quorum instead of just three members.[44]

Mason, Lee, and Adams, in their concern for separation of powers in a republican government, all focused special attention upon the judicial branch. Mason, reflecting a consensus of their ideas, detailed the structure and the functions of this part of the government in article ten of his draft plan. All of the state's judges would be selected by joint ballot of the legislature and commissioned by the governor for life tenure during good behavior with "fixed and adequate salaries." These judges could never serve in the legislature or the council. There would be three courts: a supreme court, a chancery, and an admiralty. Mason also wanted an attorney general as an exclusively judicial appointment rather than as a part of the executive department.

The committee transferred Mason's ideas into its own article fourteen. The method of appointment and tenure of judges was kept the same. The committee was more specific, though, in naming the new state courts, and it added one other court. The Supreme Court of Appeals, the general court (the addition), the chancery, and the admiralty would constitute the state's judiciary. On local justice, Mason had the county judges appointed by the governor and council. They, in turn, were to name the clerks, sheriffs, coroners, and constables. These justices of the peace and their clerks were given life tenure. The committee felt that Mason's draft left too many questions unanswered, so it made certain that the county court would remain a self-perpetuating, local bastion of gentry power by stipulating that all vacancies in county justices' positions were to be filled, and any increase in their present number made, only by "the recommendation of the respective county courts." All existing county clerks (meaning to the committee all county officers) would keep their jobs until they died, resigned, or were incapacitated. Then the justices of the peace would appoint their successors.

Article twelve of Mason's plan dealt with impeachment, or how to get rid of a state or local officer not on "good behavior." Mason conceived of a broad basis of removal from office. He felt that a man should be removed for either "maladministration" or "corruption." The committee concurred with the idea that a person could be impeached for other than criminal conduct, but it separated Mason's June 10 draft into two articles. Article sixteen dealt with only executive removal. It defined an impeachable offense as "maladministration and corruption" but added "or other means by which the safety of the State may be endangered." Article seventeen dealt with impeachment of judges and referred to the "crimes or offences before-mentioned," presumably in article sixteen.

By Saturday morning, June 22, the Cary committee had finished its deliberations on Mason's plan except for the last article on how to get the government started. Mason had written that the "representatives of the people, now met in Convention," would elect a twenty-four-member senate and then the two houses together would choose a governor and council. He had the new senate sit till the last day of March 1777 and "the other officers until the end of the succeeding session of the Assembly," that is, until the next April elections. The committee did not want to move so quickly. The governor, council, attorney general, and judges of the state courts were to be elected by the Convention, labeled as "the representatives of the people." It changed the wording to have a senate "to be first chosen by the people." The committee concluded its work that afternoon.

On Sunday, June 23, Jefferson's plan arrived in Williamsburg at Wythe's home down the street from the empty Governor's Mansion. By that time the delegates were hot, tired, and just not ready to begin the whole business of writing a constitution all over again. They were in no mood to instruct the select committee to review the Jefferson scheme and reconcile it with the committee's own completed work. The only agreement Wythe could get from the frazzled delegates on Sunday afternoon was to use it on the Convention floor that week for amendments to the committee's constitution.[45]

Fortunately, much in Jefferson's constitution meshed with what had been already done. He, too, advocated separation of powers, bicameralism with an upper house elected by the lower house, and a weak executive, called not governor but "the administrator," elected by the legislature. He, like the Convention, wanted a strong declaration of rights. Yet, despite his own conservatism on these matters at the time, Jefferson hit at the heart of a reform issue that would dominate the subsequent constitutional history of his state, representation. "It was in connection with the *basis* rather than the structure of government," Dumas Malone observed, "that

Jefferson showed himself to be more forward-looking than any of the other contemporary leaders, and an outstanding advocate of popular rule on the basis of just representation."[46]

Jefferson's legislature was the same as Mason's in structure: it had a lower and upper house. But Jefferson's lower house was to be elected by a scheme which would amount to universal adult white male suffrage. At first glance it seemed that Jefferson was still embracing the "stake in society" concept of suffrage. He asked that property requirements be retained although reduced. Instead of the colonial freehold requirement, he wanted the vote given to all adult white males who owned just twenty-five acres or a town lot. But he then stipulated that the state must immediately grant fifty acres to every person not owning land. Moreover, he wanted representation in the lower house, the General Assembly, to be apportioned according to the demographic distribution of the electorate instead of the two-per-county system. This change came from Jefferson's own sense of the potential sectional division of the state between voters living in the larger and growing counties of the interior and those remaining in the small counties of the Tidewater, a section he saw even then as "the seat of privilege and unjust power."[47]

There were other significant departures from what the committee had decided to include in the constitution. In a section on "Rights Public and Private," Jefferson demanded an end to the importation of slaves. He, like Madison, wanted to terminate all connection between church and state in Virginia. And, fundamentally, Jefferson questioned the legitimacy of the whole procedure of having the delegates write, approve, and enact a fundamental law. He asked that a statement be included in the constitution so that it could be amended by a vote of two-thirds of the people. He also went beyond the thinking of the Convention to include a broad preamble putting forth the justification for the dissolving of the royal government. Lastly, at the end of his plan, Jefferson dealt with the future of Virginia's land claims in the West.

The Convention, as Wythe reported to Jefferson, while rejecting a full consideration of his plan of government, tried to incorporate some of his ideas into the constitution. Thus on Wednesday, June 26, when the delegates reconvened in the Capitol as a committee of the whole, they had before them the Mason document as revised by the Cary committee and Jefferson's scheme for a fundamental law. The impact of Jefferson's plan on the final outcome of the Convention, despite the weariness of the delegates, was greater than many historians, and even Jefferson himself, suspected. The first, and most obvious, change in the Mason constitution was the decision on June 29 to tack on Jefferson's preamble, verbatim, as the reason for dissolving the old government and to include a part of it as a separate section, number two, as a justification for establishing a new one. Other suggestions by Jefferson were included in the text itself. Part of the section on the legislature, number three, was his handiwork, as seen in the addition of his phrase "nor shall any person exercise the powers of more than one [department] at the same time," a stronger and clearer idea of the separation of the three branches of government. On his recommendation the Convention called the men "appointed" by the legislature to the courts the judges of the Supreme Court of Appeals, judges in chancery, judges of admiralty, secretary, and the attorney general. The delegates copied with minor changes Jefferson's provision that all forfeitures that had gone to the crown would go to the commonwealth. They added, as section twenty-one, Jefferson's lengthy statement on Virginia's land claims and land titles from the Indians, in effect laying claim to the Northwest Territory above the Ohio River and to the area "westward of the Allegheny mountains." They called the upper house the senate, as Jefferson had done. They refined election procedures for the legislature's choosing the governor and the council along the lines Jefferson suggested.[48]

The delegates during this last week of June on their own initiative made further changes in the committee's draft. To compensate the western settlers for augmenting the representation of the Tidewater area by the addition, in section five, of delegates "for each of such other cities and boroughs as may hereafter be allowed particular representation by the Legislature," they stipulated that the "district of West Augusta" be given two men in the lower house. The Convention added to the prohibition on serving in the legislature and council the category of "ministers of the Gospel of every denomination."[49]

On Saturday, June 29, the constitution was read for the third time and passed unanimously. The unanimity was, of course, a facade. After adjournment there was immediate criticism of what had been done. Madison complained that having the governor elected by the legislature would cause intrigue and weaken the man's capacity to do his job. His disgruntlement over the failure to separate church and state did not diminish at all. From the conservative side, Carter Braxton made no secret of his feelings. Still sitting as a member of the Second Continental Congress, he grumbled about the dangerous novelty of the new government, in which proven institutions, such as a council functioning as the upper house, were thrown out in the midst of crisis and uncertainty. Braxton feared that the governor, especially, was too much the pawn of the lower house of the legislature, and like Madison, he believed the weak executive could hardly lead the people of the state during the war against Great Britain. St. George Tucker later wrote that the House of Delegates was too powerful. He denounced the council as being cumbersome and unnecessary. "The governor," he observed, "can constitutionally perform no one official act without their advice." Landon Carter deplored the real lack of separation of powers and predicted that soon even the judges would be corrupted by subservience to the will of the legislature. George Wythe, fed up with the end result, wrote to Jefferson in late July that the whole document should be written all over again in a constitutional convention and that Jefferson was the man best qualified to effect this "reformation."[50]

Criticisms notwithstanding, the first action of the new government was to give an appearance of its capacity to govern. In accordance with the last section of the constitution, the Convention elected the state's first governor and council. Talk about whom to choose for the executive office had been going on among the delegates since late May. About the time they were deciding the question of whether to allow bills of attainder, the Tuckahoes began to coax Patrick Henry to their camp. Although conservatives regarded Henry as an upstart, they were realistic enough to recognize that he was a man ruled more by his emotions than by intellect, character, or conviction. They knew he would bend with the popular will, whether that popular temperament be progressive or conservative. They recognized, too, that unlike Jefferson or Madison, Henry had no strong ideas personally about what the government of the new state should be. One last consideration came into play. As Dumas Malone has pointed out, Henry was universally recognized as lazy, and "during the year 1776 his health was bad." So, the Tuckahoes concluded that Henry was an easy target for preemption and then, as governor, for manipulation. He was their man.[51]

For a while though, from mid-May till late June, the Tuckahoes were in a push-and-pull match between two men for governor. Henry was the leading candidate, but Richard Henry Lee wanted Thomas Nelson of York County, "a political potentate of the old regime," in the words of Robert Meade. Lee, in a private letter, had tried in mid-May to get Edmund Pendleton to back Nelson. The sixty-year-old Yorktown planter, called "Secy.," had served as secretary of the colony (1742–76), as a York County burgess (1745–49), on the governor's council (1749–76), and then as secretary of the commonwealth (1776). Nelson, Lee wrote, therefore possesses knowledge, experience, and has already been in the dignified station." But Mason threw his considerable prestige behind Henry primarily because Henry "was the first who opened the breath of liberty to Virginia." By early June, Henry was making noises about how the governor had to be limited in power to avoid the tyrannical abuse that he had earlier, publicly, condemned in Dunmore. Such a positioning by Henry was instinctively vague, for he joined the cause of preserving liberty, which he more than anyone in Virginia that spring personified, with the idea of legislative control of the new government. In simple terms Henry told the Tuckahoes that he was willing, if not eager, to go along with their view of a limited chief executive. By supporting Henry for the governorship, the Tuckahoes expected, and got, his cooperation in beating down the attempt, which Henry at first flirted with, to separate church and state during the final discussions on the subject in early June. The vote for governor, on June 29, a Saturday, was Henry, 60; Thomas Nelson, 45; and John Page, 11. Having elected Henry as governor, the Convention then voted to install him, in impressive comfort, in the Governor's Palace. Henry, in turn, welcomed the graciously bestowed perquisite of office.[52]

Returning after a three-day break, the delegates chose a council of loyal Tuckahoes—John Page, Dudley Digges, John Taylor, John Blair, Benjamin Harrison, Bartholomew Dandridge, Charles Carter, and Thomas "Secy." Nelson. Page, who received the most votes, was its first president and, because of Henry's "physical incapacity," as Malone has discreetly referred to it, was put under an unusual burden of having to run the new government as a de facto governor during its first months. Although a friend of Jefferson's, Page was an ally of the Tuckahoes and, still glued emotionally to his inherited high social status, regarded himself as a Tuckahoe conservative. Edmund Randolph was elected attorney general the same day. On July 4 the legislature, in compliance with the constitution, divided Virginia into twenty-four senatorial districts. Then the next day they prescribed an oath of loyalty to the commonwealth which all state officers, except those who were Quakers or Mennonites, had to take. On Friday afternoon, July 5, the delegates tended to last details. They appropriated 1,000 pounds sterling to furnish the governor's residence for Henry. They voted him special powers "for the defense and protection of his colony." They prescribed the death penalty for counterfeiters, deleted all mention of the king from the litany of the Anglican church, adopted the Great Seal of the commonwealth, and adjourned until "the first Monday in October next, then to meet in the city of Williamsburg."[53]

The 1776 constitution was created with a grave error of omission. It had no provision for amendment. There was no way to reapportion the dominant branch, the House of Delegates, or to correct other weaknesses, such as the lame governorship or the restricted suffrage requirements, without overhauling the entire constitution. But the constitution perpetuated the domination of the lowland Virginia gentry, and led by Henry and the Tuckahoes, they were determined to keep it that way.

Jefferson, then Madison, nevertheless kept fighting within the House of Delegates to improve on the constitution.[54] They were able to meet with three successes, an act for establishing religious freedom, passed in final form in 1786, a revision of the state's criminal laws, and a restructuring of the courts to give common-law jurisdiction to the general court and, in the district court act of 1788, to give appellate jurisdiction entirely to the Supreme Court of Appeals."[55] In part these modifications were possible because the General Assembly became divided in the 1780s between two factions over taxation issues and reaction to the Treaty of Paris. Both matters, according to Jackson Turner Main, produced definite bloc voting in the House of Delegates beginning about December 1779.[56] Two years later the bloc pattern had firmed up, and it remained intact until the other overriding issues of the federal Constitution created new alignments of Federalists, Antifederalists, and moderates. Jefferson and Madison were able to manipulate the more liberal members of these factions to generate support for their reforms.

More was left undone in the years after 1776 than was accomplished by way of altering the conservative, gentry-dominated government of the Old Dominion. The weak governorship was accepted as a fact, and there was no further effort to redress what to Jefferson was the appalling lack of separation of powers in the constitution. The reason was simple. The gentry controlled the legislature, and the legislature controlled the governor. The judiciary, despite some reorganizing of state court jurisdictions, also remained in the hands of the gentry because the county courts stayed unchallenged as self-perpetuating family oligarchies. Jefferson tried to diminish the control of the courts over county justice in 1776 and again in 1779 by having the legislature make the sheriff an elected official no longer under the dominion of the courts and to have aldermen elected in every county. The bills failed.[57]

Legal and constitutional arguments were ineffective against an entrenched squirearchy. Not until the demography of the Old Dominion began to change could pressure by the voters to modify the structure of government be brought to bear on the legislature. Then and only then would constitutional reform become a possibility. It was not until the early decades of the nineteenth century, after a westward shift of population in the state threatened to make the old Virginia gentry an ever-shrinking minority, that some of the sons of the delegates of 1776 started to awaken to a new reality, power politics. The basic issue in Virginia, and the impetus for constitutional reform by then, was sectionalism. The spokesmen for voters in the Shenandoah Valley and Allegheny Mountains demanded the share of power in the government to which their growing numbers entitled them and which the Constitution of 1776, by its system of representation and suffrage, had denied them.

III

Sectionalism and Constitutional Reform

IN 1809, WHEN JEFFERSON stepped down from the presidency and retired to private life on his beloved mountaintop, the divisive feelings of sectionalism had replaced the harmonious, enlightened tone of the Virginia he had known and loved as a young man. In his early manhood Jefferson had seen no real social or economic conflicts in the Old Dominion, and certainly none along geographic lines. To be sure, when the delegates had gathered in the spring of 1776 at Williamsburg, a temporary geopolitical division had surfaced between the Tuckahoes and the Southsiders, and these labels reflected important contrasts in patterns of mobility and landholding in the older and the newer counties during the mid-eighteenth century. But these factions proved fragile when tested in the debates on drafting the new frame of government. The result was a constitution that, according to Richard R. Beeman, merely "strengthened the grasp of the provincial oligarchy on the politics of the state." But a generation later the consensus had evaporated. By then a sizable number of yeomen farmers and artisans had settled the Shenandoah Valley and beyond into the Allegheny Mountains. East of the Blue Ridge, though, things remained largely unchanged. So, by the first decades of the nineteenth century, Virginians were speaking in terms of sectional controversy, of East versus West.[1]

In the East descendants of the old gentry stood as tall as ever, admired and deferred to by the yeomen and black slaves. Even more than before, the leadership of the Piedmont and Tidewater, the two subregions of the East, was, in Charles S. Sydnor's view, "one large cousinhood." Across the

Blue Ridge one saw other Virginians, more independent of mind, carving homesteads in the lush and pastoral Valley where the Shenandoah, New, and Holston rivers watered their grains, fruit, and livestock. Farther west were the Virginians who farmed corn and wheat in the rugged Alleghenies, especially the deep valleys of the Kanawha, Monongahela, and Great Sandy rivers that flowed westward, away from the Old Dominion. Lurking behind the obvious physical differences between East and West was the institution of chattel slavery. Virginia in the early nineteenth century was fast becoming two societies; one based on slave labor and the plantation system, the other rapidly growing without either. A glance at map 1 tells the story. Virginia's black population by 1830 was concentrated almost entirely east of the Blue Ridge where the ratio of blacks to whites was often over two to one. At the same time, as the census data showed, the white population of the Piedmont and Tidewater was in steady, irreversible decline.[2]

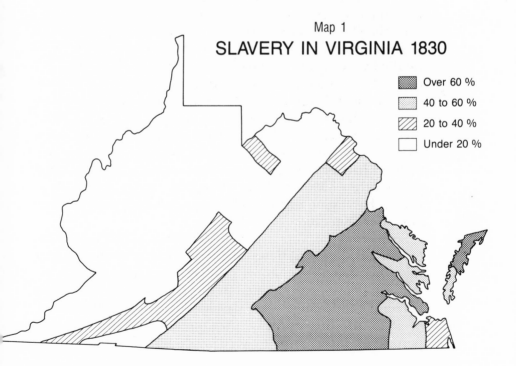

Map 1
SLAVERY IN VIRGINIA 1830

Over 60 %
40 to 60 %
20 to 40 %
Under 20 %

Slavery and the plantation system were taking their toll on the eastern gentry, on their view of themselves, their future, and their constitution. Faced with an ever-growing black population and the erosion of the numbers of their own race, they showed signs of an almost paranoia of a slave insurrection. This social neurosis probably began in the 1790s when the first gruesome details of the black revolutions in Haiti and Santo Domingo reached the Old Dominion's newspapers. Virginia planters became more and more obsessed with the possibility that their own chattels would imitate the carnage of the islands. The number of reported slave revolts in the state and elsewhere throughout the South increased the dread. The same census data that first announced the worrisome decline of the East's white population also pointed to another racial threat to white security: the large number of free blacks congregating in the eastern towns. These free blacks were more threatening than slaves because they were difficult either to supervise or to control, were thought to be a perpetual cause of crime and lawlessness, and, moreover, were the likely seedbed of a racial uprising.[3]

In the West, where there were few blacks, the mounting negrophobia was incomprehensible. Westerners took a more rational view of the "peculiar institution" and of blacks generally. They noted that the institution of slavery was in serious trouble in Virginia. A field hand by the 1820s was worth on the Richmond slave market less than one-half of his value fifty years earlier. Besides, they said, echoing a thought early advanced by Jefferson in his *Notes on the State of Virginia,* slavery tied half of the state to a ruinous system of staple crop agriculture which destroyed the fertility of the soil with repeated harvesting of the same crop year after year, generation after generation.

Such criticisms were justified. Most lowland Virginia farmers owned slaves, and even those who did not continued to raise the region's traditional products, especially tobacco. In the county of Sussex, located in the Tidewater (map 2), 62.8 percent of the families were slaveholders in 1840. The census of 1840, the first to list occupations, showed that only 1.5 percent of Sussex families were in nonagricultural manufac-

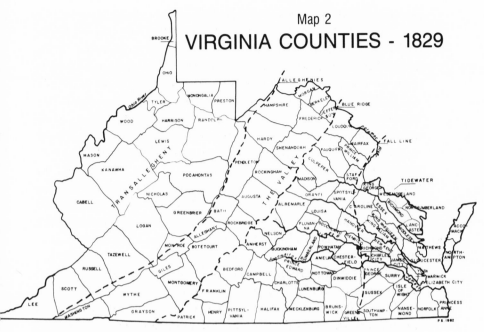

Map 2
VIRGINIA COUNTIES - 1829

Adapted from Daniel P. Jordan, Political Leadership in Jefferson's Virginia *(Charlottesville: University Press of Virginia, 1983), 5.*

turing, .05 percent were in commerce, and .08 percent in the learned professions. In the Northern Neck county of Lancaster, 99 percent of the families were in agriculture, and of these, 99 percent were slaveholders. Only one percent of Lancaster families were involved in commerce, and there were no manufacturers or professionals among them. In the Piedmont county of Halifax, 89.5 percent of the families were in agriculture, with 50 percent owning slaves. Four percent of Halifax families were in manufacturing, and none in commerce. Only .05 percent of the families made their living in the professions.[4]

While slave-based plantation agriculture was characteristic of lowland Virginia, occupational diversity was the dominant feature of the West. Small yeomen farmers and craftsmen were found everywhere. In Rockingham County in the middle of the Valley, 86 percent of the farm families owned no slaves. In Tazewell County in the southwest mountains, 72 percent of the farmers were without slaves. There were 123 slaveowning farmers living in this county, but 102 of them had less than five field hands. Nonfarming families, a rarity in the East, were seen all over the West. For example, where none of the adult white males in Lancaster County and only 1.5 percent of those living in Sussex were manufacturers, the figure in Rockingham was 19.6 percent. Similarly, adult white males engaged in the professions were more numerous in the West. In Sussex only .08 percent of the residents were professionals, none was so classified in Lancaster, and in Halifax only .05 percent were in the learned professions. In Rockingham 1 percent, of the adult white male population was professional—a ratio of 20 to 1 greater than the number of professionals in Halifax and about 12 to 1 greater than in Sussex.[5]

Differences between East and West also were present in class structure and social mobility. The tax records show that the East was a static agrarian society layered in five strata. At the bottom of the structure in the Tidewater county of Sussex were the laborers, adult white males with no taxable land or personal property. They comprised 182 families in 1830, and of that number 123 were listed as tenants. This class made up about 30 percent of the population. The next group was the lower middle class of farmers who had title to under 100 acres of land and paid personal property taxes under $2 a year. They were almost 20 percent of the county residents. The middle-class farmers, about 40 percent of Sussex families, owned from 100 to 500 acres and paid personal property taxes of $2 to $5 each year. The upper-middle-class planters, men with 500 to 1,000 acres who paid $5 to $10 in personal property taxes, constituted 8 percent of the population. At the top, the fifth layer, were the gentry. They numbered just 2 percent of the population of the county but owned over one-third of the taxable land.[6]

People in Sussex County stayed in the class in which they had been born. There was almost no vertical movement upward or downward among the classes. In this county, of fifty representative individuals who owned under $100 of personal property in 1810, only nine men, or 18 percent, showed any increase in their holdings twenty years later; and for most of these farmers the improvement was slight, that is, within class lines. Typical of this listing was Bryant Fonnell, who owned 190 acres in 1819 along with five slaves and three horses and paid a personal property tax of $2.56. He was a middle-class Sussex planter. Eleven years later Fonnell owned 250 acres, eight slaves, and four horses and paid a personal property tax of $3.12. What movement that could be detected in Sussex was not vertical but horizontal, out of the county. For example, 58 percent of the representative sample disappeared from the tax records between 1810 and 1830. Even allowing for normal attrition by death, the migration out of Sussex was extraordinarily high. Although no one can determine for sure, many of these men probably moved to the western part of the state or out of Virginia altogether.[7]

It was understandable how Sussex men might have been lured to the opportunities of the Valley or the mountains. The social profile of the Valley county of Augusta, for instance, shows a community much more fluid and mobile than anything seen at the time east of the Blue Ridge. Most residents of the county were farmers of small acreage or farm laborers, that is, of the lower class. Roughly 70 percent of all adult white males in 1830 were in this category, compared to Sussex's 50 percent. The middle class of yeomen farmers and property owners, those owning 100 to 500 acres, made up about 29 percent of the total white adult males. The upper middle class and the county aristocracy combined amounted to only about 1 percent of the total, in contrast to Sussex's 10 percent combination. And, unlike Sussex, these upper classes showed a decline in number since in 1810 when the upper-middle-class and large landowners had constituted 3 percent of the total population. During the same twenty-year period the amount of land owned by the two upper classes also decreased, indicating wider distribution of wealth in the county.[8]

The likely beneficiary of change was the Augusta middle class, which increased in numbers and wealth between 1810 and 1830. The town of Waynesboro had only forty-four members of this class in 1810, but twenty years later there were eighty-one members, only thirteen of whom had been on the 1810 list. A study of the traceable names of the lower middle class also reveals a high degree of vertical mobility. Of thirty-six residents who owned less than 100 acres of land in 1810, nineteen showed substantial property increase by 1830, some increasing their holdings over ten times. Land records for lower-class town dwellers in Augusta show that of fourteen listed in 1810 as owning plots valued at less than $50, only one remained in this class in 1830. Horizontal movement into this Valley county was great: the adult white male population increased over 30 percent in twenty years.[9]

County tax records tell something of the social structure of the Allegheny section of Virginia. The lists of Tazewell County, located in the southern mountains, show a high percentage of landless adult white males (52 percent) and propertyless residents (38 percent). The county's middle class was large—close to 40 percent of the adult white male population. Tazewell records list a greater percentage of large landowners: 3 percent of the adult white males held 500 to 1,000 acres, and 5 percent held over 1,000 acres; but most of these large parcels were held by eastern land speculators, not by residents of Tazewell. Only three individuals living in the county had personal estates valued over $1,000. Slaveholding was rare in Tazewell County, and little tobacco was raised.[10]

Social mobility in Tazewell County, both vertical and horizontal, was greater than in any of the other counties examined. Of twenty-two individuals who owned less than 100 acres in 1810, fourteen were still around in 1830. Of this number, two had doubled their holdings, five had tripled their acreage, and one had increased his lands fourteen times. Four men had not increased their property, and one had lost land. Between 1810 and 1830, 66 percent of the adult white male population moved out of the lower middle class. Most of the men moved to the middle class, which grew from only 12 percent of the adult white population in 1810 to 44 percent in 1830. Downward movement from the upper classes was marked: the upper middle class and the aristocracy both declined between 1810 and 1830. During the same twenty years the number of Tazewell adult white males involved in commerce increased four times; all the new merchants had entered the county after 1810. The white population doubled in size between 1810 and 1830, indicative of the high degree of horizontal mobility. The general picture of western society in the mountains as revealed by Tazewell County records is one of considerable mobility within the class structure and a general pattern of leveling toward the middle class.[11]

Such changes in Virginia's society broadened the base of constitutional reform beyond the legal and philosophical issues posed by Jefferson and others after the 1776 Convention. By the early nineteenth century, constitutional questions were tied to, and indistinguishable from, a sectional contest for political power. The East—gentry dominated, homogeneous, socially static, and committed to the status quo—faced a challenge for control of the state government from the heterogeneous, mobile, and forward-looking Virginians of the West. In these circumstances, the question of constitutional reform became a sectional football. At the heart of the revived interest in rewriting the fundamental law was the plain fact that the West's most pressing needs— better internal improvements and more banking facilities, for example—could be met only by reducing eastern opposition to these changes in the legislature. The way to achieve this goal, western spokesmen argued, was to change the constitution and give their region the representation in the legislature, and the corresponding political power, its ever-increasing population and wealth deserved. And the only way to do that was to call a constitutional convention.

In the beginning the focus of the sectional struggle over constitutional reform was on procedure, on the need for a convention to rewrite the law. The demand for a convention had a certain history to it by the early nineteenth century because during the Revolution both Jefferson and Madison had latched on to the idea. From the start of their collaboration to change the 1776 constitution through statute, the two men had always condemned the illegitimacy of the document because it had been spawned by a mere legislature. Jefferson,

especially, saw a specially elected convention as the foundation for a much more democratic method of making fundamental law than that followed in Williamsburg. He wanted a
convention elected by the people for the sole purpose of con-
sidering the constitution, popular ratification of the resulting
document, and a feasible process of amendment.[12] Madison,
on his part, tried twice to float the convention idea in the
General Assembly, and both times it fell flat. In 1783 he
wrote to his father that "it is generally expected [that] a convention for the purposes of reforming our Constitution will
be proposed to the people as soon as the assemble meets."
But Mason would have none of it. The powerful Fairfax
County planter felt that Virginia had to be cautious about
any tampering with what had been done seven years earlier.
Moreover, he feared what might happen if the procedure got
out of hand. Mason imagined future assemblies repeating
the process of convention calling, he wrote to William Cabell,
"until the Constitution shall have totally lost stability, and Anarchy introduced in its Stead."[13]

Madison tried one more time. In May 1784 he backed a
request for a convention submitted by Archibald Stuart of
Augusta County. Madison knew the resolution would fail,
but with the support of Richard Henry Lee behind it, he
thought it might generate some "favorable sentiments." So,
he wrote to Jefferson, "we thought it might not be amiss to
stir the matter." But Lee was ill and never showed up at Richmond, where the legislature now sat, and Patrick Henry took
a fit. The governor denounced the idea more violently than
even Madison had expected. After just two days of discussion
the resolution was trounced by a huge majority. Not content,
the Henry majority "availed themselves of their strength to
put a supposed bar . . . against a future possibility of carrying
it." A convention could not be called by a future legislature
until directed to do so by "a majority of all the free people of
the state." And that was that, as far as a convention was concerned. Madison's attention soon shifted to national events
and to reforming the national constitution. Jefferson, after
his return from Paris in 1789, focused his activities and energies on running the federal government and, shortly, toward

opposing its foreign and domestic policies. In Virginia, Henry, ever the spokesman for the gentry, crushed all efforts to reform the fundamental law.[14]

In 1802, three years after Henry's death, the first petition for a convention was sent to the General Assembly from the West, but nothing was done about it. Again in 1805 another petition was mailed to Richmond from the Valley; this time there was a debate on the issue. John Burwell of Henry County in the southwest Piedmont adjacent to North Carolina focused, as had Jefferson and Madison, on the question of representation. He said that the 1776 scheme of two delegates from each county in the lower house, regardless of the county's population, was a violation of the basic principle of the national constitution, majority rule in the House of Representatives. He also noted how expensive it was to have the state to pay for the two-delegate system; an apportionally organized legislature would need far fewer delegates. He said, as a final point, that the petition for a convention correctly called attention to the rigidity of the 1776 document. Its uniform county apportionment did not at all reflect recent population shifts toward the Valley and mountains during the last twenty years, shown indisputably in the 1790 and 1800 federal censuses. General John B. Minor of Henrico County spoke against the petition and summed up the feelings of most of his colleagues from that section in a version of Mason's caution of 1783. Minor stated that "this valuable instrument" should not be jeopardized by setting it "adrift on a sea of uncertainty." "We are well, so let us remain and not imitate him, who being well, wished to be better, took physic, and died." The vote on the petition was taken at the end of January 1805 and was defeated by an almost two-to-one vote of 98 to 58.[15]

In 1807 delegates from Patrick and Henry counties, now backed by both delegates from Pittsylvania County, again presented petitions for a convention to the legislature. This time the effort passed the lower house but was killed in the senate. In the next three meetings of the General Assembly, petitions from western counties asking for a convention failed to generate the support they had received in 1807, and during these years "no strenuous efforts were made for a convention." The hopes of the reformers were aroused briefly in 1810 when delegates from Accomack, a maritime county on Virginia's Eastern Shore, joined the cause and asked not for a convention but at least for a readjustment of representation and elimination of the freehold suffrage requirement. Encouraged by this unexpected eastern support, Valley delegates asked that the question of a constitutional convention be submitted to the people in a referendum. It was defeated in the House of Delegates by a sectional vote of 82 to 79, East against, West for.[16]

During the War of 1812 petitions regularly trickled into the legislature reiterating the demand for a convention, but with Virginians preoccupied perhaps more than any other southern state with the war, they received little attention. With the coming of peace, the issue of constitutional reform once again moved to center stage at Richmond. In 1815 the General Assembly received a package of petitions, from Patrick, Rockingham, Frederick, Hampshire, Greenbrier, Shenandoah, Ohio, and Brooke counties, all demanding a referendum on a convention. The reformers in the lower house then introduced a bill to take the issue to the people. Again the proposal was defeated by a margin of three votes, 90 to 87.[17]

The persistent stand of most eastern legislators against a constitutional convention led to a flare-up of popular expressions of dissatisfaction in the West. At Winchester in August 1816 representatives from eleven western counties attended a meeting at which they formally protested the General Assembly's refusal to respond to the need for constitutional change. That same summer other gatherings were held throughout the Valley and Allegheny counties to demand action from Richmond. In all of these meetings the proposed changes were the same: rewrite the constitution to base representation in the lower house on white population exclusively and to extend the suffrage to all adult white males.[18]

The most significant gathering of reformers that year took place at the town of Staunton, located in the center of the Valley. Here, from August 19 to 23, sixty-five delegates from thirty-five western counties discussed their grievances against the constitution and, particularly, against the eastern-dominated legislature. Indeed, the most-heard complaint by far was the now familiar charge of unfair representation in the lower house. Reformers also denounced the freehold suffrage requirement, and although not specific as to exactly what changes should be made, they agreed on the need for some reduction in the existing freehold requirement. The Staunton Convention adjourned after adopting a memorial addressed to the General Assembly which listed their complaints.[19]

The Staunton Memorial summarized forty years of objections against the 1776 constitution. It showed how the small eastern counties, with less than half of the state's white population, controlled most of the seats in the legislature. Moreover, because the General Assembly was the single most powerful body in the state under the existing constitution, the lowland minority held virtually a perpetual sway over Virginia's political life. For example, on the issues of apportionment and the franchise, any legislative change toward a more democratic system of government would, obviously, need eastern support. But this support, the reformers pointed out, would never come because for the East it amounted to political suicide. The memorial closed with a demand for a constitutional convention.[20]

The same summer that saw the strengthening of reform opposition throughout the West also saw the publication of a letter written by Jefferson on July 16, 1816, to Samuel Kercheval, a leader of the proconvention groups from the Valley. This letter became "a text for the preachers of reform." In it Jefferson sketched his early, unsuccessful efforts to revise the constitution and reiterated most of his criticisms of the document. He suggested that representation in the lower house of the legislature be based only upon white population, that suffrage be extended to all free white adult males, and that there be popular election of local officials and of the governor. Jefferson, then the revered former president and "sage of Monticello," in that single letter gave his blessing to the reform; in fact, he sanctified it.[21]

The reaction of most lowland politicians to the idea of a convention was to dig in and refuse to go along. They insisted, rather, that the Constitution of 1776 was a near perfect form of government and that to tamper with it would be to invite, at best, disorder and unrest. Besides, conservatives pointed out, there was no agreement among reformers themselves as to exactly what changes should be made. Some reformers wished to change only the system of representation and apportionment; others wanted to go beyond this to modify the suffrage requirement; and still others like Jefferson and Kercheval hoped under the cover of a constitutional convention to overthrow the time-tested institutions of county government. They lectured reformers that the venerable constitution deserved more respect than they had given it, if for no other reason than out of deference to the work of the great men of the Revolution who in their wisdom gave Virginia its fundamental law.

Not all easterners took such a patronizing line, however. Thomas Ritchie, editor of the *Richmond Enquirer* and crusader for a state system of public education, was one of these. Privately he warned his friends of the political danger of ignoring the widespread and growing discontent. Drawing a lesson from the past, Ritchie reminded his readers that they could ill afford to repeat the mistake made by the Federalists after 1800 when they ignored public opinion. No, said Ritchie, the clamor for constitutional reform must be dealt with and, more important, be controlled.[22]

This sort of pragmatic advice had effect. Although conservatives in the 1816–17 General Assembly held their ground against a convention, some joined with reformers in the passage of the first concession to the western region of the state, a bill establishing representation in the senate upon white population. In addition, eastern delegates gave the West two economic bones to chew on, promises to improve the internal transportation of the Old Dominion and to establish more branch banks west of the Blue Ridge. To the delight of lowland politicians, the appeasement worked. Petitions to the legislature for a new constitution ceased, and for a few years the focus of public attention shifted once more to national events: to policies of economic nationalism, called the American System, emanating from Congress, to the nationalistic decisions of the Marshall Court, and to the ominous implications of federal power raised by the debate over the entrance of Missouri into the Union.[23]

But this "era of good feelings" in the commonwealth was short-lived. The panic of 1819 and ensuing depression created economic distress, and eastern planters, their pockets pinched by declining prices and falling land values, questioned the feasibility of going through with their promise of expensive internal improvements for the western part of the state. To westerners, this turnabout on internal improvements was a clear sign that sectional differences were going to remain acute. The publication of the federal census of 1820 reinforced their suspicions. The census showed beyond a doubt that the white population was steadily increasing in the West, while most of the lowland country showed a decline or at best a stabilization of its white population. The data only heightened western frustration with the unfair representation in the House of Delegates. The argument of 1816 was restated: only when the West received its full share of political power would its views be respected and its needs be met by the state government, and this power could be gained only by rewriting the undemocratic Constitution of 1776. Newspapers began again to complain of the "misrule and oppression" by the East, but now a new psychological penumbra was added, race. The East was no longer referred to as a geographic or economic entity but was called the "slave-owning eastern aristocracy."[24]

As in 1816, when popular agitation for reform intensified, a few alert lowland politicians realized that once more, for political necessity, concessions were in order. Moreover, there were maverick reform pockets appearing, like cold sores, in the East. By the mid-1820s isolated areas in that section began to join the West in demanding the elimination of the freehold suffrage qualification. With dismay, conservatives read reports of meetings in support of suffrage reform in Richmond, Lynchburg, and on the Eastern Shore. At the same time petitions started to pour in regularly from western

counties demanding that the General Assembly call a constitutional convention.[25]

At Monticello the aging Jefferson gave his final effort in
the cause of constitutional reform. Writing an open letter to
the *Richmond Enquirer* in the spring of 1824, Jefferson
charged, as he had almost fifty years before, that the system
of state government was "in opposition to the principle of
equal political rights"; it was "merely arbitrary and an assumption of the minority over the majority." "Upon what
principle of right or reason," Jefferson asked John Hampden
Pleasants with infallible logic, "can anyone justify the giving
to every citizen of Warwick as much weight in the government as to twenty-two equal citizens in Loudoun?"[26]

In this atmosphere the reformers called another meeting
at Staunton in the summer of 1825. On the afternoon of July
25 over 100 delegates representing thirty-one counties denounced the eastern establishment as an "odious landed aristocracy who ruled the true majority through a violation of
true principles of a free republic." After a week of discussion
they adopted a formal resolution demanding representation
in the lower house on the basis of white population only and
the extension of suffrage to all adult white males. As before,
this assembly drew up a signed memorial and sent it to the
legislature. In the months between the second Staunton Convention and the convening of the General Assembly, the fight
over a constitutional convention became intense. Throughout the state "friends of reform" circulated the memorial in
a determined effort to put pressure on their government to
call a convention. As a result of their efforts, forty-five petitions demanding a referendum were ready for the legislature when it met at Richmond in December.[27]

During the late summer and fall of 1825 eastern conservatives fretted over the effect of the Staunton Convention and
its memorial. "I do hold it all important to disappoint that
Staunton Convention—totally," remarked Richmond attorney Benjamin Watkins Leigh. "Defeat, utter defeat, can alone
alleviate all the ill consequences of the example." He smeared
reformers as "inciters to anarchy and disunion" and "viola-

tors of the true Republican principles." Leigh, in a series of
articles published in the *Richmond Enquirer* under the name
of "Mason of '76," blasted away at the idea of constitutional
reform, the Staunton Convention, and the infamous father
of reform, Thomas Jefferson. In an effort to counter the impact of the Staunton Memorial, conservatives drew up and
circulated their own memorial. It ridiculed the reformers as
disguised Federalists and Clayite nationalists who would, if
given the chance, lead the Old Dominion away from the
"true Principles of '98," the doctrine of states' rights first articulated by those Virginians who in 1798 fought against the
hated Sedition Act.[28]

In the West the reform movement gathered more and
more support. By the summer of 1826 some eastern politicians, just as a decade earlier, talked about finding a means
of quieting and controlling the growing discontent. By re-
sourceful, calculated, and limited concessions the conservatives hoped to be able once again to calm an aroused
electorate. So, in the place of diatribes against reform and
stubborn resistance to the rise of "radical democracy," some
conservatives, again led by Ritchie, gave restrained backing
for a constitutional convention.

When the legislature met in December 1826, only Leigh,
Abel Parker Upshur, a stalwart conservative planter-lawyer
from Northampton County, and a few of their followers
stood as rigid opponents to calling a convention. Yet their
stand was more tempered than the position taken the previous autumn. Instead of immediate and outright rejection of
a bill that asked for a referendum on the convention, Leigh
and Upshur urged their supporters "to curb their opposition." Their strategy was to allow full debate on the bill so as
to give the impression that conservatives might be weaken-
ing. In the meantime Leigh and Upshur would get better
organized in the house. Then, just when reformers would
likely be most off guard, conservatives could rally not only to
defeat the referendum bill but also to call for and carry a vote
to squelch the whole idea of changing the constitution. As
planned, conservative opposition to the referendum took the

form of a series of amendments that, if a convention was called, would allow the legislature to determine its agenda. It was a camouflage.[29]

Some reformers in the house, like James M. Mason from the northern Valley county of Frederick, saw through the stalwarts' subterfuge and called upon Upshur on the floor of the house to explain the real meaning of his "agenda" amendments and to state openly his position on the convention. Having little choice, Upshur laid out the conservative argument. He, and others, believed that the reformers were grossly mistaken in their perception that Virginians really wanted to rewrite the constitution along more democratic lines. Citizens of the Old Dominion, Upshur insisted, wished to retain the freehold suffrage because of their disillusionment with the "intrigues and corruptions" that plagued other states under the "wild and demoralizing system" of universal white manhood suffrage. "Shall he who possesses no property," Upshur asked, "be permitted to dictate laws for regulating the property of others?" Upshur, at this point, left untouched the other issue of apportionment in the legislature.[30]

After a week of long, vigorous debate and behind-the-scenes maneuvering, reformers were able to defeat Upshur's "agenda" amendments by a vote of 107 to 97. Undaunted, the stalwarts then tried to postpone the referendum vote until the next session of the General Assembly, but on January 27, 1827, this measure also failed to pass, by a vote of 103 to 98. As a last resort, Upshur and the diehards introduced a technical point of who should be qualified to vote on the issue of a convention if a referendum was called for. No one had a ready answer. The result was a three-week delay on a final vote on the referendum, and because of this delay, reformers lost their momentum. Through early February, Upshur, by "emphasizing and exaggerating the demands of the extremist [reform] minority," was able to get the support of enough delegates to gain a slim conservative majority. This hastily formed coalition defeated the referendum bill in late February 1827 by a vote of 107 to 103.[31]

Exasperated, reformers decided to bypass the legislature

and to take the issue directly to the people. They would ask the voters of every county in the upcoming spring elections to select delegates to the next General Assembly with specific instructions as to how they should vote on the question of a convention referendum. The April general election, in spite of Upshur's success in the legislature, was in fact a public referendum on constitutional reform. By the time the polls closed, most candidates had received clear indications as to what position their constituents wished them to take when they went to Richmond that fall.[32]

When the General Assembly gathered in the capital in December 1827, most eastern delegates, even the stalwarts, had little hope of prolonging their opposition. It was not just that the rising popular pessure for a convention could not be controlled. If they held out any longer, things would only get worse. If a constitutional convention was delayed until after the appearance of the next federal census in 1830, which it was assumed would show the decided majority of white Virginians living west of the Blue Ridge, reformers would be in a much more formidable position. With these twin political realities in mind, some conservatives began to see advantages in having a convention before the West benefited from the most recent demographic data and gained more delegates. As a result, when a bill was introduced to give the people the opportunity to vote "Convention" or "No Convention," most conservatives gave it their support. The bill passed the lower house in January 1828 by a margin of 114 to 86 and the senate in early February by 14 to 10.[33]

Thus, after an on-again, off-again fight running over half a century, reformers at last had forced the question of a constitutional convention out of the legislature. Now they waited to see whether their efforts would be worthwhile. In the spring of 1828 the polls opened. By June the returns were in and counted; 21,896 votes had been cast in favor of a convention, and only 16,637 Virginians voted against the idea. As map 3 shows, almost all the affirmative votes came from west of the Blue Ridge while most of the East was still solid in its opposition to a new constitution.[34]

It fell to the next session of the General Assembly, meeting

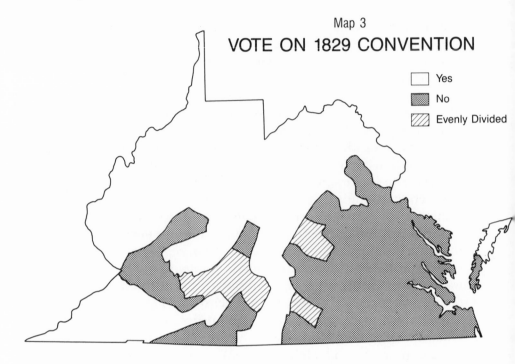

Map 3
VOTE ON 1829 CONVENTION

☐ Yes
▨ No
▨ Evenly Divided

in December 1828, to devise some acceptable plan of organizing the convention. On this problem sectional lines were again sharply drawn, for understandable reasons. Reformers, led by Philip Doddridge of far-off Brooke County, a panhandle appendage jutting up between Pennsylvania and Ohio, demanded that delegates to the convention be apportioned on the basis of white population. Such a plan, naturally, would give the more populous reform areas, even by the 1820 census figures, a higher number of delegates. Some eastern conservatives wanted representation on a county basis, while others advocated a system that took into account slaves, such as the three-fifths formula used in Congress. Reformers, however, kept a united front in their insistence on the white basis, holding caucus after caucus in order to determine consensus on the best means to defeat the conservatives.[34]

By this time a few moderate members of the eastern camp, led by William Fitzhugh Gordon, friend and neighbor of the recently deceased Jefferson, questioned the effectiveness of continued opposition to the reform position. Gordon, aided by Thomas Ritchie and the influential *Richmond Enquirer,* pointed out that the die-hard stand had only enhanced the position of the reformers in the public eye during the past years. Ritchie, always the pragmatist, argued that both reformers and conservatives should abandon their respective demands and support his compromise: use the existing twenty-four senatorial districts as the basis of electing delegates to the convention. His plan gave each district four delegates.[36]

The stalwarts in the House of Delegates, however, ignored this advice and introduced a bill in late January 1829 stipulating that the three-fifths system be used as the standard to organize the convention. But lacking the support of a number of lowland delegates who had been won over to the Ritchie plan, the measure was rejected. Next the diehards tried to have the county system, that is, two convention delegates per county, accepted, but it too failed to pass. After no fewer than twelve plans from all sides were presented, debated, and discarded, a bill providing for the senatorial district scheme was finally introduced in early February 1829. The bill passed the senate on February 10, and two days later the House of Delegates gave its approval. With this compromise the first stage of an often bitter public struggle for constitutional reform in Virginia was over. The second stage of the battle, the drafting of a new constitution in the convention itself, was about to begin.[37]

IV

The Convention of 1829–30

IT WAS A COMFORTABLE EARLY AUTUMN in Richmond when the first delegates trickled into the rooms and boarding-houses close to the Roman Capitol designed by Jefferson some forty-three years before. Fifty-three years earlier, in the sweltering summer heat of the House of Burgesses at Williamsburg, another group of Virginians had wrestled with the problems of framing fundamental law. There, however, both the atmosphere and the questions had been different than they were in October 1829. Then government had broken down, war was in the progress, and the future was dim and uncertain. The deep concerns of the Virginia gentry in 1776 were how to keep the liberties they enjoyed and to establish sovereignty in the people. They faced the challenge of how to structure a new system of government whereby tyranny would be prevented from ever again encroaching upon the rights of the governed; where power, through institutionalized checks and balances, would be limited. The task in 1776 had been to construct a constitution as a limiting document and to have it prevent tyranny and guarantee liberty. They focused, accordingly, upon a declaration of rights, control of executive power, and the preeminent authority of the legislative branch of the state government. But in Richmond in the fall of 1829 many Virginians were more concerned with questions of how to make this legislature more responsible to the will of the majority of the state's people and how to broaden the participation of those people in their government. In other words, most Virginians now wanted to expand and share power through changes in the existing constitution. Other Virginians, the eastern minority, opposed these changes.

The Convention of 1829–30 was high theater, a second gathering of the gods to some Virginians, and, indeed, many of the participants were prominent figures of national and state public life. One man had even sat in the Convention of 1776: James Madison, seventy-eight years old, weak from a recent bout of bilious fever but mentally alert. His friend James Monroe came to Richmond, fragile at the age of seventy-one, still dressed in the knee breeches of eighteenth-century vogue; the last of the three-cornered hats they called him. Chief Justice John Marshall, at seventy-four, took time off from his busy docket to ride the some eighty miles south to the Virginia capital. Two United States senators came, the pale, squeaky-voiced John Randolph of Roanoke and Littleton Waller Tazewell of Norfolk, in his fifth year in the United States Senate chamber. Governor William Branch Giles, sixty-seven years of age and at death's door, traveled with extreme difficulty from his 5,000-acre plantation in Amelia County to attend, but not to participate in, the proceedings. A future president, John Tyler, was there as a thirty-nine-year-old delegate from Charles City County. Spectators outnumbered the participants; Richmond buzzed with foreign dignitaries and visitors from far and near who crammed together in the Capitol to witness the Old Dominion's first real constitutional convention.[1]

The opening day, Monday, October 5, dawned bright and clear. At noon, the weather crisp and pleasant, the delegates took their seats. By that hour an immense crowd had packed itself into the gallery that overlooked the floor of the House of Delegates, the forum where the forensic display was to be acted out. Nothing much happened. Folks saw the tottering Madison get up to nominate Monroe, as expected, to be the Convention's president. He was approved unanimously. Monroe, even more feeble, was helped to the Speaker's chair by Madison and Marshall. The Convention immediately selected its other officers, a clerk and vice-chair, and adjourned. A few days later Monroe stepped down temporarily because of ill health, to be replaced by Philip P. Barbour of Orange County (former Speaker of the United States House of Representatives), and the delegates got down to work.[2]

Virginia's 1829–30 constitutional convention came toward the end of a series of such conventions called to rewrite the states' fundamental law. Indeed, it was "the last of the great constituent assemblies in American history," and the issues were urgent.[3] All the major constitutional questions that had divided the state into East and West were, finally, to be aired in an open forum of the people's delegates. There were the crucial reforms, demanded by the West, in legislative apportionment and extension of the suffrage. And inseparable from abstract legal arguments on either side about liberty, property rights, natural law, and democracy was the future course of two increasingly divergent ways of life. As the delegates went along, it was apparent that in the minds of most Virginians, in and out of the Convention, constitutional reform was equated with the survival of one life-style or the other. There was in Richmond that fall and winter a feeling of Armageddon. The two societies, one based on slave labor and the other largely free white, could not, many felt, exist together under the same constitution. It must be, as Abraham Lincoln phrased it thirty years later, "all one way, or all the other."

As the aged Madison sank back in his chair, he must have been struck with the contrasts between this convention and the one he attended in the prime of young manhood. Before, the delegates had been friends, of the gentry class, often related. Their goal, to build a workable republic, had been the same. Although there were loose factions, called Tuckahoes and Southsiders, the squabbles between them had been over the best means to achieve this common goal, never over the final aims of government itself. Before, there had been a large and cohesive plantation economy. Its social values were assumed rather than discussed: slavery, for example, was never seriously debated in the 1776 convention as a constitutional issue. But now, in 1829, the ninety-six assembled Virginians were men deeply divided and different, in appearance, values, interests, and in their views of the

purpose of government. Madison's own section was now led
by manipulative conservatives like Leigh and Upshur whose
objective in being in Richmond was to block all changes in
the 1776 document. So the plantation society of Virginia, to
Madison, had to appear as no longer led by the enlightened,
rational, forward-looking gentlemen of the eighteenth century, his generation of Virginia gentlemen, but rather by
young obstructionists. The other half of the state, the West,
was fed up with such conservativism and deeply resentful of
the eastern slaveholding plantation aristocracy. It was led by
the dark, phlegmatic, Scotch-Irish Allegheny orator Philip
Doddridge and by Valley delegate and moderate John R.
Cooke, a Winchester lawyer whom one eastern onlooker described as "ugly" and "his actions despicable."[4]

The men whom the people of these two sections sent to
Richmond reflected their constituency to a remarkable degree. A brief profile analysis of a few selected categories—
occupation, education, religion, and social structure—reveals a consistent parallel between the convention and the
state itself. It was, put simply, a microcosm of Jacksonian Virginia. Take the category of occupation. An occupational profile of eastern delegates showed the domination of slave-
based agriculture in that group. Almost 73 percent of the
Tidewater delegates were involved with slave-based farming
either as large planters (46 percent) or as planter-lawyers
(26.7 percent). The remaining 27 percent were lawyers, but
many of them came from plantation families. The Piedmont's voters elected 36 percent of its men from the planter
group, and 48 percent of its delegates were planter-lawyers,
so that a higher percentage (83 percent) were directly supported by slave-based agriculture than the Tidewater.

Western delegates, on the other hand, reflected that section's diversity of occupation. Just 10 percent of the Valley
delegates and 14.5 percent of the Allegheny delegates were
planters or planter-lawyers. No eastern delegates earned
their living in manufacturing, but 15 percent of the Valley
and 4.5 percent of the mountain delegates were so classified.
In commerce, the western men contrasted with the East.
Only 4 percent of the lowland delegates were merchants, but

28 percent of the West's men were in this occupation, and within that category there was considerable variety. Also among the western delegates were a banker, two physicians, a prison warden, and an evangelist. Only two easterners were earning a living outside of the planter and lawyer groups: one, William Campbell of Bedford County, was an innkeeper; the other, Samuel Clayton, was a wealthy Lynchburg tobacco merchant. Both of these men, it turned out, became mavericks who voted with the West on constitutional reforms.[5]

A second contrast was in the educational background of the two sections' delegates. The East, for over 100 years, had demanded a high level of education for its leaders, a requirement usually met by the family's hiring a tutor for the young men until they enrolled at the College of William and Mary or perhaps at Yale or Princeton. Others, if they did not go to college, most often pursued a career in law as an apprentice to some notable lawyer. In much of the West, though, education was a luxury that few could afford; one of its demands was the establishment by constitutional law of a system of general education at public expense. Early in the Convention debate, one eastern delegate openly charged that a hidden agenda of the reformers was "that the West are to be educated at the expense of the East." Not surprisingly, therefore, a significantly greater proportion of college graduates was found among the eastern delegates: 55 percent of them had received at least a bachelor's degree while among western delegates only 22 percent could claim a college education. What is more, 70 percent of the eastern college graduates had attended the same institution favored in colonial years, William and Mary, and of this number 60 percent had been at the college between 1800 and 1815.[6]

Biographies of the delegates also reflect important differences in religious and ethnic backgrounds. Eastern delegates were decidedly (63 percent) of the Episcopalian faith. Only 3 percent of the Tidewater men and 12 percent of Piedmont men were Presbyterians. There were no Baptists, Pietists, or Lutheran delegates from east of the Blue Ridge. Most eastern delegates were of British stock (83 percent), and the rest

were of mixed British and Huguenot blood. The Valley voters, however, elected only 24 percent and the Allegheny voters 5.5 percent of their delegation from men of British
ancestry. They preferred Scottish and Scotch-Irish (40 percent) men or German stock (8 percent for the Valley group
and 5.5 percent of the mountain delegation).[7]

Finally, the Convention mirrored sectional differences in
class structure and mobility. Western men, like the society
they represented, were mostly from families newly arrived,
both physically and in terms of prestige, in their localities.
Lowland delegates, however, came from families long established and influential in their communities. About 83 percent of the Tidewater and 66.6 percent of the Piedmont
delegates came from such colonial families, while just 2.8
percent from the former section and 4 percent from the latter one were newly arrived. Only 43.5 percent of Valley delegates were socially established in 1829, and only 26 percent
of the Allegheny delegates fell into this category. On the
other hand, 34.8 percent of Valley and 30 percent of the
mountain delegates were newly arrived—about fifteen times
the Tidewater percentage and eight times that of the Piedmont. Moreover, no delegates east of the Blue Ridge came
from immigrant families, but 13 percent of the Valley and 26
percent of the mountain delegates could be so classified.[8]

Before these serious sectional differences emerged to influence the course and outcome of debate on the constitution, President Barbour organized the first committees. He
divided responsibility for drafting the new document among
four committees—on the Declaration of Rights, the executive, the judiciary, and the legislature—and instructed each
of them to be ready to report back to the Convention in two
weeks. It was in the closed meetings of these four committees
that all of the real business was conducted during the first
three weeks, much to the disappointment of the impatient
public in the gallery. Although no minutes were kept of the
committee meetings, it is possible to re-create some of what
happened there from the later debates on their respective
reports on the floor of the Convention, from ongoing news-
paper accounts at the time, and from diaries kept by a young

delegate from Norfolk, twenty-three-year-old Hugh Blair Grigsby, and by a thirty-one-year-old Richmond attorney, Thomas Green.[9]

The basic question before the Committee on the Declaration of Rights, chaired by the huge, six-foot, 300-pound Samuel Taylor of Caroline County, was whether to keep the original version or to change it and include universal white manhood suffrage and proportional representation in the legislature. Robert B. Taylor of Norfolk, one of the few eastern committeemen sympathic to constitutional reform, wished to add a clause providing for these guarantees. A majority balked at the challenge and decided to keep the declaration as it was and to delay any discussion of such controversial changes until the "more practical" parts of the constitution were debated. In reporting to the Convention on October 19, the committee recommended no changes, and the Convention, acting as a committee of the whole, initially accepted the report.[10]

The Committee on the Executive, titularly under sickly William B. Giles, concerned itself with the rather innocuous idea that the executive council be abolished. Giles and committeeman Abel P. Upshur defended the privy council, as they called it, arguing that it was an essential check on executive tyranny. Reformers on the committee charged that the council was, in fact, little more than a conservative tool because it had been long dominated by the East. Western committeemen were also disgusted with the council's historic opposition to internal improvements for their section. The committee voted to abolish the council. The reformers then tried to change the way in which the governor was elected but got nowhere in committee.[11]

The Committee on the Judiciary, chaired by John Marshall, recommended only slight alterations in the existing system. Judges of the higher courts, it suggested, should be elected by joint ballot of the legislature rather than appointed by the governor. But the county court system with its appointed justices and officers should remain as it was.[12]

The Committee on the Legislature, guided by Madison, dealt with the all-important issues of representation and suffrage. Outstanding leaders of both sides offered their views. Doddridge and John R. Cooke insisted that the committee adopt the white basis of representation for the House of Delegates and extend the right of suffrage to all white adult males. John Randolph of Roanoke, Littleton Waller Tazewell, Benjamin Watkins Leigh, Judge John Green, and John Tyler took the traditional line that neither the present system of representation nor the freehold suffrage qualification should be changed. The progressive reformers, supported for a while at this early stage of discussion by Madison, had a 13-to-11 majority and adopted the white basis plan. On the suffrage issue, a memorandum written by Madison asking for basic changes in suffrage requirements was circulated among convention delegates, to the consternation of eastern delegates. Reformers, by an unrecorded vote, won a second important victory and had their position accepted by the committee.[13]

It was now the beginning of the third week in October, and despite the committee activity little substantive action upon important issues had occurred on the floor of the Convention. The public had observed only routine appointments and the comings and goings of some famous delegates. To onlookers in the Capitol who came expecting to see a dramatic debate, events had been disappointing. Late in the afternoon of October 26, a Monday, Madison asked for the floor to report the findings of the Legislative Committee. Standing in the middle of the delegation at the clerk's table, he spoke in a thin, clear voice: "Resolved, that in the apportionment of representation in the House of Delegates regard should be had to the white population exclusively." Judge John W. Green, a Culpeper planter and justice of the Supreme Court of Appeals, quickly spoke up. Strike out the word "exclusively" and add instead "and taxation combined." Here, finally, was the central question for which the Convention had been called. Time had arrived to adjourn for the day, but onlookers knew that the real debate they had come to hear would finally begin on Tuesday morning.[14]

The atmosphere surrounding the opening of full debate was apprehensive on both sides. Progressives muttered that since easterners dominated the Convention in number of delegates, because it had been elected not on the basis of population but rather on senatorial districts, the outcome was a foregone conclusion. The East would never give up the political power it had managed to retain for two generations after independence to a constitutional reform that redistricted the House of Delegates. The slaveowners would never jeopardize their property, and their own personal interest, by relinquishing control of the Old Dominion to the non-slaveholding West. Eastern delegates were uneasy. Richmond attorney John Wickham told Norfolk delegate Littleton Waller Tazewell a most upsetting piece of news. When he dined with John Marshall and other lowland delegates late in September, these gentlemen had said that while many eastern men were "opposed to a convention and friends to free-hold suffrage and the protection of slave property," they were thinking seriously about allowing a new constitution to be ratified by "the people at large" and not by just the freehold voters. Even this after-the-fact concession caused Wickham and others enormous anxiety because to them this appeasement meant the beginning of "the plundering of their property by raising their taxes and emancipating their slaves."[15]

So, before the actual arguments for and against constitutional reapportionment were articulated, the hidden issue began to surface. The power of taxation was automatically joined with reapportionment in the eastern mind to equate to a western conspiracy to destroy slavery. A gut reflex gripped the eastern delegates and clouded their thinking on constitutional rights from the beginning of the convention debates. Slavery must be defended at all costs. In a psychological sense the Virginia Convention of 1829–30 was a dress rehearsal for the entire South during the next thirty years. In the speeches and voting patterns of the lowland traditionalist could be seen the fatal southern neurosis: no change could be tolerated if it appeared to tamper with the slaveowner's control over his human property.

Some, a few, eastern delegates were more composed in early October. Tazewell told his friend Wickham to calm down. No doubt the delegates would become preoccupied with philosophical abstractions, like natural rights and majority rule, and they probably would never get around to the more crucial issues like representation, taxation, and ratification procedures. The debates, Tazewell thought, would be harmless. Besides, Tazewell pointed out, every one of Virginia's 105 counties had slaveowners, and he saw no reason why the slaveholding interests of Virginia would not contrive to stick together even if the House of Delegates was reapportioned on the basis of population. Likewise, any extension of the suffrage would have no effect on the future of slavery in the Old Dominion.

By the last week of October, though, Tazewell had changed his mind. Publicly he complained about the lack of action on the floor, stating that he was bored "heartily sick." But privately he was extremely tense. He felt that he detected, in the talk of the delegates and in the committee maneuverings, "a most determined purpose to upturn everything from the very foundation, and a sufficient force perfectly organized for the completion of such a purpose." Tazewell's hunches were sound. The debates from the start focused upon the issue of aristocracy or democracy: would Virginia continue to be ruled by a propertied slaveholding minority, or would it be governed by the popular will alone? True enough, the progressives drew heavily upon the "abstract principles" of natural rights and the Declaration of Rights, but their attention was always on changing representation and suffrage— on creating a new structure of state government which would give them control of the commonwealth. Traditionalists, likewise, pulled out the principles of conservative philosophers like Edmund Burke and David Hume to legitimize their concepts of the protection of minorities against majority tyranny, the need for continuity and experience over untried ideas, and the necessity of defending the rights of those with an interest in society as opposed to giving in to unfettered democracy. But Leigh, Upshur, and the other stalwarts knew what they were after, support for keeping the state government exactly, or almost exactly, as it was and for maintaining the continued domination of the East over the West. So it was that Leigh explained to his colleagues: "We shall want every member at his post from the word *go*."[16]

Tuesday, October 27, broke as another delightful autumn morning along the James River. By eleven o'clock, the regular time set for the Convention to convene, the first large crowd in days had congregated on the Capitol steps. Judge Green took the floor, tried to talk, but was so stagestruck he had to sit down. After an awkward silence Benjamin Watkins Leigh, short, thin, with his conspicuous spectacles, stepped forward to the center of what must have seemed to the people in the gallery a Roman forum. Not yet ready to deliver his own arguments, Leigh pulled a debater's trick. He demanded that reformers justify their position and prove that the sacred Constitution of 1776 needed to be rewritten.[17]

John Rogers Cooke picked up Leigh's challenge and walked slowly down to the well of the House. Cooke, a former member of the legislature from Frederick County and then a United States congressman, had been a leader of constitutional reform since the Valley meetings of 1816. A Bermuda-born naturalized citizen, Cooke had settled in Martinsburg sometime before 1810 and later moved to practice law at Winchester. He began by guzzling glasses of water, an annoying habit that caused one observer to note caustically that he drank enough "to quench the thirst of a camel." Cooke was, despite the quirk, an indispensable floor leader of the western delegation and one of the crucial men leading the way for changes in the 1776 document.[18]

Cooke, to start with, insisted upon rewriting the constitution to grant Virginia a democratic system of representation. He asserted, in response to Leigh, that progressives grounded their case on the ideal for which the Revolution had been fought, equality against privilege. This principle, Leigh to the contrary, was the primary "sacred truth" of Virginia's Declaration of Rights. The twin concepts of equality of men and sovereignty of the people, the premises of the reform argument, were hardly "new abstractions." Their own Virginia fathers had made mighty sacrifices in the Revolution and not just for "wild abstractions and metaphysical subtleties." No sir! The reform ideas "are the very principles which alone give *a distinctive* character to our institutions, are the principles which have the *practical* effect in Virginia, of abolishing . . . *aristocratic privilege,* substituting for them an elective magistracy, deriving their power *from* the people, and responsible *to* the people." [19]

Abel Parker Upshur then took center stage. The audience hushed. Slow, deliberate, and articulate in manner, this state judge and future secretary of state under President John Tyler made the case for the eastern delegation. It took him two days. Upshur's thrust was simple: Cooke was full of hot air. No changes should be made in the 1776 constitution because none were needed. Expanding a conservative theory of government similar to that put forth by John Calhoun the year before in his *South Carolina Exposition,* Upshur made a sharp distinction between two kinds of majorities in a democracy, a numerical majority and a majority of interest. Reformers like Cooke wanted to rewrite the constitution so as to place all power in Virginia in the hands of the first majority while at the same time, in the provision for white basis of representation, destroying the second majority. One must not, cannot, assume, Upshur intoned slowly, that the Virginia forebears meant only a simple majority of numbers when they wrote of equality before the law. They meant, beyond doubt, that "those who have the greatest stake in the Government shall have the greatest share . . . in the administration of it." [20]

Upshur cited history for proof of his belief that the majority of interest should dominate the majority of numbers. History and experience determined the best government, not some cloudy abstract moral notions like natural law and natural rights. There are no such axioms anyway, Upshur said; a priori principles do not exist and are mere absurdities. "There are no original principles of Government at all," he repeated, "no original principles, existing in the nature of things and independent of agreement, to which Government must of necessity conform, in order to be . . . legitimate." What did history say to Upshur? He saw that, always, individuals with the most permanent interest in the society were those who had the greatest share of power, and usually this interest meant property. In Virginia's case, this "feeling for property," as Upshur described it, was especially important because the feeling applied to a type of tangible property, slaves, that was abhorred by many Virginians living across the Blue Ridge. This being the case, eastern Virginians had to recognize the need to safeguard this "property" against the "tyranny of numbers," and the only reliable protection was a constitutional shield against attack by statute. More bluntly, he told his audience that the only real security, and everybody knew this fact, was "that kind of protection which flows from the possession of power." This power was given in 1776 to the majority of interest, the eastern slaveowner, and must not be surrendered.[21]

What would happen if the East capitulated to western constitutional reform? Disaster. "Give the power to the West and will there be no temptation to abuse it," Upshur ranted on in a rhetorical flourish, "no temptation to shake off the public's burdens from themselves, and to throw an unjust proportion of them upon the slaveholders?" It was foolish for any easterner to hold on to the expectation that western slaveowners would support the East in the future. They "cannot calculate on the cooperation of the slave-holder of the West, in any measure calculated to protect that species of property against demands made upon it by other interests which to the western slaveholder, are more important and immediate concern." In conclusion, Upshur returned to his original point: "That Government is best which is best in its practical results." Virginians, as they had done for more than half a century, must continue to rely upon experience and necessity as their guide to constitutional law. The galleries "in defiance of all decorum" on Wednesday afternoon gave Upshur a rousing round of applause.[22]

Benjamin Watkins Leigh was scheduled to follow Upshur on Wednesday, but he delayed taking the floor until Tuesday, July 3. In the meantime Philip P. Barbour, having surrendered the president's chair to the recovered Monroe, spoke as a delegate from Orange County. He merely endorsed Upshur's ideas. His first cousin, John Strode Barbour of Culpeper County, spoke along the same line on Monday. Leigh's peroration the next day, although forceful, was distracting because of the lawyer's "childish fretfulness that ill became a man of his distinguished excellence." He concentrated on the white basis scheme of representation. This reapportionment, Leigh said, was the "most crying injustice ever attempted in any land." Like Upshur, Leigh demanded that westerners give some justification for their plan, "not arithmetic and mathematical reasons, not mere abstractions," to help Virginians "gild the pill and disguise its bitterness." Leigh ended his speech by noting that all "true Virginians" had a mission then and there, in Richmond, to preserve the virtues of republican government as put forth in Williamsburg in the state's first fundamental law.[23]

John Scott, Jr., state senator and later judge of various Virginia courts, pointed to the grim realities of Virginia's population shifts, as far as the planter interests were concerned, and how the data translated into legislative power. Scott, a man with a 2,000-acre estate in Fauquier County and fifty-two slaves, had a vested personal interest in what he saw down the line. "What will be the effect of the principle reported by the Legislative Committee?" he asked. "It will give to the people west of the Blue Ridge, if not immediately, in a very short time, a majority in the Legislature." Why? The answer was unavoidably clear. "The increase of whites west of the Ridge greatly exceeds that of the East; and if it should continue in the same proportion, a majority will in a very short time, be found west of the Ridge." That political reality was only half of the East's problem. Most of the section's land, especially in the Tidewater, "was depleted, worn and exhausted," and therefore "the country east of the Ridge has no new lands to settle, there is no room for a great increase of population." The West was growing, the East shrinking; it was that simple.[24]

No other western reformer captured as much attention as did Philip P. Doddridge, the strange-looking delegate from far-off Brooke County. Coming down to Richmond from that sore thumb of the state which jutted up between Ohio and Pennsylvania, Doddridge looked like a creature from

another country, or planet. Sixty years old, heavy shoul-
dered, with an enormous head and a face "over-loaded with
flesh," he was described in varying terms from "uncouth" to
"Patrick Henry of the West" or a "finished demagogue."
Speaking in a broad Scottish burr, he rolled out his rebuttal
in a point-by-point refutation of the traditionalists' arguments, especially Upshur's concept of the two majorities. His
first move was an acerbic attack on Upshur's ideas as being
the equivalent of communism because the Northampton delegate had said that "it was the safest rule that a majority of
the units of the community should govern . . . only when
property was equal." And, "unless property was equal," Doddridge chided, "he did not admit the principle at all."[25]

Upshur interrupted. Doddridge was wrong, he said. He
had never argued that property must be equalized! He never
meant to infer that "the rule [of majority of interest] was safe
when the property of one individual was equal to that of another." Doddridge turned to face Upshur straight on. What
Upshur was saying, in simple words, Doddridge said, was
"that a majority of freedmen in this free land are not possessed of the right or power to govern." What was at the
heart of the question before the Convention was slave property. "But for the possession of slaves, in great masses, by the
minority, residing mostly in a particular part of the State, the
rule of the majority [of numbers] would be safe now." What
the eastern minority was trying desperately to do was to in-
vent a defense against any attack of slavery, with a state property tax, by a legislature controlled by the majority. It would
not wash. It was an absurd paranoia to predict "plunder,"
"legislative rapine," and violence if Virginia implemented
equality of representation. Look at the population figures.
They showed that such bizarre, reactionary obstructionism
was doomed to failure anyhow. In a short matter of time the
majority would be "sufficiently strong and powerful to burst
asunder any chain by which you may attempt to bind them."
So there it was. Doddridge threatened power with power.
Either the minority gave the majority in Virginia what it
wanted now, in constitutional law, or they would take it by
statute later.[26]

Doddridge's last point drove the conservatives to the wall. It was denounced as a blatant threat "of the physical force of the West against the East . . . of presenting the odds between 402,000 whites on the West side of the Ridge, and 280,000 on the East." "If threats thus bold are to be presented to us while the physical force of the West is restrained by the Constitution and the laws," said one Piedmont delegate, "with how much more force will they assail us when we shall yield up the Constitution at their bidding, and they shall have the laws under their own interpretation of it?"[27]

As debate progressed, easterners added more charges to their arsenal. They believed that the white basis would give the West the power to appropriate tax money for expensive western roads and canals. "One of the main causes of discontent which led to this convention," Leigh said, "was an overweening passion for Internal Improvements." "If we adopt the principle reported by the Legislative Committee," he warned, "representation will rise in the Mountains and overflow and drown the Lowlands; while taxation, rising in the Lowlands . . . will flow to the Mountains" to be wasted in extravagant transportation projects. Other traditionalists were equally explicit. "The object of Western gentlemen in wishing the white basis to be established was to enable them to obtain the passage of laws for the internal improvement of their country." These circumstances, William F. Gordon warned, "present a most awful question for the consideration of every member as well as every individual inhabitant East of the Ridge."[28]

For the next three weeks debate continued on the white basis. Taxation and its connection with slavery were central issues, although the controversial subject of internal improvements received the delegates' attention. Conservatives complained over and over that no men were more heavily taxed than the eastern planters. Leigh repeatedly insisted that if the white basis was adopted, the West would tax the planter into oblivion. Reformers sustained their attack on the evils of having a majority of Virginians submit to the misrule of a slaveholding minority. Recriminations mounted. Traditionalists then tried unsuccessfully to appeal to race, southern patriotism, and state pride. Drop the insistence on the white basis, they argued, because to throw out a system that protected slavery would establish a dangerous precedent for all white Virginians and for the South as well. The commonwealth, already slipping in national political power, said John Strode Barbour, could not afford to stand for a plan of representation which, if applied at the federal level, would mean abandonment of the three-fifths rule and a loss of one-third of the state's representation in Congress. Adopting the white basis would destroy the advantage "to which possession of slaves would entitle Virginia and the South." How could any real son of the Old Dominion be a party to such a foolhardy step?[29]

At this point in the deliberations John Randolph of Roanoke took the floor. Here was theater indeed. Randolph, described as a twelve-year-old boy stretched over six feet long, was the convention celebrity. He was an "unearthly-looking figure," with piercing blue eyes and a high, squeaky, sometimes melodic, voice. He gestured erratically with both arms, stabbing his spindly finger at the gallery, while constantly complaining of losing his notes. Randolph was a half-crazed aberration of Virginia conservatism. There in the all but suffocatingly packed Capitol he held forth. It was his last public speech. It was a tirade. Reformers were abolitionists. "If representation had been established upon the white basis" in 1776, he squawked, you would have seen a bill for "the emancipation of every slave in Virginia." Did not everybody know that despite the safeguards of 1776, the western lunatics were up to their sinister tricks in the commonwealth? "Sir," he purred, "have you not good reason to believe—nay do you not know—that petitions are preparing for the purpose of being presented to this body on that subject?" "I will never suffer [the abolitionist] to put a torch to my property," Randolph continued, "that he may slake it in the blood of all that are dear to me." Then came the punch line. "I will arrest his hand if I can," Randolph grumbled, "by reason if I can—but if not, by force." That was the whole question in a nutshell. If the East gave in on representation and constitutional reform, "it will be," he shouted and waved, "a declaration to all the world, that we are ready to surrender the question to the first Peter the Hermit who shall cross the mountains with 'Universal Emancipation' on his flag!"[30]

Reformers would not flinch. Regardless of what Randolph yelled and what the calmer traditionalists said, the fact remained that at the core the East wanted to continue special privileges in the state constitution in order to keep political power, and that was unacceptable. Never, said Doddridge, would the West surrender that which any government resting upon the people cannot surrender, the principle of majority rule. By mid-November more than one progressive delegate had threatened to leave the Convention. Doddridge, by then "as busy as a bee and as dirty as a hog," publicly spoke of forming another state. Popular discontent in western newspapers became just as threatening. "The people of the upper country," observed the *Alexandria Gazette,* "goaded by misrule to which they have been subjected [will] throw off at once the odious bondage in which it has hitherto been held by a small minority in the eastern and southern sections of the state."[31]

At the same time stalwarts consolidated their position throughout the East. The few eastern delegates who indicated they might be conciliatory toward the white basis were instructed by their constituents to support Leigh and Upshur or resign. General Robert B. Taylor of Norfolk was one victim of this die-hard conservatism in the Tidewater. Taylor and Littleton W. Tazewell at the time were contesting for control of the Norfolk area. Taylor was known as a reformer and a nationalist; Tazewell as a disciple of states' rights and a traditionalist. With the growth of conservative sentiment in Norfolk, Taylor became increasingly unpopular in his own bailiwick, and Tazewell effectively used the opportunity to oust him from the Convention and replace him with Hugh Blair Grigsby, Tazewell's faithful young follower.[32]

After a month of give and take, it became evident that most of the original Jeffersonian Republicans like Madison, Monroe, and Giles were too old to exert any effort toward moderation or compromise. At best these men "no longer burned with a sense of duty to correct injustices and to put into practice the democratic ideals which for decades they had so ably professed." Madison buckled to pressure from Leigh and Upshur. He reversed his earlier stand for the white basis and joined ranks with the stalwarts. Monroe was so feeble that his conduct embarrassed almost everyone. And Giles, terminally ill, backed the conservatives without question.[33]

By early December the atmosphere in the Capitol was taut. Conservatives refused to budge. They demanded a system of representation which contained a special consideration for slaveholders. Reformers were equally adamant on the white basis. The balance of power between these two deadlocked camps lay with a few as yet uncommitted delegates from counties in the western Piedmont, Benjamin W. S. Cabell of Pittsylvania, William Campbell of Bedford, and William F. Gordon of Albemarle. Realizing the importance of their votes, stalwarts began a vigorous propaganda campaign against the white basis among their constituents. Traditionalists spread the alarm that if reformers succeeded in their plans, the southern Piedmont area would, like all the East, come under the thumb of the radical West. There were bizarre reports of some dozen horsemen riding through those counties spreading the rumor that if the white basis was accepted, westerners would take slaves from the Piedmont to level the mountains! John W. Green of Culpeper County introduced a resolution to defeat the white basis, but despite the pressure on Cabell, Campbell, and Gordon they sided with the West, and the resolution was defeated by a vote of 49 to 47.[34]

The situation following the defeat of the Green resolution was serious. Reformers, despite their initial victory over Green, knew full well that the vote could not be interpreted in any way as a vote in favor of their white basis plan. Stalwarts, on the other hand, refused to be intimidated by the rejection and formulated a new amendment that they thought would pass. Upshur moved that the white population of 1829, taxation, and the "federal numbers system" (meaning three-fifths of the slaves in the state) all be combined in a formula to determine representation in the legislature.[35] Gordon, in a sincere yet desperate gesture of compromise, suggested that apportionment be assigned arbitrarily to remove the most noxious inequities in both houses without reference to any rigid plan.[36] Then John Marshall stood and gravely stated his views. "It has been argued until argument is exhausted," he said. "We have now met on the ground of compromise." Let the Convention use the average of the federal numbers combined with the white basis. For the first time, perhaps in reaction to Marshall's plea, some progressives offered an alternative to the white basis. Cooke suggested that the white basis be used only for the lower house and that the senate employ the federal numbers system. He also asked that both houses be reapportioned every ten years.[37]

Debate on these latest ideas was heated. Reform leaders like Doddridge dug in on the white basis only while other progressives leaned toward the Cooke compromise. Some delegates just gave up and said that an agreement would never be reached. Randolph, slouched in his seat, moaned melodically that it was futile to continue and that the eastern delegates should pack up and go home. Discussions dragged on. On Wednesday afternoon, December 2, Samuel McDowell Moore, a thirty-three-year-old iron and grist mill operator and member of the state legislature from Rockbridge County, "talked of war and bloodshed." Taking stock, the diehards decided that because the Gordon-Marshall plan would probably give the East a comfortable majority in both houses, they would throw their support behind it. A few reformers, led by Cooke, decided to back the same plan because it was at least an improvement on the existing system of representation for the Valley counties. Besides, it seemed to be the last chance of salvaging anything from the Convention. But most of the Allegheny delegates saw disaster, a sellout by the Valley to the East. Doddridge was beside himself. Lewis Summers, a general court justice from Kanawha, could not swallow the compromise and its impact on the mountain counties; it deprived the "men of the mountains" of their political rights. But he begged the delegates "to pause before they severed those cords of affection which had so long and so strongly bound the people of the West to those of the East."[38]

The Gordon-Marshall compromise was put to a vote on Saturday, December 5, before the committee of the whole. On that unusually mild late autumn day "crowds of delegates" arrived on the floor and spectators filled the gallery for the first time since Randolph's diatribe. After some last-minute sparring between Randolph, who could not resist performing for the crowd, and Valley delegate Chapman Johnson, the compromise vote was called by Monroe. It passed, 49 to 43. The result, figured out by one western delegate, meant that a house of 127 members was to be composed of 29 from west of the Alleghenies, 24 from the Valley, 40 from the Piedmont, and 34 from the Tidewater. Debate continued quietly for two more weeks until the compromise plan was combined with Cooke's idea of regular reapportionment. On December 16 the Convention formally considered the whole package, and two days later the delegates accepted the compromise by a recorded vote of 50 to 46. As it worked out, the plan provided that in a house of 134 delegates the West would have 56 men and the East 78. In a senate of 32 members the West would have 13 and the East 19 senators. As a final step to wrap up the representation question, the Convention on December 21 formally rejected the white basis plan by a vote of 49 to 44. On the vital issue of constitutional law as a means to political power in the sectionally divided state, the East had won.[39]

A constitutional reform second in importance to representation in the legislature was the suffrage requirement. On this issue, the West led the way in pushing for the elimination of the freehold requirement. Thirty-year-old Charles Morgan of Morgantown (who in 1831 would become the superintendent of the state penitentiary at Richmond) noted the recent reforms in suffrage in other states. Twenty-two of the twenty-four states had already adopted universal white male suffrage. Only North Carolina and Virginia stood against the expansion of democracy. Nevertheless, considerable support for extending the franchise popped up in a few Piedmont areas. The city of Richmond, for example, had sent a "Memorial of the Non-Freeholders" to the Convention, and it was presented early, without comment, by John Marshall. The petition contained perhaps one of the strongest arguments for democratizing the right to vote—patriotism. This right was the only safeguard of freedom because the right to have a say in government, couched in issues of royal taxation, was why Virginians took up arms in 1776. All other legal rights, indeed liberty itself, rested on the suffrage, "the highest prerogative of freemen." Only those citizens who have the franchise, the memorial concluded, "alone deserve to be called free" because no man can remain free who commits "his conscience or his liberty to the uncontrolled direction of others." Charles Fenton Mercer of Loudoun County, Whig congressman from Leesburg and officer of the Virginia Colonization Society, commented on another memorial sent to the Convention from adjacent Fairfax County. These Virginians, Mercer stated, argued correctly that without the vote a citizen was "a slave to the freeholders" who "alone assert and maintain in themselves the exclusive power" of making law. Mercer resurrected Jefferson again. The sage, even as a young man, had denounced the freehold requirement as "a gross injustice."[40]

Across the Chesapeake Bay in Accomack County another eastern pocket of suffrage reform support appeared. Colonel Thomas M. Bayly, a Princeton M.A., state legislator, and congressman of an old Eastern Shore family, showed how the freehold restriction handicapped his constituents. Unlike the residents of the open agricultural lands of the Tidewater and Piedmont, citizens of his county were "penned up in a peninsula." Not everyone who wanted to could obtain a freehold, "whatever his standing and means," because the "territory is small and the tracts of twenty-five acres which are necessary to make the qualification are not easily obtained at any price." Besides, Bayly stressed, "a great proportion of the Eastern Shore people earn their living by 'plowing the ocean' not plowing the land." "It is not easy" for such watermen "in their first entering into life to lay up $200 or $300 to purchase the requisite freehold to qualify them to vote."[41]

Most eastern delegates denounced suffrage reform as an

invitation to anarchy. Philip Norborne Nicholas of Richmond, son of Robert Carter Nicholas, rebutted the memorial sent by the disfranchised of that city. He called their arguments blatantly fallacious. Suffrage was no natural right, even if there were such a thing. It had its origins in "social institutions." "The Bill of Rights plainly discriminates between the state of nature and the social state" and admits "modifications" in the latter situation. Virginia's own constitution flatly modified the right to vote to give it to those with adequate permanent attachment to the community. "This sufficient evidence of common, permanent interest is only to be found in a lasting ownership of the soil of the country." Nicholas ended with a prediction of dire consequences if this suffrage requirement was altered: corruption. "Place power in the hands of those who have none, or a very trivial stake in the community, and you expose the poor and dependent to the influence and seductions of wealth." Extend the suffrage, he warned, and you immediately open the "floodgates of corruption." Both public and private virtue would be undermined, eroded. Ultimately "your boasted Republic, established by the wisdom of your ancestors . . . will share the fate of all those who have preceded it, whose gradual decline, and final extinction it has been the melancholy task of history to record." Benjamin Watkins Leigh mocked Jefferson's plea for universal suffrage. The man was a "dreamer," Leigh scoffed, "whose ideas only meant eventual despotism." It would be sheer folly to follow Jefferson and give political power to "lazy, idle, drunken men" for the sake of some abstraction. Give every white adult male the right to vote, and all Virginia would be at the mercy of "King Numbers."[42]

Other eastern delegates, as before, hit on the link between race and reform. They claimed that universal suffrage would lead to discontent and trouble among Virginia's black population. William F. Gordon, in an abrupt about-face to side with the die-hard conservatives, argued that if the suffrage was extended, the new voters "instantly would get up an interest in the state which is hostile to [slavery]." "Sir, this is not an interest to be laughed at and despised," he cautioned; "if we get up this spirit at home among our own people your state shall be sundered and severed in affection by those mountains." "Sir, I say, if they get up this on the other side of those mountains, will it not come over . . . and spread too, among all that portion of the community who are not slave-holders." "If you extend the right of suffrage, will not persons thus discontented and thus made inimical to slave-holding interest, vote for the man who will lay the highest tax upon slaves?" Robert Stanard, a tall, ungainly, and stammering Richmond lawyer and graduate of William and Mary, continued along the same line of racial holocaust. The "property which the East was trying to protect" was not "brute matter" but beings "that have passions to be inflamed, hearts to feel . . . and who are capable of catching the flame . . . of agitators" and who very easily can be aroused to bring on "the ravages of servile war." Reformers had to abandon their "callous indifference" to the "mighty dangers" to which slavery exposed the masters. If the West did not change, there would be doomsday. "Stimulated by the feelings produced by that most intolerable evil and ever-present sense of insecurity [the East] will regard [the West] with fierce and angry hostility and every collision will heat the blood" and forge sectional interest and passion into two separated masses. Then, he pictured, "the new divisions of the State will stand confronted with each other, with passions aroused [and] fraternal feelings exasperated into bitterness."[43]

Philip Doddridge tried to avoid Stanard's race equation and get debate back on constitutional and historical grounds. He saw no purpose in splitting hairs over whether the right to vote was a natural or social right. This was a "laborious enquiry" and a waste of time. The suffrage was a right whose origin was "in every human being . . . it is inherent and appertains to him in right of his existence." What was wrong with the present restrictions was obvious: "that a minority of one class have taken possession to the exclusion of a majority, not by the consent of that majority, but by consent among themselves, or by accident, or by divine right." And turning the traditionalists' own argument against them, Doddridge chided that the predictions of corruption, confusion, discord, and despotism were "all speculation and theory against the rights of man." As for Jefferson, Doddridge deplored the conservatives' attempt to make him an object of ridicule and derision. There was a time, not too distant past, when "the authority of the sage of Monticello would have stood against the world; now there are 'none so poor' as to do him reverence."[44]

Western delegate Charles Morgan, though, returned to the race issue. Ingeniously, he tried to use this eastern fear of blacks, hysterically put by Stanard, to persuade them to support unrestricted white manhood suffrage. It was a blatant appeal to white supremacy by a nonslaveowner. "Sir," he stated, "it is known that all slave-holding states are fast approaching a crisis truly alarming, a time when freemen will be needed—when every man must be at his post . . . is it not wise now, to call together at least every free white human being and unite them in the same common interest and Government?" Morgan's pitch had little effect, however, and the lowland delegates succeeded in defeating the proposed reform by a vote of 48 to 46. In the end all the reformers could achieve in the face of eastern opposition was the adoption of a seven-point resolution extending the right to vote to heads of families and certain kinds of leaseholders.[45]

Morgan's appeal to caste over sectional loyalty failed because eastern delegates opposed universal manhood suffrage out of the arithmetic of sectional interest and because the latter dovetailed into the former. If the reform had been passed, a huge number of new voters would have been added in the West while, proportionally, only a small number of new voters could be counted in the East. It was a question of the sectional balance of power. Specifically, the statistics published by the state auditor during the Convention indicated precisely the nature of the sectional demography. In the East an average of 70 percent of the adult white male population could vote under the existing property requirements—76 percent in Tidewater and 65 percent in Piedmont. In the West, however, just over half, 54 percent, could vote in 1829. So, if suffrage had been made universal, the East could have expected just a 24 percent increase in power compared to the

West's 46 percent. The eastern delegates understandably said no.[46]

The bloc voting patterns of Convention delegates reflect the overwhelmingly sectional nature of these constitutional reforms and demonstrate the way these geopolitical identifications obscured any other alignments. Table 1, showing delegate voting patterns by class on the issues of representation and suffrage, indicates how consistently the upper classes of the East voted against their western peers and how the same pattern held down the vertical line of socioeconomic strata.

The last areas of constitutional reform focused on the executive branch and the county courts. Everyone at Richmond acknowledged that Virginia's governor was the weakest state executive in the Union, a mere pawn of the legislature. Jefferson had repeatedly denounced the feebleness of the executive branch. The Executive Committee hedged, though. It recommended only abolition of the council but not popular election of the governor. On November 26 Doddridge started the floor debate by introducing a resolution that the governor be elected by the people. Immediately the traditionalists in the person of Philip Norborne Nicholas opposed him. Nicholas feared the reform meant the realization of the worst fears of the founding fathers, "inordinate authority in the hands of a single Executive Magistrate." He embraced the "idea" of a governor chosen by the people, but to him "the people" meant "their immediate representatives." Dod-

TABLE 1. Socioeconomic Class Voting by Delegates

Class	White basis of representation		Suffrage to all white male taxpayers	
	Yes	No	Yes	No
Upper	14	22*	21	5 + 10*
Upper-middle	10	14*	8 + 2*	2 + 12*
Middle	13	10*	8	5 + 10*
Lower	9	1*	6	2 + 2*
Unknown	1	2*	1	

*Eastern delegates.

dridge's point, made when he laid his resolution before the
Convention, that separation of powers demanded a popularly elected governor, was wrong. Citing the *Federalist Papers,*
No. 57, Nicholas said that it was "extremely difficult" to "prevent the powers of one department from running into those
of another." Besides, the "true meaning" of the concept of
separation of powers was that the departments of government should have no control over the acts of each other.[47]

Richard H. Henderson of Leesburg, a Princeton B.A. and
lawyer, challenged Nicholas and expounded on the reform
commitment to a governor elected by the people and responsible only to them. Nicholas, in his fear of a democratic executive, had "invested the Governor with an imaginary
splendor" and set out "to prove that this gorgeous pageant
ought not to be elected by the people." Henderson read
aloud from Jefferson's *Notes on Virginia* his warning on the
despotic effects of concentrating power in the legislative
body. "One hundred and seventy-three Despots," he quoted,
"would surely be as oppressive as one." Henderson also
brought out the *Federalist Papers,* reading from No. 47 by
Madison, which asserted that the accumulation of power in
one branch of government "may justly be pronounced the
very definition of tyranny." The legislative and executive departments of government in Virginia, to avoid such despotism and tyranny, must be elected "not by each other, but by
the people themselves." Twice the Doddridge resolution was
voted upon in the committee of the whole, and twice it was
defeated. It passed later in the Convention but was over-
turned when William F. Gordon, ever the compromise ma-
nipulator, this time for conservatives, introduced a motion to
have the governor elected, as before, by the legislature but
for a three-year term instead of annually for three years. It
passed, 50 to 46, with the support of several eastern delegates from Accomack County and the southern Piedmont
who had backed the western camp on the suffrage issue.
Their return to the fold recemented the eastern bloc. The
fate of the governor's council followed much the same sectional voting pattern. Giles's Executive Committee report
recommending its abolition twice cleared the Convention,

but on January 12, just before the Convention was to adjourn, the conservatives moved to keep the council as an advisory body reduced from eight to three men. The motion passed by 51 to 44 votes.[48]

Debate on altering the county court system was the single issue of constitutional reform where sectionalism was obscured and the earlier and reasonably persistent East-West delegate bloc voting disappeared. Discussion on local government began late, on December 1, after the progressives were losing the representation and suffrage battles. Yet some delegates, led by the Reverend Alexander Campbell, made an emotional plea for changing the self-perpetuating local oligarchies of the county courts. From the same county as Doddridge and soon the founder of the Disciples of Christ denomination, this forty-year-old Scottish immigrant and father of fourteen children did not mince words, and conservatives labeled him a "slanghanger." Campbell pointed out that the existing system of local justice, fraught with contradictions to natural and constitutional law and peppered with functional weaknesses, had an understandable historical basis. They were accepted as such "at the time of the Revolution" because of the emergency. To have tampered with these ancient local units in 1776 "would have endangered the great cause of Liberty." Because "Virginia wished to rally all her forces and to concentrate all her energies, she was willing to make an exception in favor of the magistrates" of the county courts in the first constitution. They were not subjected to the rules of separation of powers and responsibility to the people. Thomas Jefferson almost immediately had condemned the expediency as the single most unrepublican part of Virginia's government. Now, over fifty years later, it was time to make these courts secured in the constitution, not just anchored by tradition, on the same principles as the other main branches of government. The county courts must be elected and amenable to the voters. To let the local courts stand as they were would "virtually repudiate" the maxims of republican government.[49]

John Randolph, slouched deep in his seat to the left of Monroe, stared wide-eyed at Campbell across the room.

Barely moving except to hurl an arm or two to heaven now
and then, he drawled in his soprano, syrupy voice that Jefferson "has gone beyond the Ganges to the uttermost East." "On
a subject like this," he sneered, "I have not much deference
for the opinion of Mr. Jefferson." "Sir," he continued, "if
there be any point in which the authority of Mr. Jefferson
might be considered as valid, it is in the mechanism of a
plough." "So much for authority!" Besides, "not an argument has been advanced against County Courts but would
be equally good *a priori* against jury-trial." Leave it alone! The
courts were the anchor of Virginia's political and social stability. "Sir, I am for a strict adherence to the anchorage
ground of the Constitution: it has hitherto kept the Commonwealth from swinging from its moorings." "God knows
what will become of the vessel of State . . . if gentlemen succeed in introducing the newest, theoretical, pure, defecated
Jacobinism into this Commonwealth."[50]

The Judiciary Committee report asked for some change by
having the county courts incorporated into the judicial structure of the state reminiscent of Madison's plan introduced in
1784. By this scheme, which Madison later abandoned, the
justices of the county courts had their jurisdiction severely
limited and most of their criminal cases tried in the general
court.[51] Committee chairman Marshall knew that the progressives would never accept the idea because it totally
avoided the issue of an elected local judiciary, and indeed
Campbell moved to amend the report to have local elections.
The report was never voted upon. Thomas M. Bayly, Accomack County's maverick reform delegate on the suffrage
question, tried to pick up the cause of changing the courts
by moving that they could be altered in the future by the
legislature even though the new constitution might leave
their structure unchanged. John Marshall then embraced the
conservative position. The local justices, he said, acted "in the
spirit of peace-makers, and allay, rather than excite the small
disputes . . . which will arise among neighbors." So, the Convention should not circumscribe their capacity literally to
keep the peace by denying them authority to decide such
local squabbles. Look at the record of the county courts in

doing their job compared to other states, Marshall suggested. "There is no part of America where less disquiet and less of ill-feeling between man and man is to be found than in this Commonwealth, and I believe most firmly that this state of things is mainly to be ascribed to the practical operation of our County Court." Five votes were called on changing the structure of local justice, and with each roll call the conservatives picked up support. On the final vote it was decided by 74 to 23 to leave the courts alone.[52]

One last, flimsy effort at reform was made in January 1830. A suggestion for an amendment article, it came to the floor through the Declaration of Rights Committee as "miscellaneous matters." John Randolph killed the idea on the spot. Delegates in 1830, he claimed, cannot unsettle the future by providing a mechanism, an invitation, to perpetual tampering with constitutional law. One constitutional convention in his lifetime was plenty, likely too much, of meddling. This idea Randolph caustically branded as "mischievious," "nugatory," "a calamity." The reformers' "desire for new things" was a "*maggot* of innovation that did not cease to bite." "Sir," he whined, "I am against any such provision." "I should as soon think of introducing into a marriage contract a provision for divorce, and thus poisoning the greatest blessing of mankind at its very source—at its fountain head." Besides, "change is not reform." Randolph hoped only for a constitution "that will last for half a century." Even that pathetic wish, he lamented, would be denied him if an amendment provision was added. That step would be fatal. Randolph pledged to vote against the new constitution, but it might pass anyway. "If we are to have it—let us not have it with its death warrant in its very face; with the *facies hypocratica*—the Sardonic grin of death upon its countenance." The amendment resolution was voted down 68 to 25.[53]

By mid-January the Convention finished its work. A select committee, figuratively headed by Madison, was chosen to place the resolutions that had been passed into the existing document. The result was discussed briefly, slightly changed, and then on January 14 presented to the delegates for a third reading. The new constitution was voted upon on a dismal, rainy evening. At seven o'clock Thursday night, January 14, a "large crowd" poured into the Capitol and while the question was called "behaved with great decorum." It passed by a vote of 55 to 40. The next afternoon, a Friday, another damp, bleak January day, the constitution was signed by the president and secretary, and at three o'clock the Convention of 1829–30 adjourned sine die.[54]

V

The Reform Movement
Revived, 1830–50

THE SUPPORTERS OF CONSTITUTIONAL REFORM lost out in the
Convention of 1829–30. Little of substance separated the
document of 1776 and the one sent out for ratification by
the people in the spring of 1830. Indeed, Merrill Peterson
has termed it "a crushing defeat for the West and all friends
of reform."[1] The East had triumphed on the representation
issue and thus guaranteed its continued lock on the House
of Delegates. The franchise had been extended, but only
modestly, and the goal of universal white manhood suffrage
was still a generation away. At least 30,000 adult white males
were still excluded from the polls, and most of these men
lived west of the Blue Ridge. The structure of Virginia's government at the top and bottom remained the same. The governor was as before the puppet of the legislature, although
he could now perform for three years without standing for
reelection, along with a smaller advisory council. The oligarchy of local power, the county court, was exactly as it had
been for about two hundred years: self-perpetuating and un-
accountable to the people. The constitution still had no provision for amendment. The leaders of the eastern plantation
society had kept their power in the Convention of 1829–30,
but not without a fight, and they were not about to jeopardize it in the future by changing the constitution again. It
had been "a contest for power—disguise it as you will—call
it a discussion of the rights of man, natural or social," Chapman Johnson of the Valley said; they "are but the arms em-
ployed in a contest, which involves the great and agitating
question, whether the sceptre shall pass from Judah."[2]

The scepter did not pass in 1830, and the reform delegates

milling about the Capitol that dim night of January 14 knew it. Some carped at each other and blamed themselves for the conservative triumphs. Doddridge, for example, charged that easterners won because some delegates from the upper Valley, specifically John R. Cooke, had gone over to the East in return for promises of a larger number of representatives in the new legislature than their districts were actually entitled to receive. Cooke, in turn, said that the real hope of reformers, the white basis, had been killed early in the Convention and that he had been able at least to gain something for the West by compromise. This was no "corrupt bargain," he retorted, but a clear-headed and wise decision to get the best that could be had under the circumstances.[3]

The anger on the part of many western delegates, despite Cooke's rationalizations, was no small matter. That winter Doddridge tried to organize a rump convention in order to draft another constitution. The *Staunton Spectator* warned that if the constitution was ratified, all hope for the West would be destroyed. Virginians would "continue one people in name," but without a "community of sentiment, identity of interest, sympathy of feeling." The West would be "chained like conquered enemies to [the East's] triumphal car," existing only "as a kind of colonial appendage to the East." The editor of the *Wheeling Compiler,* "as mad-cap as he can be in opposition to the new constitution," led the fight against ratification in northern mountain counties. The *Wheeling Gazette* cried, "Let the WEST then call a CONVENTION of the WEST; and let that Convention appoint commissioners, to treat with the eastern nabobs for a division of the state—'peaceably, if we can: forcibly, if we must.'" In the Ohio County courthouse a public meeting unanimously condemned the constitution. The *Morgantown Republic* reported one of the most enthusiastic campaigns ever seen in that region against the document. In Lee, Russell, and Washington counties, in the southwest part of the state, opposition centered on the argument that if the document was defeated, there would have to be another convention called immediately to draw up fundamental law more favorable to the West.[4]

Surprisingly, in some places in the Valley the public was

apathetic toward the new constitution. Commenting upon the ratification contest in Frederick, Shenandoah, Hampshire, and Rockingham counties, the *Winchester Virginian* said that it "scarcely ever knew any political question about which the mass of the people manifested so much indifference." From Botetourt County came the report: "We have never witnessed as much luke-warmness and indifference on an important subject; so much so that, it is conjectured, at least one hundred freeholders left the Courthouse without even voting." Some western Virginians, fed up with all the arguing, were just plain tired of hearing about it.[5]

In the upper Valley along the Potomac River, though, a number of circumstances joined to arouse support for the 1830 constitution. In the first place, Cooke pushed for ratification as the "nearest approximation" to what he had originally wanted as "could possibly be obtained." The *Winchester Republican* reacted negatively to Doddridge's personal attack on Cooke, and for that reason alone it came out in favor of the constitution. In the mid-Valley, Samuel Kercheval, an aged and respected friend of Jefferson, lent his name to the constitution, like other Valley residents, because of simple self-interest. The formula for apportionment of the House of Delegates in this document, he explained, gave Valley counties nearly the same number of delegates they would have had under the all-white basis reform. The East had baited the Valley, and they swallowed it.[6]

Eastern Virginians were understandably pleased with the results of the Convention. Thomas Green, nephew of conservative delegate Judge Green, wrote in his diary on January 13 that "the basis of representation is to me entirely satisfactory" and predicted that "the constitution will be adopted by a large majority." Most traditionalist delegates campaigned vigorously for the document. Benjamin Watkins Leigh combed Henrico County and Richmond; Giles and Gordon were active in the upper Piedmont; Upshur and Tazewell pushed for ratification in the Norfolk area.[7]

The final results of the ratification vote were, as expected, clearly sectional. The Tidewater and Piedmont, as map 4 shows, voted heavily in favor, a few Valley counties divided

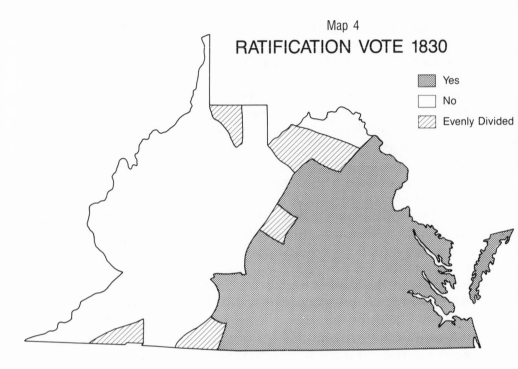

Map 4
RATIFICATION VOTE 1830

▦ Yes
☐ No
▨ Evenly Divided

evenly, and the rest of the West was almost unanimously against the constitution. The total vote was 26,055 for the document, 15,533 opposed to it.[8]

The ratification of the constitution failed to discourage the reform movement. But its acceptance did close a phase of an ongoing struggle between the forces of change and the forces of tradition which, in large measure, was a contest between two increasingly divergent ways of life. It ended this time with a victory for the conservative plantation society of the eastern lowlands and the politicians who served it. Plainly, the defeat of reform in the Convention was due in no small part to the ability of adroit conservatives who, like ancient China, were able to absorb their enemies. Through superior parliamentary maneuvering and effective organization and propaganda, they succeeded in keeping the Old Dominion straight on the path they had laid out—states' rights, defense of slavery, and steady opposition to forces of the egalitarian democracy emerging in American life.

For a time immediately after the adoption of the constitution, reformers were relatively quiet—although not silent—mainly because the document prohibited any legislative reapportionment until 1841. Even so, scattered protests from western counties were recorded in the House *Journals* in the 1830s. But as the society of this region continued to develop in ways significantly different from the eastern lowlands, demands for constitutional changes to accommodate its needs gradually intensified. The constitutional history of the Old Dominion was evermore a story of West versus East.

One reason for the continuation of sectionalism on constitutional questions was the demographic trend that was of such concern to eastern politicians in 1829: population and wealth were increasing steadily in the West. The white population of the West jumped from 318,000 in 1830 to 371,000 in 1840, and then to 534,000 by 1850. The East had 275,000 whites in 1830, only 369,000 in 1840, and just 395,000 in 1850. Blacks, while increasing slightly in the West each succeeding decade, still remained only a small portion of its residents. In the East the black population outnumbered whites by over 60,000 in 1850. In Sussex County 94 percent of the families engaged in agriculture in 1840 owned slaves, and of these over 20 percent were large planters. By 1850, 5,992 out of a total of 8,077 Sussex residents were slaves. That year 84 percent of the white farmers owned at least twenty slaves. In the Northern Neck county of Lancaster in 1840, 99 percent of the farmers were slaveowners, and ten years later the slave population exceeded the whites by 2,640 to 1,802. Similar to Sussex, 90 percent of the Lancaster farmers then owned more than twenty slaves. In contrast, the central Valley county of Rockingham, just 14 percent of the farmers were slaveholders in 1840, and ten years later the census listed only 2,331 blacks out of a total of 17,496 Virginians living there. About 20 percent of the blacks were free citizens. In Tazewell County in the southern mountains, only 7 percent of its 1,655 farm families owned slaves, and in the northern Allegheny county of Marion there were only 94 blacks (19 of whom were free) in a total population of 10,533 residents.[9]

Eastern newspapers like the *Richmond Whig* and *Richmond*

Enquirer regularly deplored another important sectional contrast, their region's "inactive" and "lethargic" economy. Planters did not show much energy. An October 9, 1845, letter from "Guilielmus" printed in the *Richmond Enquirer* noted that "men living in the low, flat country where the scenery was dull and monotonous" were lazy. The East remained tied to slave-based agriculture. In 1840 Sussex County listed 63 percent of its adults in agriculture and only 1.5 percent in manufacturing and .5 percent in commerce. Ten years later over 70 percent of the county's families were in agriculture, 13 percent in skilled crafts, 5.4 percent were laborers, and 1.5 percent in business. The remaining adults were scattered among the professions or were of unidentified occupations. The livelihoods of white Virginians in the West after 1830 continued to reflect a much more diversified economy than did those of the staple-crop, plantation East. The typical westerner of the 1840s was still a yeoman farmer or a skilled craftsman or businessman. Along the Ohio River, especially, an expanding iron, lead, and salt industry developed. Wheeling in one year produced 1,000 tons of iron and by 1835 boasted of a nail factory and two cotton and two woolen mills. The Allegheny county of Marion in 1840 had 61 percent in farming, 20 percent in skilled crafts, 3 percent in commerce, 13 percent in the professions, and 14 percent laborers.[10]

The impressive growth and diversification of the western part of Virginia had been stimulated partially by modest improvements in the state's transportation facilities during the 1830s. Petitions regularly were sent to Richmond from the West asking for more state dollars for roads and railroads. In response to these demands, the assembly appropriated money for the completion of the Baltimore and Ohio line to Harpers Ferry, the incorporation of the James River and Kanawha Canal Company, and the completion, in 1838, of the Northwestern Turnpike from Winchester to Parkersburg. The eastern-controlled legislature threw these bones to the West to keep it quiet and content.[11]

These internal improvements notwithstanding, the growing socioeconomic differences between the East and West and the unfair apportionment of the legislature continued to exacerbate sectional tensions. As the 1841 session of the General Assembly approached, western newspapers began clamoring for the authorized reapportionment. They pointed out that the 1840 census proved that the vast majority of the state's white population was now living in the West even though it had only thirteen senators and fifty-six delegates compared to the East's nineteen senators and seventy-eight delegates. Accordingly, in January 1841 the General Assembly responded to a petition from Kanawha County and authorized a special house-senate committee to investigate the possibility of reapportionment. The committee recommended a reorganization of the legislature on the basis of the number of qualified voters in the commonwealth. But the house, controlled by an eastern majority of twenty-two delegates, defeated the report. Outraged, fifty western delegates in caucus demanded that another constitutional convention be called; but, of course, this motion was defeated on the floor on a straight sectional vote.[12]

Rebuffed by the legislature, the western men in 1842 held a number of public gatherings to start another campaign for a constitutional convention. In the summer and fall meetings were convened in Clarksburg, Charleston, and Lewisburg in order to send petitions to Richmond asking for a referendum on a convention. Some western politicians argued that under existing conditions the West was paying most of the costs of internal improvements but receiving very little in return. Only a new constitution, they said, could change that. Others noted that in the event of war over the possible annexation of Texas, it would be the West which would furnish the troops because the East would be preoccupied with the necessity of protection against slave insurrections. Still other western men discussed the inevitability of the secession of their section from the commonwealth. John Fletcher, editor of the *Lexington Valley Star* wrote that if the "East are determined to refuse us justice, if they will continue to oppose the call of a convention, then we say let us separate." The choice before the assembly, he asserted, was "either a convention or a division of the State with the Blue Ridge as the dividing line." Samuel McDowell Moore, delegate to the 1829–30 convention from Rockbridge County, warned in an *Address to the People of West Virginia* that unless a convention was called and the legislature reapportioned, the future held in store only peaceful separation or civil war.[13]

At this point in the reform movement loyalty to the two national political parties for the first time appeared, albeit briefly, to play some role in determining positions on the issues. Democrats in the East by the early 1840s were anxious to bring their party into line with the Jacksonian stand of giving all adult white males the right to vote. At the same time, Thomas Ritchie, leader of the Democracy as the head of the Richmond "junto," apparently was eager to reassert his domination over the party against an insurgency of young states'-rights Democrats under R. M. T. Hunter and others.[14]

In the spring of 1840 Ritchie began to push the suffrage issue for the party. He wrote in the *Richmond Enquirer* of the immediate advantages for Virginia Democrats if large numbers of urban workers, especially in Richmond and Norfolk, could see the party as their champion of the unrestricted franchise in the commonwealth. Other Democratic editors eventually backed Ritchie. The *Lynchburg Virginian* commented sometime later that the "spirit of the age and existing grievances require that reforms should be effected" in the voting requirements. The editor of the Charlottesville *Jeffersonian Republican* endorsed universal suffrage and went even further to warn his readers to reconsider their opposition to a convention; "soon the population of the West will so far outnumber that of the East that we will be compelled to submit to any terms which the West may dictate." In the Valley the *Staunton Vindicator,* another Democratic organ, pleaded for statewide party support for "a reasonable and equitable compromise" on the organization of a convention. Yet it is important to emphasize that eastern Whigs also wanted extension of the suffrage. They were not about to be preempted in Virginia politics by Ritchie and the Democrats on that issue, especially after a divisive schism in 1841–42 between the John Tyler Whigs and the states'-rights faction of the party, many of whom were deserting to the Democrats.[15]

Contrary to Fletcher Green's belief that party spirit rather than sectionalism determined the positions on constitutional law in Virginia in the 1840s and 1850s, such party identification failed to sustain any permanent alignments for or against changes in the constitution. The data do not support the assertion that the reform movement "was largely partisan" and that the "Democratic party favored, while the Whigs opposed, a convention." The most that can be said is that national party influence in the state pulled together bisectional support for the extension of the franchise in the 1840s. When it came to the question of reapportionment, national party loyalties in the commonwealth split along sectional lines: eastern Democrats and Whigs, on the whole, refused to touch the change, while at the same time, across the Blue Ridge, both Democrats and Whigs for the most part were allies in the demand for apportioning the legislature on the white basis. For a while some Virginia Democrats engaged in a rhetorical offensive in their newspapers against the Whigs and tried to pin the label of obstructionism on them as opponents of a convention, but this ploy never really took with the voters. On the vote to call a convention, taken in March 1850, national party correlations did not appear. In the positions and votes of the delegates during the convention, Democratic or Whig alliances were meaningless. And in the ratification fight, bipartisan support for the 1851 document was found in the eastern newspapers of both national parties. All in all, then, sectional self-interest, not national party discipline, was the predominant consideration and the sustaining force in constitution making in Virginia to and through the 1850 convention and into the secession crisis.[16]

By 1845 westerners, in their fourth bid in fifteen years for a convention, started to stress the point that by then most Virginians, including eastern men, favored some sort of constitutional revision. The *Rockingham Register* pointed out in the fall of that year that only the issue of representation still really divided the state. At the same time other western leaders began to soften their demands for democratic reapportionment and to advise moderation and conciliation. State Senator Alexander Newman of the northern Valley remarked that "if one party demands all, the other will be less likely to yield even that which it has no disposition to withhold; *and* it may eventually appear to both portions of the State, that they are *injudicious friends of each who insist upon extremes.*"[17]

That same year Governor James McDowell, a native of Rockbridge County whose family had backed constitutional reform since the early 1800s, tried to put the influence of his office, such as it was, behind calling another convention. In his opening speech to the legislature he asked for a referendum on the question. The eastern-controlled legislature still refused to support any referendum that did not clearly stipulate a convention organized on the so-called mixed basis, in other words, a convention it could run. Western delegates in the house, understandably, wanted nothing to do with such a referendum because it would give control of any constitutional convention to the East. Put simply, most western men wanted no repetition of the 1829–30 meeting. Instead, hoping for a compromise on the governor's request, western representatives proposed that the referendum be on a convention for which the delegates would be allocated according to the number of qualified voters. Easterners wanted none of this formula. So nothing came of McDowell's initiative.[18]

With reform efforts bogged down in the legislature, westerners once again turned to public meetings and newspapers to generate support. They met at Staunton, the old watering hole of constitutional reform, and there sixty men from eighteen counties made their position clear. They agreed that no convention would be acceptable unless it was organized on the basis of Virginia's white population alone. They resolved, in a strategic move, to delay further action until after the next federal census, which they knew would bolster their demands for reapportionment. In the meantime, they said, they would continue to agitate the idea of a convention on the white basis. Some western meetings and newspapers were less aggressive, almost conciliatory. A meeting at the Marshall County courthouse in the spring of 1846, for instance, declared that "the West [should] unite with the East in the call of a convention as the only, and at the same time, the just way of procuring all the reforms which the West as well as the East desire." Papers such as the *Rockingham Register,* the *Augusta Democrat,* and the *Martinsburg Republican* hedged on supporting the forthright demands, and the threat, of the Staunton meeting. The *Wheeling Argus* started to classify westerners into reform types. There were those who wanted the white basis or no convention, that is, the Staunton group. There were some who talked of a convention or secession of the western counties. Others were willing to have a convention on the mixed basis. Finally, a few westerners, the editor commented, would accept a convention in Richmond on any terms. For a while, then, the reform movement balkanized and died out. Divided among themselves, name calling back and forth, the representatives of the western counties in the House of Delegates between 1846 and 1849 became impatient. Some, in disgust, flared out and condemned the whole idea of another constitutional convention as a waste of time on everybody's part.[19]

By 1849 support for a convention picked up important endorsements east of the Blue Ridge. The city of Norfolk was the significant addition to the cause of reform. For over a decade that seaport town had become increasingly bitter toward the legislature for its unwillingness to support railroad construction to that terminal and for its blatant partisanship toward the city of Richmond and other fall-line towns in preference to the seaport. Jealousy made strange bedfellows in the goal of altering the existing power base of the state government to an all-white scheme of representation. With a new legislature so structured, these Norfolk men believed their city might stand a chance of starting to compete with the burgeoning town of Baltimore and its artery to the West, the Baltimore and Ohio Railroad. So irate had Norfolk become by the late forties that it talked of getting out of Virginia altogether and linking up with North Carolina! Another eastern advocate for the western cause by then was Thomas Ritchie, editor of the *Richmond Enquirer.* His position on behalf of constitutional reform was pure politics. If the

East did not bend and compromise, the best that could happen, he predicted, was an overwhelming crunch of data from the upcoming federal census which would overwhelm any opposition to reapportionment. The worst scenario to Ritchie was disruption of the state into two separate governments.[20]

Late in the fall of 1849 some obvious signs of pressure on eastern members of the House of Delegates began to pop up all over that section. The newspapers, briefly yet specifically, started to tell their respective delegates to vote for a convention. One by one they joined ranks behind the two Richmond giants, the *Whig* and the *Enquirer*. The *Lynchburg Virginian* commented that "the spirit of the age and existing grievances require that reforms should be effected." The *Petersburg Republican* asked for a convention. The Charlottesville *Jeffersonian Republican Journal* advised the East to move fast. Accept a constitutional convention, now, on any basis and do not quibble about organizational procedures, because "soon the population of the West will so far outnumber that of the East that we will be compelled to submit to any terms which the West may dictate." That was sound advice of the type Ritchie had been dispensing from the capital. Farther south, the *Danville Register,* a conservative publication till then, changed its tune and backed the Charlottesville position. "It is the part of prudence," the editor advised, "for the East to yield cheerfully, not grudgingly, to the necessity of reform."[21]

By December 1849 western newspapers, sensing the change in the political winds across the Blue Ridge, started to push hard for unified action to get a convention. Leading the cause was the *Staunton Vindicator*. It pleaded with westerners, especially with some of the far mountain counties, to put aside their differences on the precise makeup of a convention. The time for all or nothing was over; the time for astute moves to get allies in the East had arrived. What the West must push for next year, it advised pragmatically, was "a reasonable and equitable compromise" on the organization of a convention. If it could bend a little to agree on that, then the demands for constitutional reform of representation and suffrage stood a chance. If it did not bend, if the West dug in and remained either obstinate or divided, then nothing would change.[22]

When the eastern representatives in the House of Delegates sat down in December to begin their regular 1849–50 session, they had these newspapers with them. They read the editorials and pondered their sensible warnings. It was no longer a question of opposing delegates from the western counties; on the issue of constitutional reform, it was fast becoming a matter of how to handle the voters back home. At this critical juncture in the wavering eastern attitude toward reform, John B. Floyd, the new governor and son of a former executive, called for a convention. His speech, delivered to the legislature at its opening session, was blunt and insistent. That the Constitution of 1829–30 was defective all Virginians must agree. So apparent were its inadequacies that the legislature had to recognize a new constitution as "inevitable." "Nothing short of a thorough constitutional reform will satisfy the demands of the people." And, most important, Floyd stated, "the sooner this is accomplished the better for all interests of the commonwealth."[23]

Under the governor's prodding, eastern delegates moved, slowly, to action. As a first step they introduced a resolution to refer the question of calling a convention to a select committee of the house. After a short discussion in which some of the representatives of a few Allegheny counties opposed the idea as a delaying tactic designed to kill another convention, the motion passed on December 7 on a vote of 90 to 27. The select committee then considered the various procedures for calling a convention and finally decided to put the issue to the legislature in two parts. The committee report, sent in early February to the house, recommended that the first question to be considered was whether a convention should be held at this time. If this question was answered by the delegates in the affirmative, then they should tackle the knotty problem of how to organize it. Ought it be called on the white or mixed basis?[24]

At that point some eastern delegates balked. They might be willing to think about some sort of compromise with the West; after all, pressure from hometown newspapers was growing and their own governor, himself an eastern man, was on their necks. But they were not yet ready to give away the store. They introduced an amendment to the select committee's resolution. Delete the second question, they said. Add on to the first question the idea of a convention organized on the basis of taxation (meaning taxes on slaves) and white population combined—the mixed basis. Nonsense, retorted the Allegheny delegates. The whole concept of using a mixed basis was flawed. The idea was stuck in a mistaken notion "that property with persons is a legitimate element of representation." This scheme may have been accepted in apportioning the federal House of Representatives according to the three-fifths compromise where slaves were counted, but the formula should not be applied in Virginia.[25]

The East had the votes, and the next day, February 12, the amendment destroying the compromise approach of the committee was narrowly accepted by 65 to 57 votes. Then the amended resolution was drafted into a bill for calling a convention, and on February 19 it was passed by a larger margin 78 to 42. The increase in support came from twenty Valley delegates who figured that if the bill was defeated, then there would be no convention at all. Realistically, following the advice of one of their own newspapers, the *Staunton Vindicator,* they hoped that a convention even on the mixed basis was better than the perpetuation of the status quo. On February 22 the senate without debate gave its approval by a margin of 17 to 11. A couple of days later William A. Cabell, a Piedmont planter, wrote to his uncle Joseph C. Cabell, Jefferson's old legislative advocate in creating the University of Virginia, that it seemed like 1829–30 all over again. The West was coming to Richmond angry, disgruntled at best, at the political manipulations of the East. The attitude among "the People of the West" was indeed a resentful one. They were convinced that "they are much injured by the Superior influences which [the bill for a convention] gives the East."[26]

The Convention Act, signed by Governor Floyd and dated March 4, 1850, called for a vote to be held at the same time as the regular April elections. If the results favored a convention, then 135 delegates would be chosen on the fourth Monday in August to convene in the capital on the second Monday in October. As predicted, the mixed basis gave control of the convention to the East. Counties east of the Blue Ridge were to elect seventy-six representatives and the West fifty-nine delegates, a ratio even better for the East than it had in the House of Delegates. The galling fact was, as every western politician knew, that if the white basis had been used, the West would have had seventy-four delegates, the East sixty-one. Once again, the western politicians had been done in, even before the convention started, in its attempt to write constitutional law attuned to its sectional interests.[27]

In the referendum the East came out solidly in favor of the convention. The western vote, unexpectedly, was divided. The Valley, whose population and wealth guaranteed it about the same number of convention delegates with either the mixed basis or the white basis, supported the convention. The mountain counties rejected it. They recognized that their real cause, that of reapportionment, had already been lost because of the way easterners had succeeded in structuring the upcoming convention. At the same time they saw the central issue of representation buried in talk about changes in suffrage requirements, election of the governor, and revision of the judicial system. It was the same old story. The East seemed to give in on things it had earlier opposed, suffrage for example, without jeopardizing its real position in controlling the state legislature. The incomplete but generally reliable returns from the referendum, as map 5 reveals, proved that Virginians favored a convention with the mixed basis by more than two to one. The only opposition came from the Alleghenies, where twenty of the forty-three counties rejected the convention, from the two eastern counties of Louisa and Amelia, which were evenly divided, and from the twenty voters of Warwick County, who wanted nothing to do with any kind of constitutional change.[28]

The next step was the election of convention delegates. During the interval between the vote on the convention in April and the August elections, public interest in constitutional reform was as keen as was Virginia's interest in the serious national problems surrounding the Compromise of

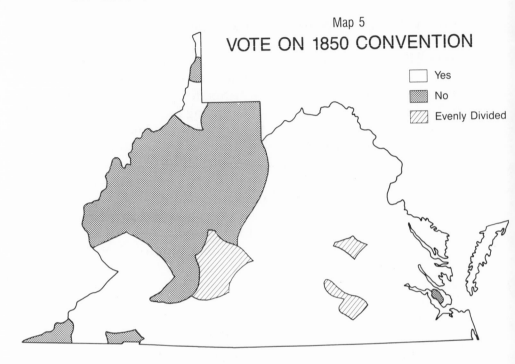

Map 5

VOTE ON 1850 CONVENTION

Yes
No
Evenly Divided

1850, then being worked out in Washington. The issues debated in the interim by the candidates and discussed by the newspapers were legislative reapportionment, universal manhood suffrage, judicial reform, restructuring of the executive branch, and a brand new constitutional question, the establishment of free public schools.

By far the most controversial constitutional change was the idea that the lower house of the legislature should be apportioned not by county but by white population. Only one candidate in the East supported the plan during the election of delegates. Henry A. Wise of Accomack County believed that the legislature should be based just upon "the will of the people." He also announced that he thought his constituents, the "Chesapeake people" he called them, were natural allies of the West. In the Valley, even though this section had supported the East in the legislature on the mixed basis for the convention itself, most of the candidates stood with the mountain counties and announced their endorsement of a constitutionally mandated legislative reapportionment. In the Alleghenies every candidate elected to the convention was committed to the white basis reform.[29]

If representation was a controversial idea during the campaign for delegate election, almost all men, including traditionalists, now approved of the need to rewrite the constitution in order to extend the suffrage. Western delegates, consistent with their stand in the 1829–30 convention and before, demanded universal suffrage for all adult white males. The East, while agreeing to a broadening of the right to vote, was initially unwilling to go as far as the West. Some, a minority of the delegates, said they wished to retain a small freehold qualification; others wanted residency requirements. Only a few, like Joseph C. Cabell, favored the progressive position on universal suffrage.[30]

In contrast to the elections for the 1829–30 convention, where most delegates wished to continue the colonial structure of the county courts, candidates in all sections in 1850 advocated sweeping changes in the oligarchic institution. Only a couple of Tidewater men defended the county courts, but even they had to admit to the need for some changes. The essential reform was Jeffersonian: eliminate the self-perpetuating nature of the courts and place them under control of the voters by having the justices of the peace and all other local officials elected. The *Richmond Enquirer* in May and the *Richmond Whig* in July proposed that the county courts be abolished altogether.[31]

Western candidates were more outspoken in support of having the governor elected by the people. Furthermore, in order to act as a check upon the legislature, they wanted him to be given broader executive powers. The executive council, they argued, should be eliminated. Eastern delegates were not so sure of the wisdom of this executive reform. Some, like James Lyons of Richmond, agreed with the need to have the governor elected directly. But others feared that this change would put the office in the hands of the more populous West and stood instead for his legislative election. Just as the East was unwilling to give up the legislature by agreeing to reapportionment on the white basis, it was also determined to hold on to control of the executive.[32]

The last important change proposed during the summer campaign was the establishment, by the constitution, of a tax-supported system of public education. The scheme, with a few exceptions, was almost entirely a western one. The argument was that because sooner or later all men would be given the ballot, steps should be taken to assure, at the very least, their literacy. Public education, they believed, as had Jefferson seventy-five years before, was one of the best guarantees against bad government. Most eastern candidates avoided the whole issue in their campaigns. Some, however, attacked the plan as a hidden scheme to overtax one part of the state, the East, for the benefit of another part, the West.[33]

On August 22 votes were cast. As returns came in, the newspapers speculated about the complexion of the convention. Some editors tried to figure out whether most of the delegates would be conservatives or reformers. The consensus was that those candidates pushing for the greatest reforms appeared to be victorious. Of the 135 delegates, there were ninety-seven lawyers, six of whom had served in the 1829–30 convention. An occupational breakdown by section shows that of Tidewater's forty-two delegates, twenty-eight were lawyers; of Piedmont's thirty-four men, twenty were lawyers; of the Valley's twenty-eight representatives, sixteen were lawyers; and of the Alleghenies' thirty-one delegates, twenty-one were lawyers. Of the remaining 34 percent of the Tidewater group, five were planters, three physicians, one was a merchant, another an editor, and another an architect. The 40 percent of the Piedmont men who were not lawyers included two farmers, eight planters, three merchants, and a planter-lawyer. The Valley's remaining 40 percent listed one farmer, three planters, two physicians, one merchant, one editor, one preacher, and a county clerk. The 33 percent of the mountain delegates who did not practice law numbered one planter, one physician, one merchant, one innkeeper, one preacher, and a millwright.[34]

On the whole, the entire delegation was a group of obscure

men compared to the two earlier conventions. Perhaps, as the brother of William Cabell Rives observed, individuals of second-rate abilities were sent to Richmond because Virginia had no men of high caliber left. Whatever the cause, "the genius of our people seems to have greatly altered." "They seem to be no longer actuated by a regard for the character of their public servants," he noted, "but rather by a low sympathy with inferior men." Another voter complained in the same vein that the representation from the Lynchburg area of the state "will be very moderate in point of understanding."[35]

VI

The Convention of 1850–51

WHEN THE DELEGATES GATHERED at the Capitol during early October 1850, there was little indication of the decade or so of sectional acrimony that had preceded the calling of the state's second constitutional convention. Routinely, as a first order of business, they chose as the presiding officer Southampton County lawyer John Y. Mason over his two rivals, George W. Hopkins of Washington County and Eastern Shore attorney Henry A. Wise. In his acceptance speech Mason, sensing the bitter sectional fight to come, pleaded for "a spirit of conciliation, mutual respect and forebearance."[1]

The rest of the afternoon and much of the second day were spent in selecting other minor officials. But even at this stage of the Convention and on such an insignificant matter the sectional reflexes of the delegates surfaced. For example, it took five ballots just to get Stephen D. Whittle elected clerk, and the last ballot showed a clear East-West profile. Whittle won the job by a margin of only 65 to 53 votes over his western opponent Rufus A. French. Three-fourths of Whittle's support came from the eastern delegates; not one of the Alleghey men gave him their vote. French, on the other hand, received 70 percent of his backing from the West's men and got only seven eastern votes. The next day, on the vote for sergeant-at-arms and doorkeeper the same warm-up exercise in sectional discipline took place, and again the West lost.[2]

The actual work on rewriting the 1830 constitution got under way when Mason appointed eight select committees with instructions to prepare specific recommendations for revisions. Then, after only two weeks in session, the West abruptly moved for a temporary adjournment. The cause of the unexpected event was a letter sent by the state auditor in which delegates were told that his office would be unable to furnish census returns until December at the earliest. Western delegates, who counted on the demographic patterns of the last twenty years to bolster their cause, asked for a recess on the technical point that the proceedings could not continue without these official data. Samuel Price of Greenbrier County, their spokesman, on October 30 accordingly proposed that the Convention reassemble on the first Monday in January 1851.[3]

Everyone knew what was going on. As expected, eastern delegates tried to keep the convention together. James Cox of Chesterfield County, their man, moved to table Price's resolution. Cox was defeated, surprisingly, by a vote of 65 to 62 with three eastern delegates defecting to the other side. Two of the mavericks came from Pittsylvania and Halifax counties along the border of North Carolina. The third delegate, John M. Botts, was a Richmond lawyer. But his breach was short-lived. On a subsequent vote, this one on whether to pass the resolution for adjournment, Botts reversed himself and fell into line with his colleagues. The other two dissenters, though, remained with the West, and the Price motion passed the Convention by a vote of 66 to 62. On the first round of the proceedings, therefore, the two camps had tested their discipline on matters at once both trivial and significant.[4]

When the Convention reconvened on January 6, 1851, the delegates for a while fussed over more petty details. For instance, some thought it essential to move the setting of the Convention from the Capitol, where the legislature was by then sitting, to the Mayo Street Universalist Church. The idea got nowhere. Other men started to wrangle over who should print the proceedings and whether the full debates should be made public. Again, nothing came of it. Finally, by January 25, they were ready to turn to the serious business of adopting a new fundamental law. On that day the first of the eight select committees named in October, the one on the Executive Department, submitted its report. Next came the report of the Committee on the Declaration of Rights, and then during the rest of the week the other committees—on representation, education, judiciary, and the county courts—all reported to the Convention.[5]

The Committee on the Executive Department, chaired by John Edmunds, a wealthy planter from Halifax County, asked for direct popular election of the governor and the expansion of his term from three to five years. It suggested the possibility of reelection for a second term after which he would be ineligible for the office. The committee also believed that there should be a lieutenant governor, popular election of the Board of Public Works and other designated state officials, and the elimination of the executive council.[6]

Floor debate in the Convention focused upon two aspects of the report, reelection of the governor and election of the Board of Public Works. Generally, eastern men were distrustful of any increased gubernatorial power. Men such as Francis Scott of Caroline County and John Meredith and Hector Davis of the city of Richmond expressed fear that if a governor could succeed himself, he would use the office to get reelected instead of disinterestedly serving the people. Scott, whose father had sat in the 1829–30 Convention, said that he "would limit the power of the governor by limiting his term of service, and thus bring him back to the people whence he sprung." Westerners and their few eastern allies disagreed. John S. Carlile of Harrison County and Henry Wise both believed that two terms and an increase of authority would enhance the dignity and the effectiveness of the office. Wise, who later became governor himself, felt that "if you allow an Executive Officer to be reelected, you at once put him on his good behavior, instead of making him a corrupt officer to prostitute the public place."[7]

The outcome was a compromise. The committee report was changed to allow the governor to be reelected after being out of office for one term. On the vote fourteen western men crossed over to side with forty-six easterners, and seven eastern delegates voted with thirty-eight western men. Two other relatively minor changes in the governorship were made in the report and accepted by the Convention. One new provision restricted his power to issue pardons or reprieves, allowing him this prerogative only after a conviction was obtained. The other change limited the governor's power to commute sentences to apply only to capital punishment cases. A weak attempt was made by some eastern delegates to abolish his powers of pardon altogether, but this idea was easily defeated.[8]

On the whole these changes created a much stronger executive branch. First of all, they made the governor, at last, independent of the legislature. Now he was able, in the words of one authority on the state's gubernatorial history, "to exert a political leadership which was destined to have a significant effect not only upon legislation but upon administration as well."[9] Thus Virginia became, as A. E. Dick Howard has written, "the next to the last state to abandon the idea of legislative appointment of the Governor."[10] To round out the updating of the executive branch, the delegates agreed that the people would also elect a lieutenant governor and an attorney general. The council of state, a fossilized advisory body since 1830, was finally eliminated.

The Edmunds committee's suggestions about the election of the Board of Public Works sparked a tangential but heated discussion on internal improvements. Western delegates favored popular election of the board in the hope of being able to influence its three-man panel, whose policies, especially in railroad building, had always favored the East. The East halfheartedly wanted to keep control of the commission by having it chosen by the legislature. The eastern delegates were not wedded to the cause, though, because that section, by 1850, had all the railroads it needed. There was no roll-call vote on the public works question; the West's view prevailed, and the new constitution provided for an elected board with increased authority. But the other changes advocated in the report, dealing with popular election of the state secretary, treasurer, and auditor, were thrown out. They would still be selected by joint ballot of the legislature.[11]

The Convention, in addition to democratizing and modernizing the executive department, enacted important changes in the judicial system. In 1831, under authority given it by the new constitution, the legislature had established circuit courts of law and chancery that met twice a year in each county under a judge of the general court. Hearing both criminal and civil cases, they frequently overlapped the county courts in jurisdiction. During the next two decades Virginians came to realize that the circuit courts and the county courts were doing essentially the same task and that the former were far superior in terms of personnel.[12]

The Committee on the Judiciary recommended, and the Convention approved with little dissent, that the circuit courts be given increased powers and that their number be expanded to twenty-one. In addition, the delegates established new district courts, ten in number, and at the top of the judicial structure they reconstituted the Supreme Court of Appeals, now to be composed of five judges from each of five judicial sections made up of two districts each.[13]

It was inevitable that such reorganization of the judiciary would kill the old county courts. Their inefficiency was both obvious and chronic. Whereas defenders of the county courts in the 1829–30 Convention had justified their existence by pointing to the fine job they had done for over two hundred years in preserving justice and order at the local level, by 1850 the aristocratic, self-perpetuating courts had become "bogged down with multitudinous executive and administrative as well as judicial duties; complicated now by the problem of an expanding population." Delegate Waitman Willey of Morgantown, speaking for westerners, moved that the county courts be eliminated and that their judicial responsibilities be taken over by the circuit courts. Richmond lawyer Robert Scott, a captain in the Mexican War, admitted the need for change but reminded the delegates of the commendable record of the venerable county institution. Be extremely cautious in any changes, he warned. The upshot of the exchange was a provision which kept the county courts but in a much weakened condition. Its members, including the clerk, would be popularly elected. The counties were subdivided into units, called districts, with one justice for each unit. A presiding judge at the courthouse would be chosen by the local district justices to direct the regular meetings of the county court. A final provision required that all county officers reside in their respective counties, except the commonwealth's attorney, and that the sheriff's tenure in office be limited in time. At last, after seventy-five years, Jefferson's desire for an elected local judiciary was realized.[14]

Democratization of the judicial system at the county level was not the only aim of the reformers; they wanted all judges chosen by the voters. While the Committee on the Judiciary was preparing its report, John Janney, a Leesburg lawyer and devout Quaker, presented it with a halfway plan. On January 10 he suggested popular election of judges of the circuit courts but continuation of the election of the Supreme Court of Appeals by both houses of the General Assembly. Another committee member, James M. Whittle, the eastern maverick from the southern Piedmont, told a friend that the committee would likely go along with the Janney plan even though the scheme fell short of direct election of the supreme court. But when the committee presented Janney's recommendation to the Convention, Robert Scott offered a truly democratic alternative. He moved for direct election of all judges and for those sitting on the highest court to serve twelve-year terms with retirement at seventy years of age. Against the opposition of some eastern delegates, the Convention accepted Scott's ideas and made the judiciary, like the executive branch, independent of the legislature but with fixed terms in the place of life tenure.[15]

The Convention not only reduced the influence of the legislature by removing the other two branches of government beyond its direct control, it also cut back significantly on the power of that body. One point of general concern was the manner in which the legislature had mishandled the state's finances. The General Assembly, most voters believed, had been irresponsibly extravagant and had increased the state debt to over $9 million, an alarming sum to Virginians. Others criticized it for meeting too frequently, thus compounding expenditures. Structural changes adopted by the Convention included biennial instead of annual sessions. Regular sessions were limited to ninety days. The senate was now allowed to introduce and amend legislation. The house was required to have a majority of the elected members present on the floor, not just a majority of those individuals who happened to attend that day, to pass money bills. A number of the outdated judicial functions exercised by the legislature, such as the granting of divorces and the direction of the estates of minors, were turned over to the state courts. The General Assembly for the first time was forbidden to bind the state for debts to private firms or to contract loans for more than thirty years. It was absolutely prohibited from emancipating the slaves. It was, by the same token, empowered to prohibit manumission.[16]

Such changes in the legislative powers were opposed only in terms of details, but there were two areas of legislative reform which brought out sharp sectional battles: taxation and reapportionment. The crux of the tax issue was the desire on the part of the East to have constitutional guarantees against future excessive taxation of its slave property. Western delegates naturally objected to the idea and insisted that such assurances, carved in constitutional law, were unnecessary. In fact, they believed any restrictions along this line were potentially harmful to the owners of other kinds of taxable property; if the state was to find itself in need of more tax revenue and if slave property was immune from further taxation, then an unfair burden would fall on all of the non-slaveowners to come up with the money.[17]

The East, however, had the majority of delegates and was able to write into the new constitution the exclusion provision. All slaves except children under twelve years of age were taxable at a rate only "equal to and not exceeding that assessed on land of the value of three hundred dollars." To offset any loss of state revenue the Convention then required a capitation tax equal to the tax levied on land valued at two hundred dollars on all adult white males, a majority of whom, as everyone knew, were in the West. To further compensate for the tax revenues lost by the limitations on slave taxes, the legislature was permitted to tax incomes and salaries. Taken as a whole, the battle on taxation was won by the East. Or, as Howard has characterized the outcome, whatever other gains the West might have made in the new constitution, "it paid for these gains in part with the constitutional provisions on taxation."[18]

Nothing in the area of tax reform matched the acrimony of the fight over the basis of representation. Even before the matter was considered by the Committee on Representation the *Richmond Enquirer* predicted serious trouble. "We hear many allusions made to the basis question," it stated; "dark spots on the horizon indicate a storm which may burst upon the Old Commonwealth." On February 6, 1851, the storm broke. On that day the chairman of the committee, George Summers, a western lawyer from Charleston, reported to the Convention that after a month of discussion it had been unable to reach agreement on a recommendation. It was evenly divided, twelve to twelve, East and West, on two different schemes of representation—the "mixed" and the "suffrage" basis. Consequently Summers felt he had no choice but to give the members of the Convention both plans for consideration. Plan A was called the mixed basis, and Plan B was designated as the "western plan."[19]

From the first weeks of debate on representation the mixed basis had the edge. "I see no signs of any faltering from the East," wrote Whittle, "and if they do not the mixed basis will of course be carried."[20] Although the oratory on both sides frequently rambled, with some like Henry Wise speaking for days on end, and was geared for constituencies at home rather than for persuasion at Richmond, two general lines of argument emerged.[21] Eastern delegates argued that because the basic principle of all good government was protection of property, the only way to assure this maxim was to grant it constitutional status in the mixed basis of representation. As in 1829, these delegates believed that there were "interests" as well as people to be considered in the state. They were still burdened with the fear that if the suffrage basis plan was adopted, the West would plunder the slaveholding interests of the East with excessive taxation for western internal improvements. Judge Scott of Richmond, for example, said he was alarmed at the "eternal clamour for the purse strings" by the West. To him the real danger lay in the "boundless wants of the West for internal improvements, and the enormous costs necessary for their construction." Like Upshur and Leigh a generation earlier, Scott combed history and law for evidence to prove that sanctity of property was the keystone of all republican governments. Robert Ridley, a Southampton County planter and lawyer, said that the right of property was "equally dear and sacred with life and liberty." Whittle further rejected the "new doctrine" where "numbers are to possess the power of this government." He claimed that surrender of the mixed basis plan would hurt Virginia's and the South's claim to existing representation in Congress. John Randolph Chambliss of Greensville County stated flatly that persons and property should be equally protected by law. George W. Purkins of Halifax County quoted Virginia's Declaration of Rights, the first reference to this "sacred document" in the debates, to show that it contained the "fixed, unchangeable principle" that protection of property was the "only just basis upon which all governments should be founded."[22]

Another line of reasoning used by eastern delegates to hold the line against the democratization of representation was the 1829–30 argument that a majority of interests as well as a majority of numbers must govern. Robert Stanard asserted that this majority of interest in Virginia had always rested with the slaveholding East. Because eastern property was worth millions of dollars, and therefore a particularly vital interest in the Old Dominion, "entire and exclusive regard should not be given to white population alone." According to Robert Scott, because the East had 401,000 slaves in 1850 as compared to the West's mere 63,000, it paid more than two-thirds of the state's revenue. If this property was not counted in representation, then, he reasoned, it should not be taxed at all.[23]

Slavery was the vital, indispensable issue in the eastern argument against democratic change. Many easterners sincerely believed that the West, like the North, was hostile to the peculiar institution and that western Virginians would destroy it if the legislature came under their control. Western men like John Letcher, then representing Rockbridge County, and Samuel McDowell Moore were accused of supporting abolitionism. Timothy Rives, a twenty-seven-year-old Petersburg lawyer, asserted that the reason the East must control the General Assembly was the overt hostility to slavery in the West. James Barbour of Culpeper coldly said that the West would not hesitate to destroy the institution. Plan B, Stanard summarized, would give power to a section "in which slavery property scarcely exists at all," and slaveowners would find themselves defenseless.[24]

Western delegates tried to persuade easterners that in a republic the majority must rule. Waitman Willey, echoing reformers of the 1829–30 Convention, said that the Declaration of Rights gave all power to the people alone, "not to people and property." Hugh Sheffey, a thirty-five-year-old lawyer from Staunton, asked how, after the East had adopted the principle of majority rule for the Convention itself and for ratification of the new constitution, it could contend that power in the legislature should rest with a "majority of interests" rather than a "majority of the community." John Carlile of Clarksburg believed that the phrase "majority of the community" as contained in the Declaration of Rights meant "nothing more and nothing less than a majority of the people." In other words, this merchant and lawyer said, a majority simply meant men of "sane minds and mature age in the community." Time and again western delegates pointed to statistical evidence to prove where this majority was in Virginia. The 1850 census, they said, listed only 401,104 whites in the East and 494,763 in the West. Furthermore, the state auditor's figures showed that the estimated percentage of taxes paid by the West between 1840 and 1850 increased considerably more than that paid by the East. The West's share had enlarged in ten years from $130,578 to $204,257, or 56.2 percent, while the East's had grown only from $268,204 to $366,237, or 36.5 percent.[25]

Another point stressed by western delegates, one close to their position on majority rule, was the un-American nature of minority rule. Henry Wise, one of the few eastern men allied with the West against the mixed basis, stated that the plan was an "aristocratic, absolute, monarchial union, part French and part English." He ridiculed an apportionment that would make one dollar of property count the same as two white men in the commonwealth. He pledged that he would forever support "liberty against mammon and the right of the people against the right of money." William Lucas, a fifty-year-old slaveowner of Jefferson County, said that he could see no justification of minority rule in Virginia and much to condemn in the "existing unequal representation . . . and other anti-republican relics." Augustus Chapman of Monroe County, a slaveowner, claimed that his Allegheny constituents would prefer to be "dogs and bay at the moon" rather than accept minority rule. Other delegates promoted Jefferson's idea that because all voters were equal under the law, all should be equally represented in the legislature. Quoting the sage of Monticello, they pointed out that as far back as 1783 he had suggested that the "number of delegates which each county may send shall be in proportion to the number of its qualified electors." Wise put the matter succinctly by stating that "qualified voters are the sovereign people and have the right to rule."[26]

Westerners time and again tried to reassure the East that their plan would not in any way endanger slave property. Hugh Sheffey claimed that there were influential slaveholders in the West, like Lucas and Chapman, and that no western politician could expect to support legislation that was hostile to the institution and survive. Western voters had just as much of a vested interest in the southern way of life as did easterners. Western men respected slave property and were "equally vigilant in protecting it, equally anxious in increasing it, and equally desirous that when acquired it shall be protected." These reassurances were never quite believable, primarily because just as eastern delegates were listening to these testimonials on the security of slavery in the Old Dominion, they heard mounting western criticism of the peculiar institution, especially in the Allegheny counties. The West's enthusiasm for Henry Ruffner's 1847 pamphlet calling for abolition in the state was still fresh in their minds. Most agreed with planter Richard Beale of Hickory Hill in Westmoreland County that the slaveholder's only security was "to organize your government as to blend the strictly personal rights with the rights of property in the majority of your electors."[27]

After almost three months of such exchanges on the issue of representation, tempers began to flare. Western delegates, realizing that the East would never give in on the issue, said they would take their section out of the state. By early May, largely because of a walkout threat by the West and the increasing number of secession resolutions coming to Richmond from western counties, some eastern men began to worry. They saw that, as the editor of the *Monongalia Mirror* wrote, the "ultimatum is, and must be, the white basis or a division of the state."[28] By May 10 one Tidewater delegate reported that some mixed-basis men were having second thoughts. To save the Convention from collapse, William Martin, a Henry County lawyer, recommended and President John Mason appointed a special Committee of Eight (four from the West, four from the East) to find a compromise solution. Five days later the committee reported out to the Convention a plan that gave the House of Delegates eighty-two western and sixty-eight eastern delegates and the senate twenty westerners and thirty easterners. The report further suggested that in 1865 the legislature be reapportioned and if then there was no agreement on the basis of representation, the question would be sent to the people. The following day, however, the plan was defeated 55 to 54. The major objection of the eastern delegates was the idea of a referendum: they wanted the question settled then and there in the Convention.[29]

Following this defeat absenteeism mounted and delegates gloomily anticipated a dissolution of the Convention and likely of the commonwealth itself. Some, like Botts and Wise, desperately maneuvered to get the assembly to accept compromise. They met only repeated frustration and defeat. Newspapers complained that the Convention was a waste of taxpayers' money. To make matters worse, instructions were sent from both western and eastern counties telling their delegates to stand firm. The break in the deadlock came somewhat unexpectedly when Samuel Chilton of Fauquier County came forth with what seemed at first just another of the many reapportionment schemes. This Warrenton lawyer proposed the same thing that the Committee of Eight had recommended but with an important modification. In the event a referendum had to be initiated in 1865, he said, the people should have a choice of four plans—total white population exclusively, population-taxes with restrictions on town representation, suffrage, and the mixed basis, or one half on the basis of white population and the other half on taxes—instead of two. He reasoned that this approach would give future voters a fair chance to express opinions on all possible ways to run their government instead of just asking them to choose between two extremes.[30]

Scott opposed Chilton's compromise but was beaten down 56 to 52. Close to midnight on May 16 the final vote was taken on the Chilton plan, and it passed 55 to 48 when eight eastern delegates supported the West: Henry Wise of Accomack County, Lewis Arthur and Gustavus Wingfield of Bedford County, Lemuel Bowden of Williamsburg, Samuel Chilton and Nathaniel Claiborne of Franklin County, William Martin of Henry County, and Thomas Jefferson Randolph of Albemarle County. In its final form the Chilton compromise provided for a House of Delegates of eighty-two westerners and sixty-eight easterners and a senate of twenty westerners and thirty easterners. In the event of a referendum in 1865, the people would be given the four plans of representation from which to choose with the option receiving the largest number of votes to be the rule of reapportionment.[31]

After the "basis question" was disposed of, the only remaining piece of unfinished business before the Convention was to change the suffrage requirement. Compared to the problem of representation, the question was quickly and easily settled. There was considerable support for some kind of liberalization of the franchise in both sections, the only dispute being whether or not to go all the way to universal white manhood suffrage. Waitman Willey had first broached the issue back in October when he asked that all adult white males in Virginia be given the right to vote. This idea, like all other proposed reforms, went to a select committee. The committee, chaired by Joseph Johnson of Harrison County, had no difficulty in reaching agreement, and on February 4 it recommended universal white manhood suffrage for all who had resided in the state for two years and in their county for twelve months. It also prohibited multiple voting.[32]

It was not until after the question of apportionment was settled that the delegates were able to devote their time to the Johnson report, and even then the debate on suffrage was sporadic. In mid-July the Convention at last decided to settle the matter. John Botts of Richmond, speaking for easterners, approved the reform even though he had hoped that the residency requirement would be more lenient. He emphasized that many in the state had worked for a long time to bring about these changes. Charles J. Faulkner of Berkeley County spoke in favor of the committee's recommendation and also emphasized the West's long fight for universal suffrage. A few eastern conservatives tried to modify the committee's report. Muscoe Garnett of Essex County attempted to add a poll tax requirement, but this was rejected 58 to 52. Thomas Flood of Appomattox County also failed to get "a revenue tax or county levy" added as a voting requirement by a vote of 59 to 50.[33] Similar efforts by Chambliss, Botts, and Scott to attach restrictions on suffrage also met defeat. On the final vote the Johnson committee report, with a few changes in phraseology, was adopted by a sizable majority of 59 to 41.[34]

The granting of universal white manhood suffrage caused little popular reaction mainly because most Virginians had anticipated the change. Besides, by midsummer with the most controversial issue, apportionment, already settled, interest in the Convention had waned considerably. Newspapers in both East and West commented favorably on the suffrage reform. Most, like the *Richmond Enquirer,* believed that because of the sensible habits of its citizens, the Old Dominion would experience none of the political troubles that had accompanied universal suffrage in other states. "There is still an overpowering conservative residium," the *Enquirer* observed, "which will effectively prevent the abuse of the right by those who exercise it."[35]

The suffrage reform completed the duties of the Convention. By late July all of the delegates were more than ready to adjourn. One observer of the proceedings remarked that by then the meeting had "become a by-word and reproach . . . a sort of levee—broken up into squads laughing and talking; while some pert orators were gesticulating, apparently in a pantomine, for the noise of the Convention drowned out their voices." On July 30 the Convention approved the new constitution by 75 to 33, with the opposition coming from eastern conservatives still disgruntled over the compromise on representation. There was a final speech by President John Y. Mason in which he reiterated his plea for patriotism and asked the delegates "to exert all your influence to allay sectional strife." On August 1 the Convention adjourned sine die.[36]

According to the terms of the new constitution, it was to be submitted immediately to the people for a full discussion of its provisions followed by a ratification vote on the fourth Thursday in October. In order to be absolutely certain that every voter would have a chance to examine the document firsthand, the governor was charged with getting it printed in newspapers throughout the commonwealth. Lastly, the constitution instructed the governor that if the people accepted the new fundamental law, he was to announce a general election in December for governor, lieutenant governor, attorney general, and the General Assembly. Then the legislature, after convening in January 1852, was to pass the appropriate statutes putting the constitution into effect.[37]

In contrast to the ratification fight twenty years before, the West was enthusiastic about the constitution and pleased with the job its delegates had done at Richmond in holding the line on representation. But western leaders took no chances, and men like Waitman Willey and John Letcher launched a vigorous propaganda campaign. Willey tried to offset any opposition to the document in the Allegheny counties because of the concession to the East on the matter of taxation of slave property. He argued that the victory over the East on the reapportionment fight was more than worth this compromise. Letcher traveled up and down the Valley extolling the reforms gained in the constitution and trying to answer questions about some of its complexities.[38]

The document picked up important endorsements from the western press. Publications such as the *Lexington Gazette*, Lexington *Valley Star, Monongalia Mirror, Staunton Spectator,* and *Winchester Virginian* praised the apportionment in the House of Delegates and predicted that in 1865 the voters would decide by referendum to base the entire legislature on white population exclusively. They all urged their readers to vote for the new constitution. They discounted the concession on slave taxation and emphasized instead the victories in suffrage reform and the democratic changes in local government. The *Lexington Gazette* even went so far as to predict a disappearance of sectionalism as a result of the constitutional reforms.[39]

Eastern reaction was mixed, understandably so given the earlier response in some areas to the compromise on the mixed basis. Some voters felt betrayed by their delegates, while others anticipated an immediate attack upon slavery from the newly apportioned legislature. Most easterners, though, accepted the changes as inevitable. Some of the revisions, such as suffrage extension and popular election of state officials, were greeted with approval. The Whig *Norfolk and Portsmouth Herald,* for instance, pushed for ratification in the Tidewater. In the southern Piedmont, the *Lynchburg Virginian* approved it. The powerful *Richmond Enquirer* gave its backing to the constitution. It noted that even though the basis of representation was unsatisfactory to some easterners, the new provisions protecting slave property from excessive taxation and limiting state credit were, in fact, geared to the needs of the Tidewater and Piedmont. "Both East and West," it observed, "will rally around this new charter [and] by an overwhelming vote, will make it the organic law of the land." The *Richmond Whig* also approved it, although with more reservations than the *Enquirer.* This paper felt the changes in state and county government had been too democratic but said that there was no point in opposing ratification because it obviously was going to be accepted by a heavy majority. "If it is the choice of the majority at all," the *Whig* conceded, "it

is better it should be adopted with a very general unanimity."[40]

The final returns bore out the predictions of the press.
The new constitution was approved by a majority of seven to
one: 75,748 voted in favor of it, and only 11,863 rejected the
document. In the West, as map 6 shows, approval was almost
unanimous. In the East only five counties voted against ratification. Three of these five counties were in the Tidewater:
Prince George, Southampton, and Warwick; the other two,
Amelia and Louisa, were in the eastern Piedmont. The large
affirmative vote was due in part to the fact that the constitution provided that all newly enfranchised Virginians could
participate in the ratification. In the vote on the calling of the
Convention, just 67,000 had participated under the suffrage
requirements of 1830; in 1851 the number had expanded by
20,000, an increase of nearly 30 percent. But even without
this newly enfranchised bloc of voters, which likely cast bal-

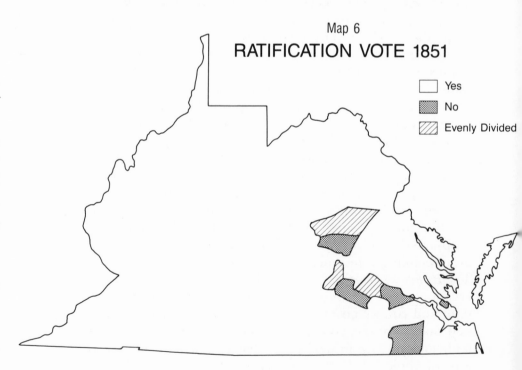

Map 6
RATIFICATION VOTE 1851

Yes
No
Evenly Divided

lots in favor of the document, the constitution would have passed.[41]

On the surface Virginia seemed to enter a period of reconciliation after the acceptance of the constitution. Joseph Johnson of Harrison County, elected governor in 1851, became the first Allegheny politician to sit in the executive chair. His victory was taken as a symbol of a new Virginia. On economic matters there also appeared to be a change in attitudes. The reapportioned House of Delegates passed legislation creating more western banks, and the Board of Public Works approved more internal improvement funds for that section. Only the seaport town of Norfolk remained openly disgruntled. But appearances were deceiving. Virginia, like the nation itself in the early 1850s, was merely enjoying a period of calm, a respite, before the reawakening of sectional divisions that, in the state and the nation, would result in a constitutional crisis over secession and a breakup, one permanent, the other temporary, of the commonwealth and the Republic.[42]

The fact is that the 1851 constitution resolved none of the emotional feelings about slavery and its protection under the state's fundamental law. As early as 1852 number of eastern slaveholders became convinced that the West, armed with its new political power, was moving to launch its first assault on the security of that property. That year western delegates in the House proposed that cattle, hogs, and sheep, like slaves, be made exempt from the state property tax. Despite assurances by the West to the contrary, this measure was seen as a blatant effort by that section to redress, if not take revenge for, past grievances. The West, it seemed, was trying to overtax the East and in the process subvert the peculiar institution.

Eastern representatives in the General Assembly were outraged. Alexander Rives of Albemarle County, for example, wrote in the *Richmond Whig* in February that he "did not think the funeral baked meats of the East were to be made the eatables of this marriage feast of the West." Charles Lewis of Harrison County put it in simple English. He said that because it was necessary to spend an inordinate amount of state money to protect the "East's institution," that section should pay more taxes. Another western representative argued that if western cattle were taxed, then eastern oysters should be, too. Tidewater delegate William B. Taliaferro succinctly expressed the eastern viewpoint: he knew the Bible said "all flesh was grass," but he was not aware that Scripture applied to tax bills. The proposed exemption amendment was defeated 67 to 64 on February 27, 1852.[43]

As western representatives placed other tax bills before the legislature, it became all too apparent that eastern slaveowners enjoyed a privileged position under the 1851 constitution. The western farmer still had to pay full taxes on his livestock, but the planter paid nothing on young slaves and paid only on a fixed value, well below the rising market value, on slaves over twelve years of age. Unavoidably sectional tension started to rise again on the tax question. The West claimed unfair discrimination, and the East feared economic exploitation. By the spring of 1852, with the constitution barely a year old, newspapers began to comment upon "irreconcilable differences" between the two sections that no constitutional reform could overcome. For example, the *Richmond Whig* wrote that if "the interests of the East and West were irreconcilable" and that if "uniform laws must operate oppressively upon one section and to the undue advantage of the other," then "to avoid external quarrels, it would seem to be the better for both sections to part in peace." The problem of unfair taxation grounded in constitutional law was never resolved. As late as the 1859–60 session of the legislature, western delegates were still complaining. In January they moved that a special house committee be appointed to investigate changing the constitution so as to have slaves subject to ad valorem taxes. Western men charged that slaveholders paid as much as a million dollars less in taxes annually than they would pay if all slaves were fairly taxed. The motion, twice offered, was tabled.[44]

Discontent over internal improvements, like the tax question, could not be contained for long. The 1851 constitution limited the power of the legislature to borrow money and by so doing placed a ceiling on the number and size of transportation improvements the assembly could give to the West. There were a couple of early concessions despite these fiscal limitations, however, such as completion of the Baltimore and Ohio Railroad on to Wheeling through Grafton and Fairmont in 1852 and the building of the Northwestern Virginia Railroad from Grafton to Parkersburg in 1857. But much of the mountain area was unaffected by these two railroads. As the *Richmond Enquirer* observed: "two-fifths of the whole Trans-Allegheny region is wholly isolated, it has no connection with the northern frontier . . . and none with eastern Virginia."[45]

The idea of changing the 1851 document on taxation matters and the joined issue of slavery was at the heart of a lingering constitutional debate. Moreover, the 1851 constitution, just like its two predecessors, had no workable amendment provision. The only thing close to an amendment clause in 1851 was the plan for an 1865 reapportionment vote. Not until 1870 did Virginians surrender the idea of a constitution as immutable law. Not until after the state itself had divided into two parts, East and West, did conservative Virginians reject John Randolph of Roanoke's 1830 condemnation of amendments as the *"rerum novarum lubido . . .* this *maggot* of innovation."[46] Even when they did write an explicit amendment procedure (either for an amendment or for another convention), the step was taken under the cloud of Reconstruction, as a "means of alleviating the harshness and obnoxiousness of this instrument foisted upon the people of Virginia." It further required, embracing Jefferson's formula of regular constitutional revision, the calling of a referendum on a convention in 1888 and every twenty years after that event.[47]

Epilogue

THE FAILURE OF THE 1850–51 CONVENTION to satisfy the West's demands for a democratic revision of the constitution and the East's mounting fear of a western attack on slavery played a crucial role in bringing about the permanent division of the Old Dominion ten years later. To be sure, many other matters help to account for the decision of the western counties to bolt the state and to stay in the Union. But the legacy of some sixty years of inability to agree upon a basic structure of government and the legitimate exercise of power within that structure was an integral, and certainly the longest-lived, part of the sectional fight that culminated in the disruption of the commonwealth and the creation of two constitutions for its people, one for the West and the other for the East.

Abraham Lincoln's election in the fall of 1860 was the event that brought about the permanent division of the state, letting loose an amalgam of constitutional, political, and economic issues that had been percolating for years, some of them for generations. Initial reaction in Virginia, unlike some parts of the South, was calm and realistic. Only the *Richmond Enquirer* urged immediate secession. Other eastern publications like the Portsmouth *Transcript* and the Tappahannock *Southerner* wanted to wait and see. Western newspapers from the start felt that the idea of a legal secession of the South was absurd.[1] Nevertheless, at the request of the General Assembly in January 1861, Governor John Letcher called a special convention at Richmond to consider the question. Lingering state constitutional matters promptly surfaced. The West would only agree to attend such a meeting if questions of the 1851 slave tax exemption and reapportionment in the senate were put on the agenda. Nor were they willing to select delegates unless the convention was based on white population exclusively rather than on the mixed basis as the governor proposed.[2]

The governor refused to give in to the West's demands about the organization of the convention, and with no alternative except refusal even to talk about the question of disunion, western counties reluctantly chose their delegates. When the February 4 election was over, it was obvious that strong sentiment against secession was found, as expected, overwhelmingly among the Allegheny and Valley delegates and in a scattering of men from the western Piedmont. The 1861 Convention, convened as scheduled on February 13, in its discussion of secession, went through three stages. At first, there was talk of a delay on a decision. Then there was a noticeable rise of secession support against any delay and, then, in April a vote to join the Confederacy. Throughout the debates distinctions were made between "moderate" and "radical" disunionism, but these labels were artificial; the vote to leave the Union fell into the same East-West cleavage that had characterized public support for or opposition to constitutional reforms since the turn of the century. Lincoln's call for troops on April 15 after the fall of Fort Sumter, beyond question, caused the final polarization. On Tuesday morning, April 16, William B. Preston of Montgomery County moved that "the constitution of the United States of America is no longer binding on any citizen of this state." The following afternoon his resolution passed by 88 to 55 votes.[3]

In looking at the secession vote, as table 2 illustrates, the old East-West pattern remained intact. The bulk of the votes for disunion was in the East: fifty-five of the eighty-eight men came from the Tidewater and Piedmont. On the other hand, forty-five of the fifty-five Unionist delegates came from west of the Blue Ridge.[4] Public reaction to events at Richmond was also sectional. The East by then was enthusiastic about secession, and it was supported by a pocket of counties in the far southwest corner of the state along the Tennessee–North

TABLE 2. Vote on Secession Ordinance

Section	For secession	Against secession
Tidewater	23	6
Piedmont	32	4
Valley	10	17
Mountain	23	28
Total	88	55

Source: Journal of Secret Convention (Richmond, 1861), pp. 10–11.

Carolina border. The greatest opposition to disunion was in the West, especially in the counties adjacent to Pennsylvania and those serviced by the Baltimore and Ohio Railroad. At the town of Grafton, for example, all potential Confederate military supplies coming through by railroad were confiscated by Union men. A southern supporter visiting Harrison, Upshur, and Doddridge counties estimated that more than two-thirds of the people there were vehemently against the Confederacy. A mass meeting on April 23 at Monongalia County resolved "their solemn protest against the Secession of the State" and affirmed that they owed "undying fidelity" to the Union. The citizens of Wetzel County, meeting at New Martinsville the same day, adopted a similar statement asserting that "Union sentiment of this people is such that we pledge our voters against any act of Secession which would sever us a State from the Federal Government."[5]

More than just opposing secession, western Virginians threatened that if the ordinance was ratified, they intended to stay in the Union and to write a new constitution and form a separate government. As early as April 22 returning delegates found local "conventions" already called in order to draft such a constitution. At Clarksburg, in Harrison County, John S. Carlile participated in one such convention that unanimously adopted a preamble recommending that "the people in each and all of the counties comprising Northwestern Virginia" appoint at least five delegates to meet in a general convention on May 13 "to consult and determine upon such actions as the people of Northwestern Virginia should take in the present fearful emergency." The Clarksburg *West-*

ern Virginia Guard endorsed the idea of a "special convention" and in addition printed an "Address of the Convention to the people of Northwestern Virginia." The address denounced secession as "contrary to the expectations of a large majority of the people of the state."[6]

By late April state and local government in some parts of the West was already collapsing. Public officials quit their jobs, and vigilante bands patrolled the roads. Groups of farmers and businessmen organized to assess the situation and to discuss copies of the Clarksburg Address as it was distributed on horseback to Weston, Kingwood, and Morgantown and by rail to Wheeling, Parkersburg, and Martinsburg. Central to the move to create another state was the historic unsuccessful battle over constitutional reform. Delegates returned from the Richmond Secession Convention to complain of the brusque way the East had rejected their sincere efforts to discuss needed changes in the 1851 constitution. Public gatherings showed that old hostilities over constitutional reforms were inseparable from the move for a new and separate government in the West: men talked of unfair taxation, unequal representation in the senate, and of the secession question all at the same time.[7]

On May 13, 436 delegates representing twenty-seven counties met at Wheeling. At Washington Hall there, they chose William B. Zinn of Preston County as temporary president and started to discuss just what sort of gathering they were holding. Some said it was just a "mass meeting" because many delegates had been elected irregularly and could not claim constitutents. In four counties delegates were literally any "good Union men" who chose to spend their own money to go to Wheeling. Others said that a mass meeting, not a convention, was what really had been intended by the Clarksburg Address. Carlile argued instead that it was a valid constitutional convention consistent with English "legal and parliamentary precedents."[8]

After a morning of indecisive debate the delegates, at three o'clock in the afternoon, gave the meeting the appearance of a formal convention by electing John W. Moss of Wood County permanent presiding officer and by appointing a doorkeeper and sergeant-at-arms. Moss then named a Committee on State and Federal Relations consisting of one delegate from each county represented. The following day this committee received resolutions from the floor that both endorsed the Clarksburg Address and condemned the secession ordinance. Carlile moved to instruct the committee to draft a recommendation proclaiming a new state government. He defended his action by arguing that in the past Vermont, Kentucky, and Tennessee had established firm precedents for such a step even though the federal Constitution forbade the formation of new states within the boundaries of existing states without the approval of the latter. Besides, he said, "it is the only legal, constitutional remedy left this people if they do not approve the action of the Virginia Convention."[9]

Other delegates, led by Waitman Willey and John J. Jackson, initially opposed the step. They wanted to see the results of the referendum on the secession ordinance and then decide whether or not to form a new state government. Willey said that Carlile's proposal was a violation of the law and against the constitutions of Virginia and the United States. It would also, he warned, bring "war and ruin upon this part of the state." Others cautioned that some of the people might refuse to accept such a precipitous move without formal approval of the voters. By the afternoon of May 15 it was generally agreed that it would be best to wait until after a referendum.[10]

Carlile then offered an amendment to his initial resolution. "In the event of the ratification of the Ordinance of Secession," he said, "this convention should re-assemble on the first Monday of June to adopt a Constitution and form of Government." The Committee on State and Federal Relations endorsed the resolution as amended, and with only two dissenting votes it was approved at an evening session of all the delegates. Meanwhile, a standing Central Committee of nine men, chaired by Carlile, was appointed by Moss "to attend to all matters connected with the objects of this convention." The delegates resolved to prepare and circulate an "Address to the People of Virginia" in which they would express opposition to the secession ordinance and summarize the results of the first "Wheeling Convention."[11]

The West, then, awaited the results of the May 28 secession vote. Because the voting was viva voce, it was hazardous for Union men to step forward in the East and equally difficult for secessionists to express themselves in the West. Consequently, the results in many counties were lopsided one way or the other. As announced by Governor Letcher, the total for what would remain as the state of Virginia was 125,950 for secession and 20,373 against it. The counties of what became West Virginia voted about 33,000 against the ordinance and only 4,000 in favor of it.[12]

Election of delegates in the West to a second Wheeling Convention then proceeded without difficulty. On the appointed date of June 11 they assembled again in Washington Hall, chose Dennis B. Dorsey of Monongalia County as temporary chairman and Gibson Cramner of Wheeling as temporary secretary, and proceeded with measures to take their section out of the Old Dominion. There were 100 delegates in attendance representing thirty-four counties, two of which were located in the far northern Piedmont next to Maryland.[13] Fifteen counties, or about one-third of the counties of what later would make up West Virginia, were not represented.

On the second day the delegates chose permanent officers—Arthur R. Boreman as president and Gibson Cramner as secretary. In the first formal action they adopted a resolution thanking the federal government and General McClellan for rescuing them from "the destruction and spoilation inaugurated by the rebel forces in our midst." The resolution repudiated the "heresy sought to be inculcated by secessionists." Then Boreman appointed a Committee of Thirteen "to prepare and report business for the Convention." On Thursday, June 13, Carlile, speaking for the committee, reported "A Declaration of the People of Virginia" which, when adopted four days later, laid the foundation of what would become a new state government.[14]

The declaration in its opening paragraph claimed that the action of the General Assembly in calling a convention to leave the federal Union had violated the will of the majority of the people of Virginia. It was, therefore, "a usurpation" which would inevitably result in "a military despotism." Carlile charged the Richmond convention with subversion of the federal Union and with inaugurating by its "usurped power" a "Reign of Terror intended to suppress the free expression of the will of the people." The declaration ended with the equivalent of a statement of independence by "imperatively" demanding the "reorganization of the government of the Commonwealth" and vacating all acts by the state of Virginia "tending to separate this Commonwealth from the United States."[15]

On June 14, the same day that Governor Letcher announced the results of the secession referendum, the second Wheeling Convention received a motion for the reorganization of the state government "on a loyal basis." Debate over the next few days focused mainly on the question of whether or not such a step violated the federal Constitution. Carlile argued, as he had in May, that other states had been created out of existing states. Delegates from Marion and Monongalia counties felt that it was too soon for such a step. But Chester Hubbard of Ohio County stated that "the case before the people of the Northwest was no longer one of choice, or even preference, but had become a matter of duty." Just before the vote was taken, Carlile urged his colleagues to move quickly; because "a Southern army is advancing upon us in two columns, we know not how soon we may have to close our doors and discussions here and seek safety elsewhere." After some last-minute debate over phraseology, the ordinance passed by a vote of 76 to 14. The next day, June 20, Francis H. Pierpont was unanimously elected governor of the "Reorganized Government of Virginia" until new elections could be held. Daniel Polsley of Mason County was also elected unopposed as lieutenant governor, as was James S. Wheat of Ohio County for attorney general. Finally, the delegates chose an executive council of five members.[16]

Pursuant to the authority given the new governor by the

second Wheeling Convention, Pierpont called the Reorganized Government into existence by convening the General Assembly on July 1, 1861. It was to be sovereign until ratification of the first state constitution of West Virginia in April 1862. Its main responsibilities centered on trying to bring some stability out of the chaotic conditions of war. It elected Waitman Willey and John Carlile to the United States Senate on the assurances of Senator Benjamin F. Butler of Massachusetts that they would be seated whether or not Virginia's senators were still in Congress. The military defeat of Northern forces that July at the battle of Manassas (Bull Run) caused many to despair of ever restoring Virginia to the Union, and newspapers such as the Wheeling *Daily Intelligencer* insisted that it was time to form a new state constitution.[17]

Accordingly, the second Wheeling Convention reconvened in August to take up the matter. On the first day the delegates authorized a special committee of one member from each county represented to "take the whole subject of division of this state into consideration" and make recommendations to the Convention. The next week, when the committee reported an ordinance for the creation of a new state, the idea met with opposition. About one-third of the delegates were deterred by the message of U.S. Attorney General Edward Bates that creation of a new state was the same as "an original, independent act of Revolution." Some delegates argued that nothing could be done until exact boundaries were determined. But most resistance to the creation of West Virginia came from delegates who wanted to be certain that the new state would outlaw slavery immediately. The editor of the *Wellsburg Herald*, for example, believed that if West Virginia allowed slavery, then he preferred "to be a citizen of a State that has a history, has territory, has population, and has resources."[18] Even so, the Convention approved the ordinance by 48 to 27 votes on August 20 and temporarily named the state of thirty-nine counties "Kanawha." The next day it authorized a referendum on the ordinance for October 24, at which time the people also would elect delegates to a constitutional convention. On that date voters cast 18,408 ballots in favor of separation and the creation of another state and just 781 against the idea.[19]

At the West Virginia Constitutional Convention, which sat from November 26, 1861, to February 18, 1862, and in a recalled session from February 12 to 20, 1863, delegates wrote a new fundamental law incorporating all the constitutional changes for which their section had fought at least since 1818. First of all the constitution provided for a legislature apportioned on the basis of white population with the suffrage vested in the "white male citizens of the state." Slavery was prohibited in the sense that new chattels could not be imported into the state. "Free Persons of Color," in a measure similar to those in effect in most northern states at the time, were also denied the right of residing in the state. Nothing was said about freeing the 18,000 slaves already living there. A plan of gradual abolition was introduced by the Reverend Gordon Buttelle of Wheeling, and this resolution was referred to a Committee on Fundamentals chaired by Peter Van Winkle of Parkersburg. But when the abolition resolution was brought to the Convention, it was tabled by a vote of 24 to 23.[20] Attention then shifted abruptly to economic matters. Believing that long-neglected internal improvements were vital to the progress of "Kanawha," some delegates proposed that the constitution authorize a bonded state debt for public transportation. Opposition of delegates from the Kanawha River valley, who felt private capital should provide such revenues, defeated the provision by a vote of 25 to 23. But in a subsequent last-minute compromise the state was in fact permitted to support internal improvements; on the last day of the session a resolution was adopted allowing the legislature to subscribe to capital stock of transportation corporations or associations provided that "such stocks shall be paid for at the time of subscribing or from taxes levied for the ensuing year sufficient to pay the subscription in full." Finally, the delegates adopted a scheme of local government that Jefferson had proposed in 1776 and 1779, in which counties were divided into townships each of which would conduct local affairs at yearly town meetings.

Their work completed, the delegates adjourned and sent the constitution to the people. When the polls closed, the results showed that 18,862 voters approved the document, and just 514 were against it.[21]

There can be little doubt that eastern Virginians, in writing and then rewriting their fundamental law between 1776 and 1851, did not want to provide a progressive and democratic government for their commonwealth. These traditionalists, at first in a majority and then in an ever-diminishing minority, controlled the state and maintained the status quo because under three constitutions they dominated the all-powerful House of Delegates. Their motives were visceral, pervasive, and persistent. This lowland agrarian leadership, increasingly beleaguered with what they perceived, accurately or not, as severe threats to their way of life from Virginians in the Valley and Allegheny counties, returned again and again to conservative constitutional principles as the shield against change. They waged a determined and largely successful fight throughout the first half of the nineteenth century to keep Virginia as they thought it had been in the eighteenth century. The result was a government geared to the needs of some but not most of its citizens.

The traditionalists, in the process of holding on to control of the state government, were willing either to pervert or to destroy their constitution as a limiting document. They paid lip service at first to the doctrine of separation of powers, but for the next seventy-five years they kept all real authority in their hands—in the House of Delegates. So, the Virginia legislature that before Independence was the instrument of popular will against expanded royal prerogative afterwards became the main barrier against the principle of majority rule. The problem began in Williamsburg when the Virginians who wrote the first constitution acted on the assumption that the legislature could do no wrong. Regardless of what they said at the time about a government based on the consent of the governed and the need for checks and balances, the 1776 constitution created a legislature almost without limitations and, to boot, included no process of amendment to redress this imbalance. Jefferson, always the sensitive observer of governmental abuse, wrote as early as 1781 that in his state the "ordinary legislature may alter the constitution itself," it was so powerful.[22]

Jefferson, as usual, was right in these matters. He knew that the first constitution hamstrung the executive branch and that the cause of the governor's impotence was a list of constitutional prohibitions on his authority. The offfice had neither power nor dignity. Furthermore, the governor's annual election by the legislature made it politically impossible for any incumbent to develop independent policy. If he was reelected, thereby providing a chance to act against the legislature, at the end of the third term he was retired for a minimum of four years. While he was in office, whatever decisions he made were dependent upon approval of the executive council, which also was chosen by the legislature. He was, of course, denied a veto. In 1829–30 the constitution did little to improve the governor's influence, only changing his annual election to a three-year term. Not until the Constitution of 1850–51 was the executive branch given some degree of authority, most significantly by placing the governor's election in the hands of the people. This document also eliminated the executive council at last and extended the governor's term of office from three to four years. However, the brief period after 1851 of a popularly elected governor with expanded powers provided little chance for those holding the office to establish real independence from the General Assembly. By 1861 there still was no effective application of separation of powers to the governor and the legislature in the Old Dominion.

The state's judiciary also was under the thumb of the traditionalist-controlled legislature. The general court in the 1790s legitimized the legislatively biased 1776 constitution by declaring that usage had validated the document even though the 1776 "convention" had not been specifically authorized to draw up a fundamental law.[23] There was no real assertion of judicial review by the Virginia courts. For instance, when the general court discussed the constitutionality of a bill which combined the jurisdictions of common law and chancery in the district courts, it left totally unclear its position on the doctrine of judicial review.[24] Later, after the principle of judicial review was asserted by the Supreme Court of Appeals in the case of *Sharpe* v. *Robinson* and the *Cases of the Judges*, the precedent was modified considerably in subsequent application by the courts because of their almost unlimited confidence in the legislature. As a quid pro quo there were no real changes in the court system by the legislature, only structural modifications to deal with complaints of inefficiency. What the West wanted but did not get for seventy-five years was an independent judiciary elected by the people. It was not until the Convention of 1850–51, when the traditionalists fell into line on the West's demand, that the popular election of judges was adopted and the courts became independent of the legislature.[25]

Just as the traditionalists were able to delay any significant alteration of the state's judicial system until 1851, they were able for the same period of time to preserve untouched the system of eighteenth-century local justice in the county courts. Despite criticism of these courts by men like St. George Tucker and Jefferson, the Convention of 1829–30 left them firmly embodied as they were in the 1776 constitution. It was not until the late 1840s, in the face of the most devastating attacks on these bodies, that things began to change.[26] In 1848 Governor William Smith recommended a complete reformation and suggested that the number of justices be reduced. In 1849 Governor John Floyd, in a speech to the General Assembly, condemned the county courts as "repugnant to the fundamental principles of Republican Government."[27] Finally, the Convention of 1850–51 placed limits on the number of county justices and officers, provided them with a set salary, and, most significantly, required them to be chosen by the people.

Over the years as more and more Virginians moved to the western counties, they felt the full impact of a government in which the legislature not only had too much power but misused this power for the exclusive benefit of the eastern planters and their constituencies. The focal point of the West's grievances from beginning to end was representation and the joined issue of slavery, even though other constitutional matters, like suffrage, and other economic problems, like internal improvements, soon were added to them. The record of the eastern-controlled legislature was perceived in the West more and more as one of perpetuating its legislative domination for the primary purpose of safeguarding white supremacy: to keep the institution of slavery from any change and to limit the number of free blacks in the commonwealth. Even though slavery spread into parts of the Valley and into some far southwestern counties by the 1820s, eastern politicians still felt compelled to protect the institution at all costs by constitutional law. The Constitution of 1850–51, for example, repeated the provisions included in the previous two documents forbidding emancipation by the General Assembly and mandating emigration of any manumitted black. For three generations slavery haunted the traditionalists' reaction to any suggestion of legislative reapportionment. They would not budge on the western demands for political democracy, for to do so, to them, meant jeopardizing the peculiar institution and their own safety.

The history of constitutional conventions in the Old Dominion between the Revolution and the Civil War, then, is a story of a sectional struggle over whether or not its fundamental law should rest upon and be responsive to the will of the people. All of the battles fought during those years—over apportionment and slavery, suffrage, a stronger executive, democratization of the courts—orbited around the hub of the concept of majority rule. Most Virginians living in the West wanted constitutional guarantees of this principle; most Virginians in the Piedmont and Tidewater did not. The underlying and increasingly divergent social and economic needs of these two sections exacerbated their respective views of the nature and purpose of constitutional law. And these socioeconomic differences were mirrored in, and determined the outcomes of, their constitutional conventions.

The conventions showed that Virginians who identified themselves with the West wanted a constitution that reflected their commitment to a republican government based on majority consent regardless of the real or imagined fears of the minority in the state about attacks on slavery. These Virginians, the progressives, from Jefferson on evoked the language of the Enlightenment embodied in the preamble of the Declaration of Independence, that all citizens had a right to be equal under the law. They condemned as an "odious distinction" a constitution that prevented some Virginians in the beginning and by 1830 most of its white adult males then living in the West from having an equitable say in their government. As a consistent theme they demanded a fundamental law based upon the will of the people, with a process of amendment, and with a workable system of checks and balances and separation of powers.

On the other hand, the eastern delegates to these conventions, the traditionalists, time after time went back to the premise that constitutions were based upon a majority of both numbers and interests. They argued that if a simple numerical majority was allowed to govern in Virginia, it would adopt laws suited only to its needs and would ride roughshod over the legitimate concerns, like the security of slave property, of the minority. Some traditionalists even denied the validity of the principle of majority rule altogether and agreed with a writer in *De Bow's Review* who stated that "the right to govern rests with a very small minority; the duty to obey is inherent in the great mass of mankind . . . such is the actual constitution of all permanent governments."[28] When all was said and done, the traditionalists had little time for any principles, either for or against majority rule. What mattered to them, they said, were the practical conditions and responsibilities of government, and these pragmatic considerations, not abstract principles or logical arguments, should determine constitutional law.

Until the Convention of 1850–51 the traditionalists were able to keep Virginia's constitution largely as it was at the time of Independence. They stubbornly resisted demands for wider participation in, and democratization of, their state government. For three generations they successfully held the line by a combination of skillful yet largely inconsequential compromises on some points in the General Assembly and adroit parliamentary maneuvering and superior floor organization at the conventions. But their success meant failure; it meant that Virginia's constitutional law failed to satisfy the legitimate demands of the larger part of its electorate. This failure and the accompanying frustration across the Blue Ridge Mountains was a crucial factor in a permanent division of the commonwealth into two separate states in the crisis of 1861.

Appendix
Notes
Selected Bibliography
Index

Appendix

Biographical data not from sources cited in the following sketches have been obtained from the *Dictionary of American Biography; Biographical Directory of the American Congress;* Lyon G. Tyler, ed., *Encyclopedia of Virginia Biography;* Thomas C. Miller and Hu Maxwell, eds., *West Virginia and Its People;* Earl G. Swem, *Register of the General Assembly;* Robert L. Scribner and Brent Tarter, eds., *Revolutionary Virginia: The Road to Independence* (Charlottesville, Va., 1973–83); United States Census, Population Schedules; Land and Personal Property Tax Records and the records of births, deaths, and marriages, Virginia State Library and Archives; and the historical archives of the Inter-University Consortium for Political Research, University of Michigan. The data on the property holdings reflect only those holdings listed on the tax rolls for the county from which the delegates were elected at the time of the conventions, or in the case of the 1776 convention at the time of the convention itself or shortly thereafter. Of special assistance in locating data on little-known delegates was information provided by Brent Tarter and Sandra G. Treadway, eds., forthcoming *Dictionary of Virginia Biography.*

CONVENTION OF 1776

ACRILL, WILLIAM (c.1731–1781), Charles City County, was born in Chesterfield County where his father sat in the House of Burgesses, 1736–38. William also served as a burgess, 1766–75, and in the House of Delegates, 1776–77.

ADAMS, RICHARD (1723–1800), Henrico Countty, son of Ebenezer Adams and grandson of Richard Adams, a London merchant-tailor who came to Virginia after 1660, was born in New Kent County. He was an Anglican and a planter-merchant until 1782 when he moved to Richmond. Sometime between that date and his death in 1800 he owned 2 town lots there as well as 41 slaves. He served in the House of Burgesses, 1752–75, House of

Delegates, 1776–78, and the senate, 1779–82. Adams was a member of the Henrico Committee of Safety. Lewis W. Bruton wrote in the *History of Henrico County* (Richmond, 1904), 184: "His means were ample and his landed possessions within the limits and in the immediate vicinity of Richmond probably were more extensive than any other, then resident."

AYLETT, WILLIAM (1734–1780), King William County, was the son of Philip Aylett and grandson of Col. William Aylett of Fairfield, burgess, 1723–26. An uncle, William, was also a member of the House of Burgesses, 1736–40. Delegate William was a cousin by marriage to Augustine Washington, brother of George. He was a planter, but no record survives of the number of slaves he owned. Aylett was an Anglican and was elected to the colonial legislature, 1772–75. During the war he was deputy commissary general for Virginia. He died at Yorktown.

BANISTER, JOHN (1734–1788), Dinwiddie County, was the grandson of a minister and botanist who immigrated to the Northern Neck from Barbados. John married Patsy Bland and lived at Battersea near Petersburg. He studied law in England at Temple Inns of Court. He served in the House of Burgesses, 1765–68, 1769–76, and was a member of Congress and a signer of the Articles of Confederation. During the war he held the rank of lieutenant colonel and served in the House of Delegates, 1776–77, 1781–83.

BERKELEY, EDMUND (1720–1802), Middlesex County, was the son of Colonel Edmund Berkeley who was a burgess from Middlesex, 1734–40. His grandfather was appointed to the governor's council in 1715 and married Lucy Burwell sometime after 1720. Delegate Edmund owned the plantation Barn Elms. He served in the House of Burgesses, 1769–71, 1772–76, and the House of Delegates, 1776. He was an Anglican, then an Episcopalian.

BIRD, ABRAHAM (born 1750), Dunmore County (renamed Shenandoah County in 1776), was born in Pennsylvania, the son of Andrew Bird (died 1750), came to the Valley as a young man, and established a plantation at Red Banks. In 1783 he owned 3 slaves. He was a burgess, 1774–75, and a member of the House of Delegates, 1776–96. He also was a justice of the peace in Shenandoah County, 1776, and a trustee of Woodstock Academy.

BLAIR, JOHN (1732–1800), College of William and Mary, was born at Williamsburg, the son of John Blair, president of the council. He attended William and Mary and the Middle Temple, London. An Anglican, he lived in Williamsburg where he practiced law. He owned 18 slaves. In 1766–68 and 1769–71 he represented the town in the House of Burgesses. He sat as chief justice of the General Court, 1776–80, then as judge of the High Court of Chancery. He was a member of the Virginia delegation to the Philadelphia Constitutional Convention and in 1788 supported ratification of the Constitution. In 1788 he was appointed to the U.S. Supreme Court; in 1796 he resigned and died at Williamsburg. See Grigsby, *Convention of 1776*, 69–72.

BLAND, RICHARD (1710–1776), Prince George County, was of the family line of Edward Bland, a prominent landowner and merchant who was one of the first settlers of the Northern Neck, coming there in 1674 to manage family plantations. He was educated at William and Mary and the University of Edinburgh, was an Anglican, and married Elizabeth Randolph. The planter served thirty years in the House of Burgesses beginning in 1745, served on the Committee of Correspondence, 1773, and was a member of the First Continental Congress. He died in October 1776 while visiting John Tazewell in Williamsburg. See Grigsby, *Convention of 1776*, 57–61.

BOOKER, WILLIAM (c.1746–1787), Prince Edward County, was the son of an Amelia County burgess. He was an Anglican planter, a justice of the peace, 1767–77, member of the legislature, 1776, and schoolteacher, 1780. He was a charter trustee of Hampden-Sydney Academy, 1776.

BOWYER, JOHN (c.1730–1806), Botetourt County, began a career as a schoolteacher in 1753 but in the 1760s became a farmer after he married. He was a captain in the Augusta County militia in 1763. He represented Botetourt County in the House of Burgesses, 1769–76, and signed the Williamsburg Association in 1772. He was a state legislator, 1776–77, 1778, 1782, 1784–86, 1789, 1791–96, 1799–1802. He was a colonel of the Rockbridge County militia, 1781, and died near Lexington. See Waddell, *Augusta County*.

BRENT, WILLIAM (born c.1724), Stafford County, was of a family dominant in the county since the 1660s. The family estate was Richland. He was an Anglican in 1776 and a member of the House of Delegates, 1776, 1778, 1784–85, and the senate, 1780–81.

BROOKE, GEORGE (born 1728), King and Queen County, lived at Mantapike, his plantation in that county. Brooke also held title to land in Orange County. He was a burgess, 1765–68, 1772–76.

BULLITT, CUTHBERT (c.1740–1795), Prince William County, was born about 1740 (his mother was Elizabeth Harrison Bullitt) and practiced law in the county. He was a member of the Committee of Safety and served in the House of Delegates, 1776–78, 1785–88. He attended the Ratifying Convention of 1788 and that year was appointed to the General Court where he sat until his death.

BURWELL, LEWIS (c.1745–1779), Gloucester County, was the son of Lewis Burwell, president of the governor's council in 1743. The family had been influential in the county since 1642. He was county sheriff in 1767. He was a burgess, 1769–74, and a member of the House of Delegates from 1776 until his death.

CABELL, JOHN (1735–1815), Buckingham County, was born in Nelson County, the third son of Dr. William Cabell and brother of Joseph and William, Jr. He inherited the Green Hill estate and was an Anglican. He served on the Committee of Safety, 1775, and in the House of Delegates, 1777–88. He was a colonel in the county militia. After the war he actively opposed the federal Constitution and then became a Jeffersonian Republican. He died at Green Hill. Main, *Political Parties*, 445.

CABELL, WILLIAM, JR. (1730–1798), Amherst County, elder brother of John, was an Anglican planter-lawyer who in 1782 owned 90 slaves and 43 buildings at Union Hill. He was a vestryman, sheriff, coroner, and presiding justice at the county court. He was a burgess, 1756–76, and a member of the senate, 1776–81, and the House of Delegates, 1781–83, 1787–88. He was a colonel in the Albemarle County militia during the French and Indian War and was a member of the Committee of Safety in 1775. See Grigsby, *Convention of 1776*, 113–20.

CAMPBELL, ARTHUR (1743–1811), Fincastle County, born in Augusta County, was captured by the Shawnee at the age of fourteen and held captive for three years in the Great Lakes area. In 1759 he escaped and provided the British with valuable military intelligence for which he was awarded 1,000 acres near Louisville. In 1776 he moved to the Holston River and was appointed a major of the Fincastle militia. His father, John, was an Irish immigrant who first settled in Lancaster, Pennsylvania, in 1724 and moved into the Valley in 1726. Arthur was educated at Liberty Hall and was a Methodist. He was a member of the House of Delegates, 1776, 1778, 1782–83, 1786–88. In 1785 he was involved in a scheme to separate Washington County from Virginia and make a new state of Franklin along with western North Carolina. The General Assembly condemned the plan as treason. He died at Royal Oak.

CARRINGTON, PAUL (1732–1818), Charlotte County, was the son of George Carrington who came to the colony in the early 1700s from Barbados and served with William Byrd on the boundary line expedition. George, who lived at Boston Hill, was a county officeholder and represented Goochland County in the House of Burgesses, 1740s-1760s. An Anglican with no higher education, Paul read law and "practiced successfully" (Main, *Political Parties*, 442). Before independence he was king's attorney, justice of the peace, and burgess, 1765–75. He was a member of the Association, a delegate to the First Continental Congress, and a member of the Committee of Safety. He served in the senate, 1776–77. He sat on the General Court and the Supreme Court of Appeals and became an active Virginia Federalist in the 1790s. He died at his home, Mulberry Hill. See Grigsby, *Convention of 1776*, 97–105.

CARY, ARCHIBALD (1721–1786), Chesterfield County, was of a family long important in the Tidewater (Miles Cary came to Virginia in 1645 and served as a burgess in the 1660s). He was an Anglican and married Mary Randolph. He was the father-in-law of Thomas Mann Randolph, Sr., of Tuckahoe and lived at the plantation Ampthill where he also operated an iron furnace. He was educated at William and Mary. He was a member of the House of Burgesses, 1748–49, 1756–70. In 1773 he was on the Committee of Correspondence. In 1776 he served in the convention as chairman of the committee of the whole and was elected to the senate where he served until his death. See Grigsby, *Convention of 1776*, 90–93.

CARY, RICHARD (1739–1789), Warwick County, was of the same influential family as Archibald. An Anglican and a large planter, Richard was county clerk, 1764, a member of the Committee of Safety, and a judge of the Admiralty Court, 1776–88. The year of his death he was appointed to the General Court.

CARY, WILSON MILES (1734–1817), Elizabeth City County, was born at Ceely in Warwick County. He was educated at William and Mary, married the daughter of John Blair (*see above*), and lived on the plantation Carysbrook. He served as a burgess, 1766–71, and as a delegate to the legislature from Elizabeth City County, 1776, 1780, 1795, 1796, Fluvanna County, 1777, and Warwick County, 1783–86. He died in Fluvanna County.

CLAPHAM, JOSIAS, Loudoun County, immigrated to Virginia from Wakefield, England, after 1749 in order to claim an inheritance from his uncle of 1,135 acres. He was a burgess, 1774–76, and member of the House of Delegates, 1776–81, 1787. Main, *Political Parties*, 442.

CLAYTON, WILLIAM (c.1726–1797), New Kent County, was born in England. His grandfather, John Clayton (1665–1737), an English barrister, was educated at Inner Temple, came to Virginia as a judge of the Admiralty Court, and served as a burgess from James City County, 1720–28. William was a planter and an Anglican who was a burgess, 1766–71, member of the Committee of Safety, 1776, and House of Delegates, 1776, and delegate to the Ratifying Convention of 1788. He was also county clerk from time to time.

COCKE, ALLEN (c.1736–1780), Surry County, was born in Goochland County, great-grandson of Richard Cocke (1600–1665) of Bremo who emigrated to the colony in the 1620s and served in the House of Burgesses, 1634, 1654. His father, Benjamin Cocke (1710–1758), also was a burgess from Goochland, 1742–47. Allen was a planter who served as a burgess, 1772–75, and in the Committee of Safety, 1775, and the House of Delegates, 1776, 1779–81. He was a colonel of the Surry County militia. He lived at his plantation Bacon's Castle.

COWPER, WILLIAM (born 1735), Nansemond County, was an Anglican, a justice of the peace, 1772–76, and served in the House of Delegates, 1776. He owned 1,000 acres and was a partner with his brothers Willis and John in a shipbuilding and mercantile operation in Portsmouth.

CRALLE, JOHN, JR. (born c.1731), Northumberland County, was born in England and was a planter at Heath's Hill and member of the legislature in 1776. His son, Mattrone B., was a county clerk of Northumberland. He stood for election to the House of Burgesses in 1765 and 1768 but lost both times.

CURLE, WILSON R. W. (born 1726), Norfolk Borough, was of a family line which settled in Sussex County in 1688. He lived in the town of Hampton and served in the House of Delegates, 1776–79, and then as a judge of the Admiralty Court. He also was on the Elizabeth City County Committee of Safety in 1774.

DANDRIDGE, BARTHOLOMEW (born 1737), New Kent County, was the son of Colonel John Dandridge and brother of Martha, the wife of George Washington. He was an Anglican planter who in 1785 paid taxes on 37 buildings. He served as a burgess, 1774–76, and in the House of Delegates, 1778. Douglas S. Freeman, *George Washington* (New York, 1949), 2: 294–94, 298n.

DIGGES, DUDLEY (1730–1790), York County, was the son of Cole Digges, a member of the council. The family line included Edward Digges, governor of Virginia in 1656. He was educated at William and Mary and was a planter-lawyer and an Anglican. He represented York County in the House of Burgesses, 1752–56.

DIGGES, WILLIAM, JR. (c.1742–after 1806), York County, was a nephew of Dudley. He was an Anglican planter who lived at Denbigh. He was a member of the House of Burgesses, 1772, and House of Delegates, 1776, from York County. He also represented Warwick County in the house, 1790–93 and 1800–1805. He took the designation Jr. to distinguish himself from his uncle William, brother of Dudley.

DREW, WILLIAM (born c.1748), Berkeley County. He was the first clerk of Berkeley County, 1772.

EDMONDSON, JAMES (c.1734–1791), Essex County, was a planter who served in the House of Burgesses, 1769–76.

FARMER, LODOWICK (c.1730–1780), Lunenburg County, was a native of Chesterfield County who moved to Lunenburg County in 1770. He was a planter who in 1783 owned 5 slaves. He was a vestryman, a justice of the peace, county clerk, a burgess, 1769–71, and a member of the House of Delegates, 1776.

FAULCON, NICHOLAS, JR. (1736–after 1803), Surry County, replaced his father-in-law, Hartwell Cocke, as a burgess in 1773 and served until 1774. He was a member of the Committee of Safety, 1774, and a captain in the Surry County militia. He served in the House of Delegates, 1776, 1794–99, and in the senate, 1799–1803.

FIELD, HENRY, JR. (c.1734–1785), Culpeper County, was the son of the first vestryman chosen in Germanna, 1731. He was an Anglican who succeeded his father as vestryman in 1762. He was a planter, a burgess, 1768–70, and justice of the peace, 1775, a member of the Committee of Safety, 1775, and a delegate to the legislature, 1776–79, 1781–82. Philip Slaughter, *History of St. Mark's Parish, Culpeper County, Virginia* (Baltimore, 1877).

FITZHUGH, WILLIAM (1726–1808), King George County, was born at Eagle's Nest, son of Henry and Lucy Carter Fitzhugh, a daughter of Robert ("King") Carter. He was educated by private tutors and at William and Mary. He was a planter-lawyer and an Anglican with two estates, Chatham near Fredericksburg and Ravensworth in Fairfax County. Main describes him as "one of Virginia's wealthiest men" (*Political Parties*, 442). He served as a burgess, 1772–75, on the Committee of Safety, 1775, in the House of Delegates, 1776–77, 1780–81, 1787–88, and in the senate, 1781–85, and was a member of Congress, 1779–80. Freeman, *Washington*, 1:2, 6, 8, 2:100, 101n, 225–26, 338, 439–44, 487–88.

FLEMING, WILLIAM (1747–1824), Cumberland County, was born in Powhatan County, the son of Colonel John Fleming of Mount Pleasants. He was educated at William and Mary, where he became a close friend of Thomas Jefferson, studied law, and practiced in Cumberland County. He was a burgess, 1774–76, and a member of the Committee of Safety, 1775, and the House of Delegates, 1779–81. In 1780 he was appointed to the circuit court and in 1788 to the Supreme Court of Appeals where he sat until his death in Chesterfield County.

FULGHAM, CHARLES (born c.1746), Isle of Wight County, was of a family that patented estates on the Rappahannock River in 1643 and supported Nathaniel Bacon during Bacon's Rebellion. He was a planter, a captain in the county militia in 1775, and a member of the House of Delegates, 1776–78.

GARLAND, DAVID (c.1723–1783), Lunenburg County, was an Anglican planter who owned 27 slaves in 1783. He served in the House of Delegates in 1776.

GEE, HENRY (c.1733–1781), Sussex County, was an Anglican and a burgess, 1774, a member of the Committee of Safety, 1775, county justice, 1776, and legislator, 1776–79.

GILMER, GEORGE (1742–1795), Albemarle County, was the second son of St. George Gilmer of Scotland. He was educated at William and Mary and studied medicine at the University of Edinburgh. He practiced first in Williamsburg, 1766, then in Charlottesville, and finally at his residence Pen Pash where in 1783 he owned 10 buildings. He served in the House of Delegates, 1778–79. He was a close friend of Thomas Jefferson. See Malone, *Jefferson*, 1:99, 240, 367, 2:246, 301; Boyd, *Jefferson Papers*.

GOODE, BENNETT (born 1744), Mecklenburg County, the son of John Goode, Jr., at Falls, a plantation in Chesterfield County, and grandson of John Goode, Sr., an English immigrant. John Jr. married Thomas Jefferson's aunt Martha. Bennett was a wealthy planter who served as a member of the House of Delegates, 1776, and in the Ratifying Convention of 1788. He was also a member of the Virginia delegation to the federal Constitutional Convention of 1787.

GORDON, JAMES, JR. (born c.1752), Lancaster County, was born in that county, the son of James Gordon, immigrant in 1738 from Scotland (Scott, *Orange County*). His father was a planter and merchant and a Presbyterian, a brother-in-law of the "Blind Preacher" James Waddell. He represented Richmond County in the house, 1776–77, 1782, 1786–88, and was a delegate from Orange County in the 1788 Ratifying Convention. See A. C. Gordon, *The Gordons in Virginia* and *William F. Gordon;* Freeman, *Washington*, 1: chap. 4.

GRAY, EDWIN (1744–1813), Southampton County, was the son of a burgess, 1754–68, Colonel Joseph Gray, of the line of Thomas Gray who came to Virginia in 1608. He was an Anglican planter and a burgess, 1769–76, and a member of the House of Delegates, 1776, 1779, 1787–88, 1791, the senate, 1777–79, and the U.S. Congress, 1799–1813.

HARVIE, JOHN, JR. (1747–1807), West Augusta County, was the son of an immigrant from Gargunnock, Scotland, who came to Virginia in 1742 and settled in Albemarle County. John Jr. attended William and Mary, was a lawyer, and owned 15 buildings in 1782. He represented West Augusta in the legislature in 1776, Albemarle County in 1777, and the city of Richmond, 1793–94. He was an Indian commissioner in 1774 and secretary of the commonwealth in 1788. He was killed by a fall from a ladder in Richmond.

HARWOOD, SAMUEL (c.1740–1778), Charles City County, was born at Weyanoke. Both his father and grandfather had been burgesses from the county. An Anglican planter, shipbuilder, and graduate of William and Mary, he served in the House of Delegates only in 1776.

HENRY, PATRICK (1736–1799), Hanover County, at the 1776 Convention was a spokesman for Southside delegates but became a willing compromiser with the Tuckahoes after being advanced as their candidate for governor. He was chosen governor again in 1784 and 1785.

HITE, ABRAHAM (1720–after 1808), Hampshire County, was the son of Jost Hite, a native of Strasburg, Germany, who came to Pennsylvania in 1732, then to the Valley the following year. He was a farmer and a Baptist. He was a burgess, 1769–71, and a member of the House of Delegates, 1776–79, 1782–83, and moved to Fairfield, Ohio, in 1783. Wayland, *Shenandoah County,* 609–10.

HOLT, JAMES (1711–1779), Norfolk County, was the son of Thomas Holt of Hog Island, Surry County, a burgess, 1699–1700. He was a planter-lawyer who in 1782 owned 12 slaves and in 1785 paid taxes on 9 buildings. He served in the House of Burgesses, 1772–74, House of Delegates, 1776, and senate, 1776–79.

JOHNSON, THOMAS, JR. (born c.1734), Louisa County, was the son of a planter at Chericoke and of a family line, including burgesses, going back to 1645. He was a planter, a burgess, 1769–72, 1774–76, and a member of the Committee of Safety and of the House of Delegates, 1776, 1779–81, 1783, 1785–86. Johnson was a strong supporter of Patrick Henry.

JONES, JOSEPH (1727–1821), King George County, was the son of James Jones, a building contractor and burgess from King George. He was a planter who was trained at Middle Temple, 1751. He lived in Fredericksburg. His niece, Elizabeth, married James Monroe. He was a member of the House of Burgesses, 1772–75, the Committee of Safety, 1775, the House of Delegates, 1776–77, 1780–81, 1783–85, and Congress, 1777–78, 1780–83. He was a delegate to the Ratifying Convention of 1788. In 1789 he was appointed a judge of the General Court. Freeman, *Washington,* 1:52n.

KENNER, RODHAM, III (1740–after 1785), Northumberland County, was born of a family that went back to Richard Kenner, a prominent English merchant who came to Virginia in 1660. He was educated at William and Mary and was an Anglican planter.

He was a burgess, 1773–76, and a member of the 1776 House of Delegates. He signed a Westmoreland County protest against the Stamp Act.

KING, HENRY (born c.1736), Elizabeth City County, was the son of Michael King, who came to Nansemond County about 1690. He was an Anglican, a justice of the peace, 1769, and a member of the House of Burgesses, 1772–74, and House of Delegates, 1776.

LANKFORD, BENJAMIN (c.1743–1810), Pittsylvania County, was an Anglican vestryman and a planter (400 acres), sheriff, and justice of the peace. He was a burgess, 1774, and a member of the Committee of Safety, 1775, and of the House of Delegates, 1776, 1779, 1780–90. He opposed the ratification of the federal Constitution and later was a Jeffersonian Republican.

LEE, HENRY (1727–1787), Prince William County, was the third son of Henry Lee of Lee Hall. He was educated at Princeton and was an Anglican and a planter at Leesylvania. He served as a burgess, 1758–76, and a member of the senate, 1776–87, and was a justice of the peace. He married Mary Bland and was the father of "Light-Horse Harry" Lee and grandfather of General Robert E. Lee. Freeman, *Washington,* 1:11, 94, 99, 207; Hendrick, *Lees of Virginia,* 76, 97, 329–31.

LEE, RICHARD (1726–1795), Westmoreland County, was the second son of Henry Lee of Lee Hall. He was an Anglican vestryman and a planter known as "Squire Richard" Lee. He was a bachelor, a justice of the peace, a burgess, 1756–75, a signer of the Westmoreland Resolutions, and a member of the House of Delegates, 1777–90, 1792–94. Freeman, *Washington,* 1:3, 6, 11, 91, 488–89, 527; Hendrick, *Lees of Virginia,* 66, 97, 135, 209.

LEE, RICHARD HENRY (1732–1794), Westmoreland County, was the third son of Thomas Lee of Stratford Hall, president of the governor's council. He was educated at Wakefield Academy, Yorkshire, England, 1751, and was an Anglican planter at Chantilly. He served as justice of the peace, as burgess, 1758–75, and as a member of the House of Delegates, 1777, 1780–84. He was a member of Congress, 1774–80, and of the Confederation Congress, 1784–87. He was against the ratification of the Constitution. In 1789 he was elected to the U.S. Senate where he served until 1792. Hendrick, *Lees of Virginia,* 80, 85–87, 91–105, 123–25, 127–29, 166, 180–91, 197–210, 211–13, 367.

LEE, THOMAS LUDWELL (1730–1778), Stafford County, was the oldest living son of Thomas and Hannah Ludwell Lee of Stratford Hall. He was a lawyer and an Anglican who served as a burgess, 1758–65, as a member of the Committee of Safety, 1775, and in the senate, 1776–78. He was educated in England at the Middle Temple and lived at his plantation near Bellview in Stafford County.

LEWIS, CHARLES (born 1740), Albemarle County, was the son of Robert Lewis of Belvoir. He served in the House of Delegates, 1776. He lived at North Garden, his estate in Albemarle County.

LEWIS, THOMAS (1718–1790), Augusta County, was born in Donegal County, Ireland, and came to Pennsylvania in 1731, then to Augusta County in 1733. He was an Anglican planter, surveyor, and bookseller. He was on the Committee of Safety and in the House of Delegates, 1776. Grigsby wrote that "Lewis was representative of the people of the extreme west" (*Convention of 1776*, 110). His plantation, Lewistown, was located adjacent to the Shenandoah River.

LOCKHART, PATRICK (c.1740–c.1813), Botetourt County, was born in Scotland and came to Virginia before 1748. He served with Braddock in 1754 and also fought Indians at Point Pleasant and was a captain in the seige of Yorktown. He was a justice of the peace, 1773, and served in the House of Delegates, 1776–78. He was a tavern owner and merchant.

LYNCH, CHARLES, JR. (1736–1796), Bedford County, was the son of an Irish immigrant who came to Virginia about 1720 as an indentured servant to a Louisa County planter, Christopher Clark. Charles Sr. married Clark's daughter in 1733 and moved to Goochland County in 1740, then to Albemarle County in 1745 where he became a county justice and burgess, 1748–49. Charles Jr. studied law and was a burgess, 1769, 1774–75. He was a member of the House of Delegates, 1776–77, and the senate, 1784–89. He acquired 4,393 acres between 1756 and 1781. He was a Quaker. Lynch lived at Green Level near the Staunton River. His youngest son, John, founded Lynchburg.

LYNE, WILLIAM (born c.1738), King and Queen County, was the son of William Lyne, a British immigrant who had first settled in North Carolina and then moved to Stratton Parish, King and Queen County. He was an Anglican planter at his estate Lyneville and served as burgess, 1769–71, and in the House of Delegates, 1776, 1787–88. He was on the Committee of Safety, 1775, and saw duty as a colonel in the county militia during the war.

McCARTY, CHARLES B. (born 1741), Richmond County, was born of a family line traceable to Dennis McCarty who came to Virginia about 1670 and died in the county in 1694. His father, Daniel, owned extensive acreage and served in the House of Burgesses, 1705–6, 1715, 1718, 1720–23, twice being elected Speaker. Charles was a justice of the peace, 1770 on, an Anglican vestryman, and a planter with an estate at Lylel's Swamp; he was in the House of Delegates, 1776.

McDOWELL, SAMUEL (1734–1818), Augusta County, was born in Ireland. His father, a surveyor, came to Pennsylvania in 1736, then to Virginia where he was killed by Indians in 1742 near the James River. Samuel was privately taught and was a lawyer who served in the House of Delegates, 1776–77, for Augusta County and for Rockbridge County, 1778, 1780–81. He was a burgess, 1772–75. He moved to Kentucky in the 1780s and was chosen circuit judge.

MACLIN, FREDERIC (c.1739–1808), Brunswick County, was born in Scotland and came to Virginia in 1725. He was a county judge, a burgess, 1774–76, and member of the legislature, 1776–77, 1782.

MADISON, JAMES (1751–1836), Orange County. President of the United States, 1809–17, Madison was first elected to public office to serve as a delegate to the Convention.

MASON, DAVID (1733–1785), Sussex County, was the grandson of Captain John Mason (died 1755). He was an Anglican planter noted as a breeder of racehorses. In 1782 he owned 38 slaves. He was justice of the peace of Sussex, a burgess, 1760–76, and a member of the House of Delegates, 1779, and the senate, 1776, 1779–81.

MASON, GEORGE (1725–1792), Fairfax County, was the author of the Virginia Declaration of Rights and an important member of the federal Constitutional Convention of 1787.

MAYO, JOHN (1740–1786), Cumberland County, was the son of a surveyor who came from England in 1723 to make a map of the Northern Neck. He was an Anglican planter who served as a burgess, 1768–76, and legislator, 1776. He was the grandfather of the wife of General Winfield Scott.

MERCER, JAMES (1736–1793), Hampshire County, was the son of John Mercer, an Irish immigrant lawyer from Dublin who came to Virginia in 1720 and established a plantation, Marlborough, in Stafford County. He was a graduate of William and Mary, a lawyer, and an Anglican. He was a burgess, 1762, 1774, and a member of the Committee of Safety, 1775, and of Congress, 1776–80. From 1780 to 1789 he was on the General Court and the Court of Appeals.

MERIWETHER, GEORGE (1745–1782), Louisa County, was the son of Nicholas Meriwether and member of a large landowning family. He was an Anglican and served in the House of Delegates, 1776–78. In 1782 he planned to move to the site of the future town of Louisville, Kentucky, but died before he arrived there.

MONTAGUE, JAMES (1741–1781), Middlesex County, was of a family going back to Peter Montague who came to Virginia in 1621 and represented Nansemond County in the House of Burgesses until moving in 1654 to Middlesex County which he represented in the house until his death in 1659. The family had extensive landholdings in the Northern Neck. James was an Anglican planter and justice of the peace who was a burgess, 1772–76, and member of the House of Delegates, 1776–77, 1780–81.

MOORE, WILLIAM (born c.1741), Orange County, was the son of John Moore of Albemarle County who in 1745 owned about 5,000 acres and several town lots in Charlottesville. He was an Anglican vestryman and planter, justice of the peace, member of the Committee of Safety, and delegate to the legislature, 1776–77, 1781–83. In 1782 he owned 2,000 acres and 50 slaves.

MUSE, HUDSON (born c.1740), Richmond County, was an Anglican vestryman, merchant, and planter who represented the county in the Virginia legislature for one year, 1776.

NELSON, THOMAS, JR. (1738–1789), York County, was the son of Thomas Nelson, secretary of the colony and president of the governor's council. He was educated at Eton and at Trinity College, Cambridge (B.A.), was an Anglican, a planter-merchant, and a member of the House of Burgesses, 1761, Continental Congress, 1775–77, 1779, and House of Delegates, 1777, 1783, 1786–88. During the war he was a colonel in the 2d Virginia Regiment and commanded at the seige of Yorktown. He died at his plantation Offley in Hanover County. Freeman, *Washington,* 1:117, 236.

NEWTON, THOMAS, JR. (1742–1807), Norfolk County, was a burgess, 1765–76, and a delegate representing the county, 1779–82, 1795, and the town of Norfolk, 1783, 1794, 1796. He was a graduate of William and Mary. He was a member of the senate, 1797–1805. He was a member of the Committee of Safety, 1774, and the Naval Board during the Revolution. He was educated in the schools of the town and served as its mayor, 1780, 1786, 1792, 1794.

NICHOLAS, ROBERT CARTER (1728–1780), James City County, was the son of Dr. George Nicholas and Elizabeth Carter Nicholas, daughter of Robert ("King") Carter. He was a graduate of William and Mary, was an Anglican, and married Anne Cary. His son was Governor Wilson Cary Nicholas. A lawyer by profession, he served as burgess from York County, 1756, and James City County, 1765–76, where he supported the Stamp Act Resolutions but opposed Henry's views of 1765, was treasurer of the colony, 1766–76, and was a member of the Committee of Correspondence. He was a member of the legislature for one term, 1776. Grigsby, *Convention of 1776,* 61–69.

NORVELL, WILLIAM (c.1726–1802), James City County, was a descendant of Hugh Norvell, an "early immigrant" to Virginia. He was a planter who was a burgess, 1774–76, and served in the House of Delegates, 1776–92.

PAGE, MANN, JR. (born 1750), Spotsylvania County, was born at Rosewell in Gloucester County, the grandson of Mann Page (1691–1730), an Oxford-educated member of the governor's council, 1715. He was the half brother of Governor John Page. He was a graduate of William and Mary and an Anglican planter at Mannsfield near Fredericksburg. In 1776 he married the daughter of John Taylor. He served as a burgess, 1772–76, in Congress, 1777, and in the House of Delegates, 1776, 1778–87. He died at his plantation. Freeman, *Washington,* 1:34.

PATTESON, CHARLES, Buckingham County, was the son of David Patteson who patented land in 1714 in Henrico and Chesterfield counties. He served on the Committee of Safety, 1775, and the House of Delegates, 1776–77, 1781–82, 1784–85, 1787–88. He attended the Ratifying Convention of 1788.

PENDLETON, EDMUND (1721–1803), Caroline County, was a member of the Virginia Committee of Correspondence and the first Continental Congress. He was the leading opponent of Patrick Henry as president of the 1776 Convention. Pendleton was first Speaker of the House of Delegates and after 1779 president of the Supreme Court of Appeals until his death.

PENN, GABRIEL (born 1742), Amherst County, was of a family which had come to Virginia in the 1630s from Maryland. He was an Anglican planter whose will of 1798 shows him owning a 1,640-acre plantation. He was a colonel in the Amherst County militia, 1776–81, and a member of the House of Delegates, 1776–78. He was a kinsman of John Penn of North Carolina, a signer of the Declaration of Independence. In 1782 he owned 1,491 acres and 42 slaves.

PEYTON, FRANCIS (c.1745–1815), Loudoun County, was born in Powhatan County, fifth son of Valentine Peyton, Jr. (1688–1751), burgess, sheriff, and justice of the peace, and grandson of Valentine Peyton who came to Westmoreland County about 1650. Francis was a planter, a county justice, and an Anglican vestryman of Shelburne Parish. He served as county clerk, 1781–82, 1789–90, in the House of Burgesses, 1769–71, 1772–75, in the House of Delegates, 1776, 1779–82, 1784–87, in the senate, 1798–1803, and on the executive council, 1797.

PICKETT, MARTIN (1740–1806), Fauquier County, was a justice of the peace, a member of the House of Delegates, 1776–81, and a delegate to the Ratifying Convention of 1788. In 1787 he owned 287 slaves in Prince William County. He was a prosperous merchant, lived on his estate Paradise, and was a vestryman for Hamilton Parish.

POYTHRESS, PETER (c.1734-c.1776), Prince George County, was born in an old family traced to Captain Francis Poythress (his grandfather) and Major Francis Poythress (his father) of Charles City County. He was a planter at Flower de Hundred in Prince George County. He was a burgess, 1768–76, and a member of the legislature, 1776. He was the son-in-law of Richard Bland.

RANDOLPH, EDMUND (1753–1813), Williamsburg, was the nephew of Peyton Randolph. He was a member of Congress, 1779–82, governor of Virginia, 1786–88, and delegate to the federal Constitutional Convention. He was elected as an alternate for

George Wythe who was in Philadelphia at the Second Continental Congress and did not return to Williamsburg until ten days before adjournment of the Convention. Later he served in Washington's cabinet as attorney general, 1789–93, and secretary of state, 1794–95.

RANDOLPH, THOMAS MANN, SR. (1741–1793), Goochland County, was the son of William Randolph, of the Tuckahoe Randolphs, and childhood companion of Thomas Jefferson. He was an Anglican planter who married Anne Cary, daughter of Archibald Cary; among their many children was Thomas Mann Randolph, Jr. (1768–1828), who in 1790 married Martha Jefferson, the daughter of Thomas Jefferson. He was a burgess, 1769–76, and served in the House of Delegates, 1780–81, 1783, 1784–88, and the senate, 1776–78, 1791–93. For a genealogy of the Tuckahoe Randolphs, see Dumas Malone, *Jefferson and His Time* (Boston, 1948–81), 1:428.

READ, THOMAS (1732–1817), Charlotte County, was of the family of Colonel Thomas Read, an officer under Cromwell who came to Virginia about 1660. His father, Clement, was active in Lunenburg County, being county clerk, 1745–65, and a burgess. He was educated at William and Mary and began public life as deputy clerk of Charlotte County in 1765, the year it was formed from Lunenburg. He was an Anglican and the brother-in-law of Paul Carrington. A planter, he owned 35 slaves in 1782. He was against the Stamp Act, opposed the Constitution in 1788, but before his death became a follower of Jefferson. He served, besides in the Ratifying Convention, in the House of Delegates, 1776, 1794–1800. Grigsby, *Convention of 1776*, 104–8.

RIDDICK, WILLIS (born c.1726), Nansemond County, was the son of a Nansemond burgess and county clerk. He was a burgess, 1756–69, 1771, 1774, and a member of the House of Delegates, 1776–79, 1784–1801. He attended the Ratifying Convention of 1788. He was county clerk, 1756–71, 1775–76.

ROBINSON, WILLIAM, JR. (born 1751), Princess Anne County, was born at the family estate, Bunker Hill, in Richmond County, the son of a county clerk and burgess. He was a lawyer and a burgess, 1774, and a member of the House of Delegates, 1776–79, 1782.

ROSCOW, WILLIAM, Norfolk Borough. No extant data available.

RUSSELL, WILLIAM (1735–1794), Fincastle County, was born in Culpepper County and lived at Saltville on the Clinch River and owned 2 slaves in the 1770s. He was a lieutenant colonel of the Culpeper County militia and in 1774 commanded at the battle of Point Pleasant; he was promoted to brigadier general in the Virginia militia during the Revolution. He was a delegate from Washington County, 1784–86, and in the senate, 1788–89. Russell County in what is now West Virginia was named in his honor.

RUTHERFORD, ROBERT (1729–1803), Berkeley County, was born in Essex County and moved to the Northern Neck with his father, Thomas, who had purchased land from Lord Fairfax and served as the first sheriff of the county, 1743. An Anglican merchant-planter at Flowering Springs, he owned only 2 slaves in 1782. He was a burgess from Frederick County, 1766–73, and Berkeley County, 1772–76. He sat in the senate, 1776–90, and was a member of Congress, 1793–97, until his defeat in the election of 1798.

SAVAGE, GEORGE (1739–1791), Northampton County, was of a family line going back to Ensign Thomas Savage who came to Virginia in 1608 and established a plantation on the Eastern Shore before 1619. Family members served as burgesses regularly beginning in the 1660s. He was an Anglican planter, probably on rented lands, with an estate worth over £360 at Savage's Neck adjacent to the courthouse and served in the legislature in 1776. In 1782 he owned 24 slaves, 17 horses, and 30 cattle.

SAVAGE, NATHANIEL LYTTLETON (c.1730–after 1794), Northampton County, was a planter, land speculator, and merchant who served on the Committee of Safety, 1774–76, and was a member of the House of Delegates, 1776–77. In 1777 he retired to his plantation in New Kent County.

SCOTT, JAMES, JR. (1742–1779), Fauquier County, was the son of Rev. James Scott of an estate named Dipple in Scotland who came to Virginia about 1739. James Jr. was a planter, burgess, 1769–76, and member of the House of Delegates, 1776–79. He died of exposure while serving as a captain in the Virginia militia.

SELDEN, JAMES (born c.1745), Lancaster County, was the son of Richard Scott Selden, king's attorney for Elizabeth City County, justice of the peace, and burgess. His great-grandfather Samuel

Scott was an English barrister who settled in Elizabeth City County in 1695. James was an Anglican planter, a burgess, 1774–76, and a member of the Committee of Safety.

SIMMS, CHARLES (1751–1815), West Augusta County, served in the House of Delegates in 1776. He attended William and Mary and was a lawyer and land speculator who owned 3,031 acres near Pittsburgh in 1775.

SIMPSON, SOUTHY (died 1793), Accomack County, was a prominent landowner on the Eastern Shore. He was a burgess, 1761–65, 1766–68, 1769–71, 1772–74, and a member of the House of Delegates, 1776, and the senate, 1777–78. Whitelaw, *Virginia's Eastern Shore.*

SMITH, ISAAC (born 1725), Accomack County, was an Anglican planter, merchant-shipper, and burgess, 1774. He was in the senate, 1776, and the House of Delegates, 1778, and was a captain of the Accomack County militia.

SMITH, MERIWETHER (1740–1790), Essex County, was the son of Colonel Francis Smith of Bathurst. He was an Anglican planter-merchant who in 1783 owned 67 slaves. He served as a burgess, 1774, was a member of the Westmoreland Association against the Stamp Act, 1765, and was a delegate to Congress, 1778–82, and to the Ratifying Convention of 1788. Richard Henry Lee called him "the Fiddle," implying that he was only in harmony with himself at the Convention.

SPEED, JOSEPH (born 1750), Mecklenburg County, was the fifth son of Joseph Speed, Sr., sheriff of Mecklenburg County, and served in the House of Delegates, 1776–77. He was a merchant and tobacco planter who owned 534 acres of land. After 1778 he moved to North Carolina.

STARKE, BOLLING (1733–1788), Dinwiddie County, was a justice of the peace, 1763–76, sheriff, 1763, burgess, 1769–76, and member of the legislature from Dinwiddie County, 1776–77, and Prince George County, 1780–81. He was state auditor, 1776. Starke owned extensive land along the James River and was a shipowner.

STROTHER, FRENCH (c.1730–1800), Culpeper County, was the son of James Strother (died 1761) and the grandson of William

Strother of Richmond County. He was vestryman of St. Mark's Parish, lieutenant colonel of the county militia, 1763, and a planter who in 1771 purchased a large estate from an heir of Robert ("King") Carter. He was a member of the House of Delegates, 1776–91, the senate, 1791–1800, and the Ratifying Convention of 1788. Freeman, *Washington*, 1:58.

SYME, JOHN, JR. (c.1729), Hanover County, was half brother of Patrick Henry. His father, John, a colonel of the Hanover County militia and a burgess, 1722, died in 1730; his mother then married John Henry. John Jr. was an Anglican planter, burgess, 1756–68, 1773–75, and member of the House of Delegates, 1776–78, 1781–82, and the senate, 1784–88.

TABB, JOHN (1745–1798), Amelia County, was the son of Thomas Tabb of Clay Hill, a wealthy merchant. He was educated in England in the law. He inherited Clay Hill and in 1770 married the daughter of John Peyton. He was the father-in-law of Governor William B. Giles. He was a burgess, 1772–76, and a member of the Committee of Safety, 1775, and of the House of Delegates, 1776, 1782.

TALBOT, JOHN (born c.1736), Bedford County, was the youngest of four sons of Matthew Talbot, an immigrant planter who came to Virginia from Maryland about 1720 and formed a shipping partnership near the site of Lynchburg. John owned 45 acres in 1784. He was a county justice, 1773, burgess, 1761–65, member of the legislature, 1776–82, and captain in the Virginia militia. Early, *Campbell Chronicles*, 508–9.

TAYLOR, HENRY, JR. (1731–1781), Southampton County, was a burgess, 1769–76, and member of the House of Delegates, 1776–77. His father was a burgess from Isle of Wright County, 1752–55.

TAYLOR, JAMES, III (born c.1733), Caroline County, was the son of James Taylor II (1700–1736) and the grandson of James Taylor I (born 1635), of Carlisle, England, who came to Caroline County in 1665. He was the uncle of John Taylor of Caroline. He was an Anglican planter who in 1772 owned 8,500 acres in Orange County. He was a burgess, 1774–75, and served in the House of Delegates, 1776, the senate, 1777–83, 1789–91, and the Ratifying Convention of 1788.

TAYLOR, RICHARD SQUIRE (born 1730), King William County, was a justice of the peace, 1755–64, sheriff, 1764–73, and served in the House of Delegates, 1776. He was a shipping agent and in 1782 lived on a large plantation of 1,238 acres and owned 56 slaves.

TAZEWELL, HENRY (1753–1799), Brunswick County, the son of Littleton Tazewell, Brunswick County clerk, was a graduate of William and Mary and a lawyer. He served in the Virginia legislature, 1776–85, and was a judge of the General Court, 1785–93, and the Supreme Court of Appeals, 1793. From 1794 until his death he was a U.S. senator and supporter of Jefferson. Grigsby, *Convention of 1776*, 79–82; Peterson, *Tazewell*, 2, 3, 5, 6, 10–12, 14–16.

TERRY, NATHANIEL (born c.1730), Halifax County, was an Anglican planter. W. J. Carrington, in *Halifax County*, 189, wrote: "Colonel Terry was a very influential and wealthy gentleman in colonial days, and after the Revolutionary War had enormous land grants (extending along the Bannister river from Pittsylvania down through Halifax) . . . for services rendered in the war." He was a burgess, 1758–65, 1768–75, county sheriff, 1765–68, a justice of the peace, 1752–54, a member of the legislature, 1776–78, and a colonel and aide to General Washington.

THOROWGOOD (or THOROUGHGOOD), JOHN, JR. (1745–1804), Princess Anne County, came from a long line of burgesses. He was an Anglican planter who owned 840 acres and 13 slaves. He served in the House of Delegates, 1776–83, 1786–87.

THORNTON, GEORGE (c.1730–1781), Spotsylvania County, was born at Fall Hill sometime between 1730 and 1749, the son of Francis Thornton (1704–1749), burgess of the county. He was an Anglican planter and merchant who served in the legislature in 1776. During the war he was a major in the Continental line.

TIPTON, JOHN (1731–after 1796), Dunmore County (renamed Shenandoah County in 1776), was a vestryman and planter who in 1783 owned 4 slaves. He was a burgess in 1775 and a member of the House of Delegates for Dunmore County, 1776–77, and Shenandoah County, 1778–81. He moved to North Carolina and then to Tennessee where he represented Washington County in that state's constitutional convention of 1784. He died in Tennessee sometime after 1796.

TRAVIS, CHAMPION (1747–1806), Jamestown, was the son of Colonel Edward Travis, burgess from Jamestown, 1752–65. The family line went back to 1637. He was educated at William and

Mary and was a planter. He was a burgess from the "city" of James-town, 1769–76, and served as sheriff and justice of the peace for James City County and represented the county in the House of Delegates, 1781–82, 1800–1806. He was a colonel in the state regiment as well as a member in 1776 of the state Naval Commission.

WASHINGTON, JOHN AUGUSTINE (1736–1787), Westmore-land County, was the younger brother of George and served as the alternate to Richard Henry Lee who was in Philadelphia as a member of the Second Continental Congress. He was an Anglican planter who for a brief period of time managed George's estates. He served in the House of Delegates in 1776 and 1779. See Free-man, *Washington*.

WATKINS, BENJAMIN (c.1725–1780), Chesterfield County, was born of a Welsh family which came to Virginia in the 1620s. He was a planter and surveyor (in 1761 he surveyed the towns of Gatesville and Manchester) and served as county clerk, 1749–79, burgess, 1772–76, and delegate, 1776. He married into the Cary family of Warwick County.

WATKINS, MICAJAH (1744–1801), Halifax County, was the son of William Watkins (died 1762) of Prince Edward County. He served in the House of Burgesses, 1774–76, and the House of Delegates, 1776–79.

WATTS, WILLIAM (1743–1803), Prince Edward County, married Mary Scott, daughter of Thomas Scott. He was a justice of the peace, 1765–75, a planter-lawyer, and an Anglican who served in the House of Delegates, 1776–77. In 1787 he moved to Botetourt County and then, in 1796, farther west to Campbell County where he had purchased land in 1790 on Flat Creek. By 1775 he owned 1,365 acres near Mountain Creek in Prince Edward County.

WEST, JOHN, JR. (c.1732–1777), Fairfax County, was the son of Hugh West, a Fairfax burgess, 1752–54, and great-grandson of John West who came to the Northern Neck about 1690 from York-shire. He was a speculator in Ohio lands and an Anglican planter who owned land adjacent to Mount Vernon and represented the county in the 1776 House of Delegates.

WHITING, THOMAS (c.1712–1780), Gloucester County, was born at the family estate, Elmington. He was an Anglican planter, burgess, 1755–76, member of the House of Delegates, 1776, and chairman of the Naval Commission during the Revolution.

WILKINSON, NATHANIEL (c.1740–1808), Henrico County, was a justice of the peace, 1770, sheriff, 1771–72, vestryman, and planter who served in the House of Delegates, 1776–94, 1807–8. In 1783 he owned 1,686 acres, a town lot in Richmond, and 39 slaves.

WILLIAMS, ROBERT (born c.1741), Pittsylvania County, was a planter who owned 3,866 acres by 1782 as well as 52 cattle and 36 slaves. He served one term in the House of Delegates, 1776.

WILLS, JOHN SCARSBROOK (c.1745–1794), Isle of Wight County, was born at Bedingfield Hall, the son of a burgess. His grandfather, Colonel Henry Wills, an Oxfordshire immigrant, founded the town of Fredericksburg in 1727. John was a burgess, 1774, and a member of the House of Delegates, 1776–87, and the senate, 1787–93. During the war he rose to the rank of brigadier general. He was an Anglican and a planter.

WINN, JOHN (born c.1738), Amelia County, was of Welsh stock and was a burgess, 1769–76.

WOOD, JAMES, JR. (1741–1813), Frederick County, was born at Glen Burne, the son of the founder of the town of Winchester. He was an Anglican planter. His public service included deputy clerk and surveyor, 1760, burgess, 1766–75, member of the executive council, 1776–99, and lieutenant governor, 1796–99. He was a brigadier general during the war and fought at Yorktown. Wood County in what is now West Virginia was named in his honor. See Russell, *What I Know about Winchester,* 178.

WOODSON, JOHN (1731–1789), Goochland County, was a descendant of Dr. John Woodson who came to Virginia in 1619 with Sir George Yeardley. He married Dorthea Randolph, an aunt of Thomas Jefferson. He was a vestryman and planter who served as a burgess, 1769–76, and a member of the legislature, 1776–77, 1781–82.

WYTHE, GEORGE (1726–1806), Williamsburg, was elected by the voters of Williamsburg to the 1776 Convention but was absent most of the session in Philadelphia as a delegate to the Second Continental Congress. He returned to Williamsburg in late June where he introduced Jefferson's scheme of government to the Convention. He was appointed one of four members of a committee to develop a seal for the new state, and the committee's report was approved by the convention.

ZANE, ISAAC, JR. (1743–1795), Frederick County, was the son of a German immigrant who settled in Pennsylvania in 1735. He was a Quaker who donated land in Winchester for the building of a meetinghouse. Isaac operated a flour mill in that city. He was a close friend of James Wood, Jr. He was a burgess, 1773–76, and a member of the House of Delegates from Frederick County, 1776–82, and Shenandoah County, 1782–95. He owned the Marlboro Iron Works twelve miles west of Winchester close to his 20,000-acre estate at Cedar Creek.

CONVENTION OF 1829–30

Eastern Conservative Delegates

ALEXANDER, MARK (1792–1833), Mecklenburg County, was born and raised in that county and educated at the University of North Carolina. An Episcopalian planter-lawyer, in 1830 he lived on a plantation of 982 acres with 125 slaves; he was married, with 3 children. He was a member of the House of Delegates, 1815–19, and Congress, 1819–33, and was a presidential elector, 1816. His father had served in the Virginia legislature in the 1790s, and his brother, Nathaniel, was a member of the House of Delegates in the 1820s and 1830s. He was "an intimate friend" and messmate of John Randolph while both were congressmen (Bruce, *Randolph*, 624). Grigsby described him as "extremely neat in person" (Diary, no. 1).

BARBOUR, JOHN STRODE (1790–1855), Culpeper County, was born and raised in that county and earned a B.A. at William and Mary, 1809. He was an Episcopalian and a commonwealth's attorney. He is not listed in the land records for Culpeper, Madison, or Orange County. He owned 8 slaves and 2 horses in Culpeper County in 1830; he was married, with 9 children. He was known as "an able exponent of States-Rights republicanism of the period in the halls of the Federal Congress" (Gordon, *William F. Gordon*, 52). A member of the prominent Barbour family, he was a first cousin of James and Philip P. Barbour. See Lowery, *James Barbour: The Biography of a Jeffersonian Republican.*

BARBOUR, PHILIP PENDLETON (1783–1841), Orange County, was born and raised in that county and received a B.A. from William and Mary, 1803. An Episcopalian planter-lawyer, in 1830 he lived at Frascati, a plantation of 623 acres, owned 61 slaves and 22 horses, and was married, with 3 children. A member of the House of Delegates, 1812–14, and Congress, 1814–27, he was Speaker of the House of Representatives in 1821 and was appointed to the U.S. Supreme Court by President Jackson in 1836. He was known as an opponent of internal improvements and the tariff and was president of the Free Trade Convention held in Philadelphia, 1831. See Lowery, *James Barbour: The Biography of a Jeffersonian Republican.*

BATES, FLEMING (1778–1831), Northumberland County, was born and raised in that county of a seventeenth-century Quaker family. He had no formal education and was a planter and county clerk. He lived on a small farm of 230 acres in 1830 with 16 slaves and 4 horses; he was married, with 3 children. His brother, Elisha, was elected to Congress in 1827 as an Adams man, but Fleming opposed him as a states'-rights advocate and an admirer of John Randolph. Elisha Bates to Fleming Bates, May 20, 1827, Bates Papers, Virginia Historical Society.

BRANCH, SAMUEL (1788–1847), Buckingham County, was the son of an active supporter of internal improvements in Botetourt County in the 1790s. He was educated at Hampden-Sydney and William and Mary. In 1830 he lived at Woodlawn in Buckingham County with 42 slaves; he was married, with 1 child. He was an officer in the War of 1812 and a trustee of Hampden-Sydney, 1820–47. Robert D. Stoner, *A Seed-Bed of the Early Republic: Early Botetourt* (Radford, Va., 1932), 157; *William and Mary Quarterly*, 1st ser., 9 (1909): 198.

BRODNAX, WILLIAM HENRY (1786–1834), Dinwiddie County, was born and raised in Greensville County, was educated at Hampden-Sydney, and was awarded an honorary M.A. by William and Mary in 1830. An Episcopalian planter-lawyer, in 1830 he lived at Kingston, a plantation of 590 acres, with 41 slaves; he was married, with 3 children. A member of the House of Delegates, 1818–19, 1830–33, and a presidential elector for Crawford, 1824, he was a member of the Virginia Colonization Society and took a middle position in the 1832 General Assembly debate on slavery between Thomas Jefferson Randolph and John Floyd. See Brodnax Family Papers, Virginia Historical Society.

CLAIBORNE, AUGUSTINE (1784–1841), Greensville County, was born and raised in Sussex County and had no formal higher education. A Methodist planter-lawyer, in 1830 he lived at Chestnut Grove, a New Kent County plantation of 762 acres, with 33 slaves, 14 horses; he was married, with no children. He was a member of the House of Delegates, 1830–31. His father was Colonel Augustine Claiborne (1721–1787), a burgess from Sussex County and state senator from Chesterfield County. He was related to the Harrisons through his mother and was the brother-in-law of John Hartwell Cocke of Bremo. Grigsby commented that "he is a methodist and was elected by religious men," as a lawyer he was "possessed of no talent," and he was "extremely ugly" (Diary, no. 1).

CLOPTON, JOHN BACON (1798–1860), New Kent County, was born and raised in St. Peter's Parish in that county; he attended William and Mary, 1818. An Episcopalian planter-judge, in 1830 he owned a farm of 602 acres, with 19 slaves and 4 horses; he was married, with 4 children. He was a member of the state senate, 1821–30, and a Jeffersonian Republican in Congress, 1795–99. Grigsby believed that Clopton "was a reformer in every vein and artery of his system; but voted with the East" (Diary, no. 1). Upton, "Road to Power," 261–64.

COALTER, JOHN C. (1769–1838), King George County, was born in Rockbridge County but moved to Williamsburg in 1809 as a tutor to the family of St. George Tucker; he attended Washington and Lee College, 1788–89, and William and Mary, 1789–90, where he studied law under George Wythe, 1789. An Episcopalian planter-lawyer-jurist, in 1830 he lived on 2,173 acres at Chatham near Fredericksburg, the largest slaveholder in the area with 92 slaves and 13 horses; he was married, with 6 children. He was clerk of Augusta County, commonwealth's attorney, 1803–9, judge of the General Court, 1809–11, and judge of the Supreme Court of Appeals, 1811–30. He supported Adams in 1828. He came to the Convention on November 23 as a replacement for John Taliaferro. He was related by marriage to Fleming Bates; his father-in-law was St. George Tucker; his brother-in-law was John Randolph. Elizabeth Coalter Bryan (1805–1856), Diary, Virginia Historical Society, contains a sketch of the life of her father.

DROMGOOLE, GEORGE (1795–1847), Brunswick County, was born and raised in Lawrenceville, in that county, of Methodist parents; he graduated from William and Mary, 1817, and studied law at Richmond. A planter-lawyer, in 1830 he lived on a farm of 117 acres with 20 slaves; he was married, with no children. He was a member of the House of Delegates, 1826–29, state senate, 1829–38, and a Democrat in Congress, 1835–41, 1843–47. He was a Jackson man in 1828. His father was Edward Dromgoole, a Methodist minister and co-founder of Ebenezer Academy (Randolph-Macon College) in 1793. Grigsby commented that he "showed much spirit . . . was ready to terminate any speech in a fight of any kind" (Diary, no. 1). Dromgoole Family Papers, University of North Carolina.

GARNETT, JAMES MERCER (1770–1843), Essex County, was born and raised in Essex and Caroline counties. An Episcopalian planter, in 1830 he lived at Elmwood, a plantation of 1,195 acres, with 83 slaves and 11 horses. He was a member of the House of Delegates, 1824–25, and Congress, 1805–9, as a Quid. He was for Jackson in 1828. In the 1820s he opened on his estate a school for young women in which he taught English. He was a founder of the United States Agricultural Society and for twenty years was president of the Fredericksburg chapter. A close friend of John Randolph, John Roane, and Hugh B. Grigsby, he was related by marriage to Thomas R. Dew. He was a longtime opponent of protective tariff and the idea of constitutional reform in Virginia. Davis, *Intellectual Life*, 44, 112, 422; Bagby, *King and Queen County*, 294; Garnett-Randolph Papers, University of Virginia Library.

GILES, WILLIAM BRANCH (1762–1830), Amelia County, was born and raised in that county and graduated from Princeton, 1781. An Episcopalian planter-lawyer, in 1830 he owned a plantation of 4,990 acres, with 98 slaves and 13 horses. He was a member of the House of Delegates, 1798–1800, 1816–17, 1826–27, and a Jackson man in 1828. He was governor of Virginia, 1827–30. See Anderson, *Giles*.

GOODE, WILLIAM O. (1798–1859), Mecklenburg County, was born and raised in that county at Inglewood; he graduated from William and Mary, 1819. A planter-lawyer, in 1830 he lived at the family homestead with 10 slaves and 3 horses; he was married, with 2 children. His father, Samuel Goode (1756–1822), was an Adams Federalist in Congress, 1799–1801. He began law practice in Mecklenburg in 1821. Dr. Thomas Massie, delegate to the Convention from Nelson County, was his father-in-law. He was a member of the House of Delegates, 1822–23, and Congress, 1841–43. Grigsby noted that he was "a handsome man, quite juvenile in appearance . . . took no part in great questions of government that agitated the Convention" (Diary, no. 1). He also served as a delegate to the Constitutional Convention of 1850–51. G. B. Goode, *Virginia Cousins.*

GORDON, WILLIAM FITZHUGH (1787–1858), Albemarle County, was born and raised in that county, attended James B. Wadell's school in Fredericksburg, and read law under Benjamin Botts there. A Presbyterian planter-lawyer, in 1830 he lived at Edgeworth, a plantation of 978 acres, with 44 slaves and 11 horses; he was married, with no children. He was a member of the House of Delegates, 1819–29, and the state senate, 1829–30. See Gordon, *William F. Gordon.*

GREEN, JOHN WILLIAMS (1781–1834), Culpeper County, was born and raised in that county and had no formal higher education. An Episcopalian planter-lawyer-judge, in 1830 he lived on a 400-acre plantation, with 42 slaves and 30 horses; he was married, with 7 children. He was a member of the state senate, 1815–19, and a judge of the Supreme Court of Appeals, 1822–27. He served in the War of 1812. He was related by marriage to delegate James Mason. See du Bellett, *Prominent Virginia Families*, 399; Thomas Green, Diary.

GRIGSBY, HUGH BLAIR (1806–1881), city of Norfolk, was born and raised in that city and attended Yale, 1824–25. A Presbyterian, he was the son of Rev. Benjamin Porter Grigsby, pastor of the First Presbyterian Church of Norfolk. A lawyer, he was a member of the House of Delegates, 1828–30. He was a close friend of John Tazewell, son of Littleton Waller Tazewell. See Alden G. Bigelow, "Hugh Blair Grigsby, Historian and Antiquarian" (Ph.D. diss., University of Virginia, 1957).

HOLLADAY, WALLER (c.1795–1858), Louisa County, was born and raised in Spotsylvania County of an established colonial (since 1671) family; he had no formal higher education. A Presbyterian planter, in 1830 he lived at Prospect Hill, a plantation of 404 acres, with 7 slaves; he was married and had 1 child. He was a member of the House of Delegates, 1819–20. He strongly feared slave uprisings in the Louisa County area and reported to the governor evidence of threatened insurrections. Holladay, *Fincastle Presbyterian Church; Calendar of Virginia State Papers*, 10:436.

JONES, JOHN W. (1791–1848), Chesterfield County, was born and raised in that county and had no formal higher education. An Ep-

iscopalian planter-lawyer, in 1830 he lived at Dellwood, a plantation of 1,435 acres, with 7 slaves and 12 horses; he was married,
with 4 children. He was attorney of the General Court, 1815–35, a
member of Congress, 1835–39, 1843–44, and speaker of the
House of Representatives, 1843–44. A Democrat, he was noted as
a distinguished lawyer. He was a trustee of Chesterfield Academy.
He received the highest number of votes in the election of delegates to the Convention of 1829–30 from his district. Grigsby
wrote that Jones "spoke on trivial matters" at the Convention and
was "large, well-formed, and handsome in countenance" (Diary,
no. 1). Lutz, *Chesterfield,* 153.

LEIGH, BENJAMIN WATKINS (1781–1849), Chesterfield
County, was born and raised in the Tidewater; he earned a B.A.
from William and Mary, 1802, and was granted an honorary LL.D.,
1835. An Episcopalian lawyer, in 1830 he lived in Richmond and
owned property valued at $8,000 and 11 slaves; he was married,
with 5 children. A member of the House of Delegates, 1811–13,
1830–31, and the U.S. Senate, 1833, he was a vocal War Hawk in
1812 and a Jacksonian in the 1820s but turned against Jackson in
the nullification crisis. In 1833 he went to South Carolina to postpone action on nullification until Congress had time to act. He was
permanently lamed as a result of a childhood injury. Grigsby wrote
that there was "something in his manner that displayed a childish
fretfulness, that ill became a man of his distinguished excellence"
and that he "did much to ensure the adherence of the Fauquier
delegation to eastern interests" (Diary, no. 1). Lutz, *Chesterfield,*
161, 182–83, 195, 200; see also Steiner, "The Prelude to Conservatism."

LEIGH, WILLIAM (1773–1871), Halifax County, was born and
raised in Chesterfield County (brother of Benjamin Watkins Leigh)
and graduated from William and Mary, 1804. An Episcopalian
planter-lawyer-judge, in 1830 he owned 127 acres, 58 slaves and 5
horses; he was married, with 11 children. He was a judge of the
circuit court, 1831–58, and a captain in the War of 1812. "Most
intimate friend" of John Randolph (Bruce, *Randolph,* 613, 651), he
took care of Randolph's business affairs in the 1820s, visiting him
almost weekly at his Caroline plantation, and was executor of Randolph's will. Grigsby described him as "short and thin" with spectacles (Diary, no. 1). William Leigh to James M. Garnett, May 6,
1818, Garnett-Randolph Papers, University of Virginia Library;
Lutz, *Chesterfield,* 183, 205.

LOGAN, RICHARD (1775–1831), Halifax County, was born in Roanoke the son of Rev. Robert Logan, a Presbyterian minister. Richard was a member of the Greensville Polemic Society, 1827–30, which met regularly to discuss current political questions. A planter and the father of 5 children, in 1830 he owned 1,605 acres and 12 slaves. He was a member of the House of Delegates, 1819–20, and a strong supporter of Andrew Jackson in the elections of 1828 and 1832.

LOYALL, GEORGE (1789–1868), city of Norfolk, was born and raised in that city and earned a B.A. from William and Mary, 1808. A lawyer, in 1830 he owned 5 town lots valued at $7,910 and 8 slaves; he was married, with 4 children. A member of the House of Delegates, 1817–27, and Congress, 1831–37, he was a Jackson supporter in 1828. He began law practice in 1822 in Norfolk; before then he was the legal representative of a European commercial house in Norfolk. William F. Gordon and Loyall zealously pushed in the Virginia legislature for the establishment of the University of Virginia. "A warm friendship sprang up between Gordon and Mr. Loyall, which was illustrated by the former's giving one of his sons, born in 1829, the name of his friend" (Gordon, *William F. Gordon,* 117). He was a strong supporter of free trade, opposing Clay and the American System, and was a close friend of Hugh Blair Grigsby (Diary, no. 6). His political opponent in the Norfolk area, Robert B. Taylor, was his cousin. As a naval agent for the federal government (appointed by Jackson in 1836), he "disbursed more than $14,000,000 of public money without loss of a cent to the treasury" (Forrest, *Norfolk,* 366). *Virginia Magazine of History and Biography* 22 (1914): 325.

MACRAE, JOHN (1775–1830), Prince William County, was born and raised in Dumfries and had no higher education. A planter, in 1830 he lived at the 6,000-acre Effingham plantation on Quantico Creek, with 17 slaves; he was married, with 10 children. He was a member of the House of Delegates, 1816–17, and served in the War of 1812. Grigsby called him one of the "leading citizens" of Prince William County (Diary, no. 6). Writer's Program, *Prince William,* 90, 113, 153.

MADISON, JAMES (1751–1836), Orange County. The Convention of 1829–30 was Madison's last important public appearance. His advanced age prevented his taking an active role, except at the beginning, in the procedures.

MARSHALL, JOHN (1755–1836), Richmond, was Chief Justice of the U.S. Supreme Court. He was a strong influence for compromise on the apportionment question during the final weeks of the Convention.

MARTIN, JOSEPH (c.1775–1832), Henry County, was born in Albemarle County, the son of planter Joseph Martin who came there in the 1740s, and had no higher education. An Episcopalian planter, in 1830 he owned 1,875 acres at Scuffle Hill, 58 slaves, and 25 horses; he was married, with no children. A presidential elector in 1816 and 1832, he was a "great supporter of Madison and the resolutions of 1798" (Early, *Campbell Chronicles*, 93). Clement, *Pittsylvania County*, 48, remarks that "he purchased a plantation in Pittsylvania on Leatherwood Creek to which he moved. He was active in Indian affairs along the frontier, and acted as an Indian agent for Virginia for a number of years."

MASON, JOHN YOUNG (1799–1859), Southampton County, was born and raised in that county and earned a B.A. from the University of North Carolina, 1816. An Episcopalian planter-lawyer, in 1830 he owned 314 acres, 48 slaves, and 11 horses; he was married, with 4 children. He was the nephew of both Charles F. Mercer and William Fitzhugh. A member of the House of Delegates, 1823–33, and the Congress, 1831–37, in 1837 he was appointed judge of the federal district court of Virginia. He had a large and lucrative law practice at Hicksford and was a trustee of Union Academy in Sussex County, president of the James River and Kanawha Canal Company, 1849–53, and president of the Constitutional Convention of 1850–51. He died in Paris. Noted as a follower of Thomas Ritchie, he was a local leader of the "Virginia party" along with George Dromgoole, William Goode, and William C. Rives. Grigsby observed that he "lacks force of character" and "his mind lacks body, as they say of a certain kind of beer" (Diary, no. 1). *Virginia Magazine of History and Biography* 5(1897): 188; Ambler, *Ritchie*, 111.

MASSIE, THOMAS, JR. (1783–1864), Nelson County, was born in that county, was educated in Edinburgh, Scotland, first practiced medicine in Chillicothe, Ohio, and returned to Virginia in 1810. In 1830 he owned the 1,509-acre Blue Rock plantation, 61 slaves, and 8 horses; he was married, with 6 children. A member of the House of Delegates, 1824–27, 1829–30, he was an anti-Adams man. His father, Thomas, was a very large landholder with plantations in Nelson, Frederick, and Amherst counties. He was related to John Hartwell Cocke of Bremo by marriage and was the father-in-law of William O. Goode. He was a surgeon in the War of 1812 and a trustee of Washington College, 1826–42.

MONROE, JAMES (1758–1831), Fauquier County, was president of the United States, 1817–25. Ill health made it impossible for him to participate in the Convention except in a symbolic way as a representative of Virginia's lost "Golden Age."

MORRIS, RICHARD B. (1778–1833), Hanover County, was born and raised in the Hanover area and had no formal higher education. An Episcopalian planter, in 1830 he owned a plantation of 3,281 acres, 58 slaves, and 25 horses; he was married, with 4 children. He was a member of the House of Delegates, 1819–25, 1830–31. William C. Bruce wrote that Morris was a Quid "who had he lived longer might have left a truly illustrious name in the history of Virginia" (*Randolph*, 1:623). A sketch of Morris in the *Southern Literary Messenger* 18 (1851): 50, said that he was "more likely to allow himself to be carried away by the tide of his own eloquence than any other public speaker we recollect ever to have heard. . . . During the greater part of his life he had . . . no taste for politics, and no desire even to practice in the Court of Appeals . . . passionately devoted to rural pursuits."

NEALE, AUGUSTINE (born c.1780), Lancaster County, was a planter who in 1830 lived in Richmond County on a farm of 279 acres with 27 slaves; he was married, with 4 children.

NICHOLAS, PHILIP NORBORNE (1775–1849), city of Richmond, was born and raised in the Tidewater, the son of Robert Carter Nicholas; he had no formal higher education. An Episcopalian lawyer, in 1830 he owned 8 properties in Richmond valued at a total of $7,589 and 13 slaves; he was married, with 2 children. He was a presidential elector, 1809–32, a Junto member, and a Jacksonian. He wrote states'-rights pamphlets along with Philip P. Barbour and William B. Giles. A promoter of the Bank of Virginia, during the War of 1812 he advocated expansion of domestic manufacturing. Grigsby said that he was a "singular compound of buffonery and good sense . . .a perpetual smile on his face so that some thought he was in jest when debating a very serious subject" (Diary, no. 1). Davis, *Intellectual Life*, 406.

PERRIN, WILLIAM K. (born 1785), Northumberland County, lived in Gloucester County and had no formal higher education.

An Episcopalian planter, in 1830 he owned 1,011 acres, 79 slaves (largest slaveholder in the county), and 13 horses; he was married, with 2 children. He was a member of the House of Delegates, 1810–12, 1821–22, 1830–31.

PLEASANTS, JAMES, JR. (1769–1836), Goochland County, was born and raised in the Piedmont of Quaker parents and remained in that section as an adult; his higher education is unknown. A planter-lawyer, in 1830 he owned 501 acres, 22 slaves, and 7 horses. He was a member of the House of Delegates, 1803–11, Congress, 1811–19, and the state senate, 1819–22, and was governor, 1822–25. He supported states' rights and was president of the Board of Public Works, 1822.

PRENTIS, JOSEPH (1783–1851), Nansemond County, was born and raised in that county and received a B.A. from William and Mary, 1801. An Episcopalian lawyer, in 1830 he lived in Lawrenceville, owned 2 town lots valued totally at $3,500 and 6 slaves, and was married, with 6 children. He was commonwealth's attorney and county clerk. He was the son of Joseph Prentis, a prominent Tidewater politician of Williamsburg who was known as an Antifederalist, a personal friend of Patrick Henry, and a member of Governor Henry's executive council.

RANDOLPH, JOHN (1773–1833), Charlotte County, was the brilliant and pithy spokesman for the extreme conservative views at the Convention. He was a member of the U.S. House of Representatives when elected as a delegate to the Convention.

ROANE, JOHN, JR. (1766–1838), King William County, was born and raised in the Tidewater. A planter, in 1830 he owned 1,350 acres in Culpeper County and paid taxes on 2 horses and 2 carriages but no slaves. A member of the House of Delegates, 1821–24, 1825–26, and Congress, 1809–15, 1827–33, he was a presidential elector for George Washington and a member of the Ratifying Convention of 1788. He was a close friend of John Randolph. He was related to Abel P. Upshur through his mother and to Thomas Ritchie and Patrick Henry through marriage. His cousin was the renowned states'-rights apologist Spencer Roane. *William and Mary Quarterly*, 1st ser., 18 (1900): 275.

ROSE, ALEXANDER (born c.1775), Northumberland County, was born and raised in the Northern Neck. An Episcopalian planter, in 1830 he owned 726 acres on the Potomac River, 37 slaves, and 22 horses; he was married, with no children. He was a member of the House of Delegates, 1816, 1820, and the state senate, 1821–22, 1825–26. His brother married the youngest sister of James Madison.

SCOTT, JOHN, JR. (1782–1850), Fauquier County, was born in that county and educated at Dickinson College. An Episcopalian planter-lawyer-judge, in 1830 he lived at Oakwood, a plantation of 2,000 acres, with 52 slaves and 33 horses; he was married, with 1 child. He was a member of the state senate, 1811–13, and judge of the circuit court, 1831–32, and General Court. His father was an Anglican missionary. He was a close friend of John W. Green (Thomas Green, Diary).

STANARD, ROBERT (1781–1846), Spotsylvania County, was born in the Tidewater but moved to Richmond in 1816; he earned a B.A. from William and Mary, 1798. A Presbyterian planter-lawyer-judge, in 1830 he owned a 700-acre plantation on the James River outside Richmond, with 35 slaves. A member of the House of Delegates, 1810–17, 1835–36, and Speaker, 1815–16, 1835–36, he was a U.S. district attorney, 1821–31, and a judge of the Supreme Court of Appeals, 1839–46. Grigsby observed that he "always stammered, but had a head wonderfully clear . . . was tall, ungainly" (Diary, no. 1). Monroe boarded with Stanard while at the Convention. Thomas Green, Diary, Oct. 2, 1829.

TAYLOR, SAMUEL (1781–1853), Chesterfield County, was born in Southampton County, taken to Kentucky as a small boy, and at age sixteen came back to Cumberland County, Virginia, to study law at the school of Chancellor Creed Taylor. A lawyer, in 1830 he owned 357 acres in Chesterfield County, 20 slaves, and 14 horses; he was married, with 3 children. A member of the House of Delegates, 1816–19, 1825–26, and the state senate, 1826–30, he aided in the establishment of the University of Virginia and was an original trustee of Manchester Academy. In the 1820s and 1840s he was involved in coal-mining operations in the Richmond area. Grigsby noted that he "spoke when any topic touching the Bill of Rights was under discussion . . . large man; over 6 feet and weighed about 300 pounds" (Diary, no. 4).

TAYLOR, WILLIAM P. (1791–1863), Caroline County, was born in Fredericksburg and had no formal education. A planter, in 1830 he owned 1,275 acres, 66 slaves, and 3 horses; he was married, with

4 children. He was a member of the House of Delegates, 1829–30, a states'-rights Whig to Congress, 1833–35, and a presidential elector, 1845. In the 1840s he followed Calhoun back into the Democratic party. Ambler, *Ritchie*, 214; Gordon, *William F. Gordon*, 277.

TAZEWELL, LITTLETON WALLER (1774–1860), city of Norfolk, was born in Williamsburg and earned a B.A. from William and Mary, 1792. An Episcopalian lawyer, in 1830 he owned 7 town properties in Norfolk valued totally at $183,000 and 12 slaves; he was married, with 7 children. He was a member of the House of Delegates, 1796–1800, 1804–17, and U.S. Senate, 1816–26, and was governor, 1834–37. A protégé of John Marshall, he began law practice in 1796. Jeffersonian and anti-Hamilton in the 1790s, he supported the Virginia and Kentucky Resolutions. A warm friend of William Wirt when Wirt lived in Norfolk in 1803, he was a follower of John Taylor of Caroline and his theories of government. An opponent of the War of 1812 and liberal banking, he was a Jackson man in 1828, working hard with John Floyd to carry the state for Jackson. He favored nullification and Calhoun. He was the chief opponent of a constitutional convention in the legislature in 1816. He was an "intimate friend of the Madison family," (Grigsby, *Tazewell*). Ambler, *John Floyd*, 136; Toombs,"Early Life of Tazewell"; Tazewell Papers, University of Virginia Library; Peterson, *Tazewell*.

TOWNES, GEORGE (c.1790–1850), Pittsylvania County, was born and raised in the Danville area and had no higher education. An Episcopalian planter, in 1830 he owned 2,343 acres and 30 slaves; he was married, with 4 children. A member of the House of Delegates, 1818–19, 1848–49, and the state senate, 1829–30, he promoted the Roanoke and Danville Railroad along with Benjamin W. S. Cabell in 1838. He was known as a "gracious planter" (Clement, *Pittsylvania County*, 229).

TREZEVANT, JAMES (c.1785–1841), Southampton County, was born and raised in Sussex County, the son of Dr. John Trezevant, a surgeon in the Revolution who came to Virginia from South Carolina in the 1770s. A planter, in 1830 he owned 793 acres, 43 slaves, and 11 horses; he was married, with 4 children. He was a member of the House of Delegates, 1807–8, state senate, 1808–12, and Congress, 1825–31, and was Sussex County sheriff, 1812–14. Grigsby wrote that he was "certainly not very eminent in intellect . . . there was little about him to [command] esteem" (Diary, no. 1).

TYLER, JOHN (1790–1862), Charles City County, was president of the United States, 1841–45. Governor of the state, 1825–27, in 1830 he was serving in the United States Senate and owned 831 acres and 29 slaves. Tyler played no significant role in the Convention debates.

UPSHUR, ABEL PARKER (1790–1844), Northampton County, was born and raised in that county of a family with deep colonial roots, attended Yale, 1805–6, and Princeton, 1806–7, and read law under William Wirt at Richmond, 1808–10. An Episcopalian planter-lawyer, in 1830 he owned 180 acres but no slaves at Valcuse in Northampton County. He was a member of the House of Delegates, 1812–13, 1824–28, and secretary of state under President Tyler. See Hall, *Upshur.*

URQUHART, JOHN B. (1783–1843), Southampton County, was born and raised in that county and graduated from William and Mary, 1816. An Episcopalian planter, in 1830 he owned 10,977 acres valued at $69,775 at Oak Grove plantation, 73 slaves, and 27 horses. He owned a line of steam packets that went between Smithfield and London. Grigsby said that he was a "rich old man, very goodhearted and a rich old farmer" (Diary, no. 1).

VENABLE, RICHARD N. (1763–1838), Prince Edward County, was born and raised in the Tidewater, attended Princeton in 1782, and graduated from William and Mary, 1785. A Presbyterian planter-lawyer, in 1830 he owned 676 acres at Slate Hill, 23 slaves, and 5 horses; he was married, with 1 child. A member of the House of Delegates, 1797–98, 1820–21, 1830–31, he began law practice in Pittsylvania County in 1786. He was a Jeffersonian Republican, later supported the War of 1812, and was a Jacksonian in 1828. He was president of the Upper Appomattox Canal Company, a trustee and promoter of Hampden-Sydney College, and an officer of the Prince Edward Presbytery.

Reform Delegates and Their Allies

ANDERSON, WILLIAM (1788–1850), Shenandoah County, was born in that county of Scottish immigrant parents from Glasgow and had no formal higher education. A Presbyterian woolen manufacturer, in 1830 he owned 198 acres, 8 slaves, and 2 horses; he was married, with 6 children. He was a member of the House of

Delegates, 1824–27. Wool manufacturing was a family concern. He was active in promoting Shenandoah College and a friend of Briscoe Baldwin and Samuel Kercheval. Later in life he moved to Pendleton County. Wayland, *Shenandoah County,* 221.

BALDWIN, BRISCOE GERARD (1798–1853), Augusta County, was born and raised in Winchester and earned a degree from William and Mary, 1807. A Baptist lawyer-judge, in 1830 he owned 270 acres and a town lot in Staunton and 17 slaves; he was married, with 4 children. He was a member of the House of Delegates, 1818–20, and a judge of the Supreme Court of Appeals, 1842–53. He practiced law with Chapman Johnson. "In every important civil cause, these gentlemen were arrayed . . . against each other, and it was an intellectual treat of a high order to witness the forensic contest of these two giants in their profession" (Peyton, *Augusta County,* 322, 376–77). He was a cousin of delegate Archibald Stuart. Archibald Stuart to Eleanor Stuart, Nov. 17, 1820, Stuart Papers, University of Virginia Library.

BAXTER, JOHN (born 1790), Pocahontas County, was born in North Carolina, came to Bath County, Virginia, in 1800, and then moved to Pocahontas County. A Presbyterian county politician and landowner, in 1830 he lived at Sulphur Springs, owned 4,500 acres, no slaves, and 6 horses, and was married, with 7 children. He was a justice of the peace, a colonel of the 127th Regiment, and a leader in the organization of Pocahontas County in 1822. Grigsby remarked that he "was a simpleton . . . as a member of the convention he manifested a great reluctance . . . he remained in Richmond after the convention hoping to obtain office by hook and by crook" (Diary, no. 1).

BAYLY, THOMAS M. (1775–1834), Accomack County, was born and raised in St. George Parish of an old colonial (1667) family and earned an M.A. from Princeton, 1794. An Episcopalian planter, in 1830 he owned 1,377 acres, 49 slaves, and 33 horses; he was married, with 9 children. He was a member of the House of Delegates, 1798–1801, 1819–20, 1828–29, the state senate, 1801–9, and Congress, 1813–15. His family was Federalist. He was a colonel in the War of 1812. "He never lost an election and very rarely ever had one closely contested . . . as a politician was ever found on the side of popular rights" (tombstone inscription, *William and Mary Quarterly,* 1st ser. 7 [1899]: 107). His son Thomas succeeded him in the House of Delegates in 1836 as a Whig. He was related to the Custis family. Ambler, *Sectionalism*, 93; Stratton Nottingham, ed., *Wills and Administrations, Accomack County, Virginia, 1663–1800* (Onancock, Va., 1931).

BEIRNE, ANDREW P. (1777–1845), Monroe County, was born in Roscommon County, Ireland, and settled in Virginia in 1793 and remained in what became Monroe County. A merchant, in 1830 he owned 2,591 acres, 19 slaves, and 14 horses. He was launched "on a mercantile career when a countryman named Flanagan became his security for a few hundred dollars of goods." In 1800 the firm of A.G. Bierne was organized with his brother, George Beirne. It was "very successful . . . without parallel" (Morton, *Monroe County*, 308–10). A member of the House of Delegates, 1807–8, and the state senate, 1831–36, he was a follower of Jackson and Van Buren. Grigsby said that he was "one of the wealthiest men west of the mountains . . . warmhearted old gentleman" (Diary, no. 1).

BOYD, ELISHA (1767–1841), Berkeley County, was born and raised in the lower Valley, attended Liberty Hall Academy, 1785–86, and studied law under Colonel Philip Pendleton. A lawyer, in 1830 he owned 2,925 acres near Martinsburg, 24 slaves, and 87 horses; he was married, with 4 children. He was a member of the House of Delegates, 1795–96, 1797–98, 1804–5, 1813–14, and the state senate, 1823–27, commonwealth's attorney, and a Federalist. He was a brigadier general of the Virginia militia and an associate of Briscoe Baldwin in law practice in the Valley. Aler, *Martinsburg and Berkeley County*, 145, 185–188; Col. Elisha Boyd to Briscoe Baldwin, March 28, April 19, 1822, Stuart-Baldwin Papers, University of Virginia Library.

BYARS, WILLIAM (1776–1856), Washington County, had no higher education. A Methodist planter, in 1830 he owned 2,742 acres, 47 slaves, and 28 horses; he was married, with 11 children. A member of the House of Delegates, 1807–11, and a justice of the peace, 1810, he was noted as a good farmer; "by diligent and excellent management of farming operations he accumulated wealth, much of which he used in founding and promoting the interests of Emory and Henry College" (Summers, *A History of Southwest Virginia; Washington County*, 774).

CABELL, BENJAMIN W. S. (1792–1866), Pittsylvania County, was the son of Joseph Cabell of Repton and moved to Pittsylvania County in 1820. He attended Hampden-Sydney College. An Episcopalian planter, in 1830 he lived at Bridgewater plantation on the Dan River near Danville, owned 27 slaves, and was married, with 5 children. A member of the House of Delegates, 1823–30, and the state senate, 1831–32, he was a strong advocate of branch banks and more state-supported internal improvements. *Calendar of Virginia State Papers*, 10:471–72.

CAMPBELL, ALEXANDER (1786–1866), Brooke County, was born in Scotland and immigrated to Virginia in 1809; he attended the University of Glasgow, 1808–9. An evangelist, he founded the Disciples of Christ. In 1830 he owned 855 acres, 8 slaves, and 6 horses; he was married, with 14 children. He founded Bethany College. He later wrote that he was reluctant to go to the Convention of 1829–30 because he had never been directly involved in politics. Grigsby, writing to John Tazewell during the first weeks of the Convention, said of Campbell: "I never saw such a slanghanger before. He completely drew down upon himself the sympathy of his western friends, while he received a full portion of contempt and ridicule from those of the East; he has ruined himself forever" (Hugh B. Grigsby to John Tazewell, Oct. 31, 1829, Tazewell Papers, Virginia State Library). Campbell, *Memoirs*, 1:305; see also Lindley, *Apostle of Freedom*.

CAMPBELL, EDWARD (born 1788), Washington County, was born at Hell's Bottom in Washington County, a brother of Governor David Campbell; he "received academic education and was admitted to the bar" (Summers, *Washington County*, 776, 815). A Presbyterian planter-lawyer, in 1830 he owned 2,260 acres, 22 slaves, and 21 horses; he was married, with 10 children. He was a commonwealth's attorney. He had a Federalist family background. Aler, *Berkeley County*, 145; Fischer, *American Conservatism*, 370.

CAMPBELL, WILLIAM (c.1775–1844), Bedford County, was born and raised in Botetourt County where his father operated an inn. A Presbyterian innkeeper, in 1830 he owned 262 acres, 40 slaves, and 7 horses; he was unmarried. He was a member of the House of Delegates, 1816–21, and state senate, 1830–44. Stoner, *Seed-Bed*, 166.

CHAPMAN, HENLEY (1779–1864), Giles County, was born and raised in that county and had no formal higher education. A Presbyterian planter-lawyer, in 1830 he owned 6,152 acres, 27 slaves, and 15 horses; he was married, with 5 children. He served in the state senate, 1812–16. His father came to Giles County in 1768 from Shenandoah County and settled on the New River. He began law practice in Tazewell County in 1802 and was its first common-wealth's attorney. He was related to delegate Andrew Beirne by marriage. Morton, *Monroe County,* 300.

CLAYTON, SAMUEL (born 1795), Bedford County, a tobacco merchant, in 1830 lived in Lynchburg, owned 160 acres and 5 slaves, and was married, with 3 children. He was a "leading citizen" of Lynchburg and served on various city committees (Christian, *Lynchburg,* 72, 84, 93). He married into a wealthy commercial family, the Murrells. Yancey, *Lynchburg,* 376.

CLOYD, GORDON (1775–1833), Montgomery County, was born in the Montgomery County area of a pioneer family (his father, Joseph, came to the county in 1774, built a Presbyterian church, and fought as a major in the Revolution); he had no formal education. A lawyer and a cattle raiser, in 1830 he lived in Newburg, owned 28,491 acres in Giles County and 3,091 acres in Montgomery County, 59 slaves, and 38 horses, and was married, with 3 children. He was sheriff, 1816, county surveyor, county clerk, and a major general of the Virginia militia. *Calendar of Virginia State Papers,* 8:367–68, 10:159–60; Cloyd Family Papers, Virginia Historical Society.

COFFMAN, SAMUEL H. (c.1795–1841), Shenandoah County, was born and raised in that county and had no formal higher education. A Mennonite merchant, in 1830 he lived in New Market, owned 26 properties valued at $300 and renting at $25 each, 6 slaves, and 3 horses, and was married, with 10 children. He served in the War of 1812 and was a promoter and founder of the Valley Pike Company. His grandfather was a Mennonite minister. Grigsby remarked that he was a "sensible dutchman . . . a merchant and wealthy withal" (Diary, no. 1); Wayland, *Shenandoah County,* 392.

COOKE, JOHN ROGERS (1788–1854), Frederick County, was born in Bermuda, settled in Martinsburg sometime before 1810, and had no formal higher education. An Episcopalian lawyer, in 1830 he lived at Winchester, owned 672 acres, and 6 slaves, and was married, with 5 children. A member of the House of Delegates, 1814–15, he was a Whig candidate for Congress in 1835 and "barely won over Colonel Edward Lucas 372–365" (Bushong, *Jefferson County,* 77). He was the brother-in-law of delegate Philip P. Pendleton and a close friend of Elisha Boyd. Grigsby wrote: "his mind appears to be well trained, but his person is ugly and his actions despicable. While speaking he could use enough water to here quench the thirst of a camel" (Diary, no. 3). Cooke's diary, Virginia Historical Society, is extremely sketchy until after 1830. Aler, *Martinsburg and Berkeley County,* 102–3.

DODDRIDGE, PHILIP (1773–1832), Brooke County, was born in Pennsylvania (Bedford County) and studied law. A Methodist lawyer, in 1830 he owned 56 acres on the Ohio River and 2 slaves, and was married, with 6 children. He was a member of the House of Delegates, 1815–20, the state senate, 1804–9, and Congress, 1829. His father, a blacksmith and carpenter, came to Virginia from Pennsylvania in 1765, and the family followed in the mid-1770s. Philip began law practice in Wellsburg and was recognized as "the best lawyer in western Virginia." In 1808 he was active as a Federalist in the Old Dominion. He pushed for a general system of public education in the state. Lambert, *Pioneer Leaders,* 126–39.

DONALDSON, WILLIAM (c.1765–1848), Hampshire County, was born in Ireland and came to America with his father sometime during the Revolution; he had no formal education. A Presbyterian planter, in 1830 he owned 492 acres, 12 slaves, and 5 horses and was married, with 3 children. He was a member of the House of Delegates, 1805–6, and the state senate, 1833–37.

DUNCAN, EDWIN S. (1790–1858), Harrison County, was born in Ireland and came to Virginia "in early manhood." A Baptist lawyer-judge, in 1830 he lived at Clarksburg, owned 2,235 acres, 5 slaves, and 11 horses, and was married, with 3 children. He was a member of the House of Delegates, 1812–13, and state senate, 1820–24, and a judge of the circuit court, 1831–58. "He represented his country in England under President Monroe" (Bernard L. Butcher, *Genealogical and Personal History of the Upper Monongahela Valley, West Virginia* [New York, 1912], 689). He was an officer of the Board of Public Works. "Edwin S. Duncan, afterwards Judge Duncan, was from Harrison County. Duncan and his elder half-brother John J. Allen, were law partners" (Maxwell, *Randolph County,* 214).

FITZHUGH, WILLIAM HENRY (1792–1830), Fairfax County, was born and raised in the Fairfax area and graduated from Princeton, 1808. A Presbyterian planter, in 1830 he lived in Stafford County, owned 10,412 acres valued at $52,372, 50 slaves, and 21 horses, and was married, with 10 children. He was a member of the House of Delegates, 1811–16, 1828–29, and state senate, 1819–23. His father was a friend and supporter of Washington and the Federalist party. William was vice-president of the Virginia Colonization Society and directed that his slaves be freed and sent to Africa after his death. Brother-in-law of Robert E. Lee, he was a close friend of William F. Gordon. Du Bellett, *Prominent Virginia Families*, 558; *Virginia Magazine of History and Biography* 7 (1900): 95–110; Gordon, *William F. Gordon*, 44–45.

GEORGE, JOHN B. (c.1775–1850), Tazewell County, was a Presbyterian merchant. In 1830 he lived at Jeffersonville, owned 2 properties valued at $100 each, 290 acres, 9 slaves, and 35 horses, and was married, with 3 children. He was a member of the House of Delegates, 1817–28, sheriff, 1812–15, 1842–44, and justice of the peace, 1816. A major in the Virginia militia, he was the owner and proprietor of "John B. George & Co" and had a "fine farm" (Harman, *Tazewell County*, 1:359).

GRIGGS, THOMAS, JR. (1780–1860), Jefferson County, was born in that county and had no formal education. A Methodist planter-lawyer, in 1830 he lived at Charles Town, owned 640 acres, 49 slaves, and 4 horses, and was married, with 3 children. He was a commonwealth's attorney and a member of the House of Delegates, 1811–12, and Congress, 1835–37. His father came to Jefferson County from Lancaster County in 1770 and became a wealthy planter. A "lawyer pre-eminent for his commanding intellect" and the president of the Valley Bank of Virginia at Charles Town for thirty-six years, he had a Federalist family background (Bushong, *Jefferson County*, 77). Norris, *Lower Shenandoah Valley*, 658–59.

HARRISON, PEACHY (1777–1848), Rockingham County, was born and raised in that county. A Lutheran physician, in 1830 he owned 151 acres and 4 slaves and was married, with 4 children. He was a member of the House of Delegates, 1816–17, a presidential elector, 1816, sheriff, 1824–26, and on the Jackson ticket, 1828. He was said to have been a leader of the Democratic party in the Valley (obituary, MSS, University of Virginia Library). In 1807 he wrote a history of Rockingham County for the Philadelphia Medical Museum. He supported Van Buren and was against nullification, serving as head of a committee which asserted the supremacy of the national government and called the nullifiers "rash, misguided . . . dangerously unconstitutional" (*Staunton Spectator*, Jan. 7, 1833). He was the father of Gessner Harrison (born 1807), professor of Latin and Greek at the University of Virginia. Grigsby described him as "a dark looking man" (Diary, no. 1).

HENDERSON, RICHARD H. (1781–1841), Loudoun County, received a B.A. from Princeton, 1802. A Presbyterian lawyer, in 1830 he lived at Leesburg, owned 53 acres, 7 slaves, and 3 horses, and was married, with 7 children. He was on the Leesburg town council. He worked with Charles F. Mercer, also of Leesburg, on community projects. Wayland, *Shenandoah County*, 285.

JOHNSON, CHAPMAN (1779–1848), Augusta County, was born in Louisa County and graduated from William and Mary, 1802. An Episcopalian lawyer, in 1830 he lived in Richmond, owned 432 acres, 33 slaves, and 2 horses in Augusta County, and was married. He was a member of the House of Delegates, 1834–35, 1846–48, and the state senate, 1810–26. He first practiced law in Staunton; in 1824 he moved to practice in Richmond but retained a summer home in Staunton. He "was too hardworking and studious a lawyer to find much leisure for the pleasures of society" (Peyton, *Augusta County*, 78, 379). He had one of the most extensive legal practices in the state. He was mayor of Staunton, 1808, on the Board of Visitors, University of Virginia, 1819–45, and rector, 1826–45, and an Adams man in 1828. "His ambitions were legal rather than political" (Gordon, *William F. Gordon*, 116). He was in favor of extensive state support of internal improvements. *Virginia Magazine of History and Biography* 19 (1911): 157, 25 (1917): 161–62, 246–50; Broadside to Freeholders, March 20, 1816, University of Virginia Library.

JOYNES, THOMAS R. (1789–1858), Accomack County, was born and raised in that county and had no formal education. An Episcopalian planter-lawyer, in 1830 he owned 1,275 acres valued at $20,928, 27 slaves, and 8 horses and was unmarried. He was a member of the House of Delegates, 1811, commonwealth's attorney in the Supreme Court of Appeals, 1825–28, and county clerk, 1828–45. A self-made man, he started as a clerk in a village store in the town of Accomac. He was a captain in the War of 1812.

LAIDLEY, JOHN OSBORNE (1781–1863), Cabell County, was born in Philadelphia of Scottish immigrant parents, raised in Morgantown, and had no formal higher education. A Methodist lawyer, in 1830 he owned 362 acres on the Ohio River and 4 slaves and was married, with 8 children. He was a member of the House of Delegates, 1819–20, 1823–25, and a Jacksonian. He moved to Cabell County in 1815 and became prosecuting attorney. He was a cousin of delegate Joshia Osborne. Wallace, *Cabell County*, 42.

McCOY, WILLIAM (1768–1841), Pendleton County, was born in Augusta County and had no higher education. A Presbyterian merchant, in 1830 he owned 4,221 acres, 11 slaves, and 16 horses and was a widower, with 5 children. He was a member of the House of Delegates, 1798–1804, and Congress, 1818–33, and a Jacksonian. He was a trusted friend of President Jackson and chairman of the Ways and Means Committee. A merchant at Franklin, he suffered a stroke in 1833. Grigsby portrayed him as "a good deal baldheaded . . . honest old fellow . . . deemed the watchdog of the treasury" (Diary, no. 1); Morton, *Pendleton County*, 258.

McMILLAN, ANDREW (born c.1775), Lee County, was a Presbyterian small farmer. In 1830 he owned 240 acres valued at $1,447.20, no slaves, and 3 horses and was married, with 3 children. He was a member of the House of Delegates, 1811–29. Mentioned in Wallace, *Cabell County*, 308.

MASON, JAMES MURRAY (1798–1871), Frederick County, was born on Mason's Island near Washington, D.C., graduated from the University of Pennsylvania, 1818, and studied law at William and Mary, 1819–20. An Episcopalian lawyer, in 1830 he lived at Winchester, owned 151 acres and 7 slaves, and was married, with 5 children. He was a member of the House of Delegates, 1826–31, Congress, 1837–39, and U.S. Senate, 1847. He was a presidential elector on the Jackson ticket, 1832. He practiced law and was a bank president at Winchester. A grandson of George Mason of Gunston Hall, he married in 1824 the daughter of Judge Chew, chief justice of Pennsylvania Supreme Court. He became a strict constructionist in the 1840s and a follower of Calhoun and was sent to England by the Confederacy in 1861. See V. Mason, *James Murray Mason*.

MATHEWS, JOHN P. (c.1775–1842), Wythe County, was born in Staunton and had no formal higher education. A Presbyterian lawyer, in 1830 he lived in Evanstown, owned 63 acres and 12 slaves, and was married, with 11 children. His grandfather came to Staunton from Ireland in 1739 and was a merchant. His father, George, was also a merchant and a "hot Federalist" (Waddell, *Augusta County*, 191). John "was one of the best known and highly respected men in Southwest Virginia, well informed and possessed of excellent social qualities, and greatly esteemed by the court and bar" (Johnston, *Old Virginia Courts*, 404). He was a friend and fellow attorney with delegate Gordon Cloyd and suffered an attack of pleurisy and was confined to bed during the first weeks of the Convention. Gordon Cloyd to David Cloyd, Oct. 18, 1829, Cloyd Family Papers, Virginia Historical Society.

MERCER, CHARLES FENTON (1778–1850), Loudoun County, was born and raised in that county and received an M.A. from Princeton, 1797. An Episcopalian lawyer, in 1830 he was unmarried, lived in Leesburg, and owned 578 acres valued at $35,855 and no slaves. He was a member of the House of Delegates, 1810–17, and Congress, 1816–40. He was the grandson of an Irish immigrant. His father, James, was a member of the Convention of 1776 and a Federalist friend of Washington. Charles was also an "open Federalist" (Fischer, *American Conservatism,* 384–85). Antislavery, he was an officer of the Virginia Colonization Society. He supported general public education and favored internal improvements, serving as the president of the Chesapeake and Ohio Canal Company. Against the Bank of the United States, he was a proponent of agricultural reform. He was a strong nationalist Whig in Congress. Garnett, *Charles Fenton Mercer.*

MILLER, FLEMING BOWYER (1793–1874), Botetourt County, was born in Fincastle in that county and was educated at Washington and Lee College, Yale, and the Litchfield Law School in Connecticut. He practiced law for a year in Nashville, Tennessee, and then returned to Fincastle. In 1830 he was married, with 6 children; he owned 138 acres, 9 slaves, and 3 horses. He was a member of the House of Delegates, from 1825, with brief interruptions, until 1837, the Convention of 1850–51, and the Secession Convention. He was U.S. district attorney for western Virginia, 1853–61. He voted for secession on April 17, 1861. He was a member of the state senate, 1866–67, and commonwealth's attorney of Botetourt County, 1870–73. Early in 1874 he moved to Augusta County where he died. Stoner, *Seed-Bed,*438.

MOORE, SAMUEL McDOWELL (1796–1875), Rockbridge County, was the son of General Andrew Moore of that county and was educated at Washington College. A Presbyterian lawyer-manufacturer, in 1830 he owned 150 acres, 3 slaves, and 8 horses and was married, with 6 children. He was in the House of Delegates, 1825–33, 1836–37, and state senate, 1845–47, and was a Whig member of Congress, 1833–35. He was elected lieutenant governor of Virginia in 1859. He was of a Federalist family background. He was described as a "rank Federalist" (Grigsby, Diary, no. 1) and "an avowed Adams man" (Simms, *Rise of Whigs*, 266). He was involved with iron and grist mill operations in the county. He was a member of the Convention of 1861 and voted for secession. In 1863 he was elected to the Confederate lower house and resigned the lieutenant governor's position to serve there 1864–65. After serving again in the House of Delegates, 1874–75, he was elected judge of the Eighth Judicial Circuit and served as a justice until his death. Morton, *Rockbridge County*, 268; Montague, *Peter Montague*, 311–12.

MORGAN, CHARLES (1799–1859), Monongalia County, was born and raised at Morgantown and had no formal higher education. A Methodist politician and penitentiary warden, in 1830 he owned 83 acres and no slaves. His father was a justice of the peace and sheriff of Monongalia County for many years. Charles retired from politics in 1832 to become the superintendent of the Virginia penitentiary at Richmond.

NAYLOR, WILLIAM (c.1785–c.1858), Hampshire County, was a lawyer who in 1830 lived in Romney, owned 6,717 acres and 9 slaves, and was married, with 10 children. He was a member of the House of Delegates, 1817–18. Admitted to Winchester bar in 1812, he was well known as a successful lawyer in the county. He is listed in Kercheval, *The Valley*, as one of seventeen outstanding citizens of Hampshire County in 1833. Grigsby wrote that "Naylor was a rank Federalist" (Diary, no. 1). Maxwell and Swischer, *Hampshire County*, 494.

OGLESBY, WILLIAM (1785–1866), Grayson County, was a Lutheran merchant. In 1830 he owned 307 acres, 11 slaves, and 5 horses and was married, with 1 child. He was a member of the House of Delegates, 1838–39. He had a business partnership with the Nuckolls family, one of the most influential in the area, in the "goods business," at Grayson Courthouse (Lambert, *Pioneer Leaders*, 89).

OSBORNE, JOSHIA (c.1790–1830), Loudoun County, was a Baptist and a farmer who in 1830 owned 915 acres valued at $14,335 near Hillsborough. He served in the House of Delegates, 1824–25. He supported Jackson in the election of 1828.

PENDLETON, PHILIP C. (1790–1860), Berkeley County, was born and raised in that county and had no formal higher education. A Presbyterian lawyer-judge, in 1830 he owned 298 acres and 13 slaves and was married, with 4 children. He came from a Federalist family. In 1831 he represented Virginia at the National Republican Convention in Baltimore. He was on the Board of Visitors for the University of Virginia, 1818. His father-in-law was delegate Elisha Boyd; his brother-in-law was John R. Cooke. Aler, *Martinsburg and Berkeley County*, 145; Simms, *Rise of Whigs*, 43.

POWELL, ALFRED HARRISON (1790–1831), Frederick County, was born and raised in Loudoun County, was educated at Princeton, and studied law in Alexandria. A Presbyterian lawyer, in 1830 he lived near Winchester, owned 433 acres valued at $9,465 and 17 slaves, and was married, with 4 children. He was a member of the state senate, 1812–19, and Congress, 1825–27. He had a Federalist family background and was deeply convinced that the national government has the power to finance internal improvements. He was related by marriage to Elisha Boyd. Fischer, *American Conservatism*, 376–77; Dingledine, "William Cabell Rives," 94; Powell, *Powells in America,*171–72.

SAUNDERS, JAMES (c.1785–c.1840), Campbell County, was born in the Campbell–Prince Edward County area. A Methodist physician, in 1830 he lived in Lynchburg, owned 205 acres, with no slaves, and was married, with 8 children. He served in the state senate, 1825–30. He made money on tobacco and had "one of the loveliest homes in Lynchburg" (Yancey, *Lynchburg*, 44–45). Saunders's family was nationalist-Whig. Early, *Campbell Chronicles*, 188.

SEE, ADAM (born 1767), Randolph County, was born in Pennsylvania. A Presbyterian planter-lawyer, in 1830 he lived on 4,379 acres along the Elk Valley River and owned 26 slaves and 27 horses. He was a member of the House of Delegates, 1797–98, 1800–1802, 1809–10, 1814–16, 1822–23. The See family came to America in 1734 to escape religious persecution in the Palatine and first settled in Bucks County, Pennsylvania. Adam was the son of German-speaking Marshall See who moved to Virginia sometime after 1765. Adam began law practice in Randolph County in 1793 and was prosecuting attorney of the county, 1798. Bosworth, *Randolph County*, 30; Maxwell, *Randolph County*, 203, 206, 232, 457.

SMITH, WILLIAM (1774–1859), Greenbrier County, was born and raised in Madison County. "Without education . . . he was only able to write his name and that mechanically for he could write nothing else" (Johnston, *Middle New River Settlements*, 174). A Presbyterian farmer, in 1830 he owned 600 acres on Mill Creek, 3 slaves, and 1 horse; he was married, with 4 children. A member of the House of Delegates, 1819–20, 1828–29, he was a Clay supporter. His father, Isaac, served in the Revolution. William was justice of the peace in Mercer County, 1837–49. He was a candidate for the state legislature twelve times. Grigsby remarked that he was "a good republican . . . he was an ugly man, very. He has no points of character" (Diary, no. 1). Early, *Campbell County*, 29.

STUART, ARCHIBALD, JR. (1795–1855), Patrick County, was born in Lynchburg and studied law and maintained a practice in that city. He was an officer in the War of 1812. In 1830 he lived with his family at Laurel Hill, a plantation of 3,389 acres valued at $27,754 and 19 slaves, near Lynchburg. He served in the Virginia House of Delegates, 1830–31, the state senate, 1852–53, and was a Whig in Congress in the House of Representatives, 1837–38. Stuart was also a delegate to the Constitutional Convention of 1850–51 representing Patrick County.

SUMMERS, LEWIS (1778–1843), Kanawha County, was born in Fairfax County. A Presbyterian lawyer-manufacturer-judge, in 1830 he owned 387 acres on the Kanawha River, 14 slaves, and 5 horses; he was married, with no children. He moved to Ohio in 1808 and served in the Ohio legislature; he returned to Virginia in 1814 and settled permanently in Kanawha County. He was admitted to Cabell County bar, 1816, and was a member of the Board of Public Works, 1816. A warm follower of Jefferson, he was an Adams man in 1828, serving on the electoral ticket along with delegates Chapman Johnson and Archibald Stuart, Jr. He operated salt furnaces and other business pursuits. Simms, *Rise of Whigs*, 30.

TAYLOR, ROBERT B. (1774–1834), city of Norfolk, was born in Smithfield and graduated from William and Mary, 1793. A lawyer-judge, in 1830 he owned 9 properties in Norfolk valued totally at $91,000, 9 slaves, and 2 horses; he was married, with 3 children. He was a member of the House of Delegates, 1788–99, and a judge of the General Court, 1831–34. He was a Federalist. A brigadier general, he defended Norfolk against the British in 1815. He opposed the Virginia and Kentucky Resolutions and the doctrine of states' rights. *Southern Literary Messenger*, 17 [1841]: 302; Bigelow, "Hugh Blair Grigsby," 34.

THOMPSON, LUCAS P. (c.1804–1866), Amherst County, was born in Nelson County. A lawyer-judge, in 1830 he owned 225 acres and 11 slaves and was married, with 3 children. He was a member of the House of Delegates, 1826–30, and a judge of the circuit court, 1831–66. In 1830 he moved from Amherst County to Staunton and lived next door to delegate Briscoe Baldwin. He operated a law school in his home. He was elected a judge of the Supreme Court of Appeals in 1866 but died before assuming the position. "One of the younger men at the Convention, he achieved later a position second to that of none of the many great nisi-prius judges of his generation in the state by his administration through a long series of years of duties" (Gordon, *William F. Gordon*, 158).

WILLIAMSON, JACOB (1779–1874), Rockingham County, was educated at Philadelphia Medical College. A Lutheran physician, in 1830 he owned 1,233 acres valued at $27,504, 20 slaves, and 18 horses. He was a member of the House of Delegates, 1817–18. An Adams man in 1824, he supported Jackson in 1832 (on electoral ticket). He was sheriff, 1841. He worked with Samuel Coffman to promote the Valley Turnpike and was a trustee of New Market Academy, 1817–51. He was related to delegate Peachy Harrison by marriage. Grigsby wrote that he was an "honest sensible farmer . . . studied medicine when young at Philadelphia" (Diary, no. 1). Wayland, *Shenandoah County*, 25.

WILSON, EUGENIUS M. (born c.1795), Monongalia County, was born in Morgantown and raised in Randolph County by his immigrant parents (his father came to America from Scotland in 1755). A Presbyterian merchant, in 1830 he owned 20 acres and 2 slaves; he was married, with 2 children. His father, Benjamin, was "one of the acknowledged leaders of the Federal party in western Virginia until the War of 1812" (Bosworth, *Randolph County*, 293–96; Maxwell, *Randolph County*, 409). He was related to Philip Doddridge by marriage and a cousin of delegate Edwin S. Duncan.

CONVENTION OF 1850–51

Tidewater Delegates and Their Allies

BEALE, RICHARD L. (1819–1893), Westmoreland County, was the son of Major Robert Beale of Hickory Hill. He was educated at Dickinson College and the University of Virginia School of Law. He was a lawyer and planter who owned land valued at $20,000 and 38 slaves in 1850. He was a Democrat in Congress, 1847–49, 1879–87. He served in the state senate, 1857–61, and was a general in the Confederate army.

BOTTS, JOHN MINOR (1802–1869), Henrico County, was born in Prince William County and moved to the city of Richmond at the age of nine. He studied law and was admitted to the bar in 1820. He owned 21 slaves, but there is no record of his property valuation in 1850. He was a Whig, strongly opposed to Jackson. He served in the House of Delegates, 1833–40, and Congress, 1837–43, 1847–55. He was a Unionist opposed to secession in 1861.

BOWDEN, LEMUEL J. (1812–1864), Williamsburg, was educated at William and Mary, studied law, and practiced in the town. He owned property valued at $2,000 but no slaves in 1850. He served in the House of Delegates, 1849–51, and in 1861 was a presidential elector.

BRAXTON, CORBIN (1792–1852), King William County, was born at Elsing Green, the son of Carter Braxton (Convention of 1776). He was a planter with an estate valued at $35,000 and owned 67 slaves in 1850.

BURGES, ALBRIDGETON S. H. (1792–1864), Southampton County, was born in St. Luke's Parish, Isle of Wight, the son of "Parson" Burges, head of Millfield Academy. He attended the academy along with William Henry Harrison. He was an Episcopalian. He studied medicine in North Carolina and began practice in Raleigh. He owned property valued at $3,500 and 15 slaves in 1850.

CHAMBLISS, JOHN RANDOLPH (1809–1864), Greensville County, was born in Hicksford, the son of an Episcopalian minister. He was educated at West Point Military Academy and was a lawyer by profession. He owned land valued at $964 but no slaves in 1850. He was married, with 2 children. He was a governor's aide, 1856–61, and while serving as a brigadier general in the Virginia militia was killed in battle in 1864.

CONWAY, EUSTACE (1818–1857), Spotsylvania County, was born in Stafford County of a prominent local family. He attended Fredericksburg Academy, studied law, and practiced in Fredericksburg. He was an Episcopalian. In 1850 his property was valued at $5,450, and he owned 12 slaves; he was married, with no children. He was a Democrat in the House of Delegates, 1847–50, and state senate, 1852–56. In 1856 he was elected a judge of the circuit court. He also was on the William and Mary Board of Visitors from 1849 until his death.

COX, JAMES H. (1810–1877), Chesterfield County, was born at the family seat of Clover Hill, attended Hampden-Sydney, and studied law. He taught at Tallahassee Academy in Florida, 1829–32, and then became a planter and businessman. In 1832 he opened Clover Hill Coal Mines in the southwest part of Virginia. He was active in railroad construction, building the Clover Hill Railroad and promoting the Atlantic Coastline Railroad system. In 1850 he was living in Fluvanna County with property valued at $1,000 and 5 slaves; he was married, with 8 children. He was a Douglas Democrat in 1860 and served as temporary chairman of the Secession Convention. He opposed secession unless the South was invaded.

DAVIS, HECTOR, city of Richmond, in 1850 owned 2 lots valued at $3,000 and $2,500.

DOUGLAS, BEVERLEY (1822–1878), King William County, was born in New Kent County, was educated at Hanover Academy and William and Mary, then read law with Judge Beverley Tucker. He moved to King William County in 1846 to begin his practice. In 1850 he owned an estate valued at $7,500 and 19 slaves; he was married, with 1 child. He was a Democrat in the state senate, 1852–65, and a major in the Confederate army.

FINNEY, LOUIS C. H. (1822–1884), Accomack County, came from an old Eastern Shore family going back to the 1660s. He was educated at Montgomery Academy, Washington and Jefferson College, Pennsylvania, and Harvard Law School. His estate of 392 acres was valued at $5,488 with no slaves in 1850. He served in the Confederacy as a lieutenant colonel. Whitelaw, *Virginia's Eastern Shore*.

GARNETT, MUSCOE (1808–1880), Essex County, was born in King and Queen County and attended the school of Thomas Fax in Hanover County. After about eight visits to Kentucky as a young man, he settled in Essex County and studied law. He was a Baptist. A planter-lawyer, he owned property valued at $110,000 and 40 slaves in 1850. He was a member of the House of Delegates, 1842–50, 1865, and a county judge, 1870–80. He was buried at his plantation Ben Somond.

GARNETT, MUSCOE RUSSELL HUNTER (1821–1864), Essex County, the son of James M. Garnett (Convention of 1829–30), was born at Elmwood. He attended the University of Virginia, class of

1842, and studied law. He was a Baptist. He owned property valued at $20,000 and was among the largest slaveowners—100 slaves—in the county in 1850. He was a neighbor and friend of Robert M. T. Hunter. He was a member of the House of Delegates, 1853–56, and a Democrat in Congress, 1856–61, and went to the Democratic National Convention in 1852 and 1856. He served in the Confederate Congress until his death.

HALL, ADDISON, Lancaster County, was a Baptist minister. In 1850 he owned 212 acres valued at $3,170.

JONES, JAMES A. (1822–1894), Petersburg, was born in Mecklenburg County, the son of James B. Jones, was educated at Randolph-Macon (B.A.) and University of Virginia (M.A.), and then studied law in Richmond under Conway Robinson and settled in Petersburg in the 1840s to practice. In 1850 he owned 2 lots there valued at $300 and $1,400. He served in the state senate, 1853, and was a trustee of Richmond College. His career as a lawyer in the Supreme Court of Appeals was "one of the ablest in the state" (*Cyclopedia of Virginia Biography*, 3:299).

LYONS, JAMES (1801–1882), city of Richmond, was educated at William and Mary and admitted to the bar in 1820. He was prosecuting attorney for the circuit court in Richmond. He was president of the Virginia Agricultural Society and an Episcopalian vestryman of St. James Church. His grandfather had been a judge of the Supreme Court of Appeals. In Richmond he owned 6 properties with values of $982, $985, $1,450, $24,962, $11,850, and $9,900 in 1850. He was a states'-rights Whig in the U.S. Senate until 1852 when he became a Democrat. He was a member of the Confederate Congress and a personal friend of Jefferson Davis.

McCANDLISH, ROBERT (born 1789), Williamsburg, was a lawyer who owned an estate in 1850 valued at $47,000; he was married, with 5 children.

MASON, JOHN YOUNG, Southampton County: *see* Convention of 1829–30, Eastern Delegates. In 1850 he owned a 314-acre estate valued at $2,413 and 83 slaves.

MEREDITH, JOHN (1814–1882), city of Richmond, was born in New Kent County, was educated at the University of Virginia (M.A., 1833), studied law under Conway Robinson, and practiced in Richmond after 1835. He lived in a mansion on the corner of Franklin and 8th streets, across from the home of delegate Robert

Stanard. His properties in 1850 included lots valued at $4,500, $5,715, $40, and $40. He was commonwealth's attorney for Hanover County, state senator, 1852, then judge of the circuit court, 1852–60.

NORRIS, EDWARD W. (born 1822), Hanover County, was a lawyer with property valued at $7,000 in 1850; he was married, with 1 child.

PETTY, JOHN (born 1822), Princess Anne County, was a planter with property worth $1,000 and 54 slaves in 1850.

RIDLEY, ROBERT (born 1812), Southampton County, was a lawyer who owned property worth $22,000 and 64 slaves in 1850; he was married, with 3 children.

RIVES, TIMOTHY (1807–1865), Prince George County, was a lawyer who practiced for a few years in Sussex County and then settled near Petersburg. In 1850 he owned land valued at $8,376 and 17 slaves; he was married, with 1 child. He was a member of the Secession Convention of 1861. Rives was a Unionist and voted against secession on April 4, but he voted for secession on April 17. Rives served in the Confederate army as a captain and took part in the battle for Petersburg on June 9, 1864. He was captured in that action and was confined for several months at Point Lookout, Maryland. After his release, he returned home and died near Petersburg. Childs, *Rives*, 644–45.

SCOTT, FRANCIS W. (born 1808), Caroline County, was the son of John Scott (Convention of 1829). An Episcopalian lawyer, in 1850 his property was valued at $18,070, and he owned 20 slaves; he was married, with 6 children. Wingfield, *Caroline County*.

SCOTT, ROBERT G. (1820–1894), city of Richmond, a brother of Francis, was educated at William and Mary, studied law under his father John Scott (Convention of 1829), and was admitted to the bar in 1841. He was a vestryman and owned 2 town lots worth $7,876 and $50 in 1850. He was a captain of the Richmond Grays during the Mexican War. In 1855 President Pierce appointed him consul to Brazil. In 1861 he moved to Alabama, returning to Richmond in 1870 to continue his law practice.

SMITH, ARTHUR R. (1805–1866), Norfolk County, was born in Nansemond County, the son of an attorney. He was educated in the Norfolk city schools and attended the University of Virginia and the Jefferson School of Medicine in Philadelphia. In 1848 he moved to Deep Creek, Norfolk County, to practice medicine. He was a Democrat in the state senate, 1856–60, and a supporter of Governor Wise. He attended the Democratic National Convention in Charleston in 1860 as a supporter of Letcher. During the war he served as a surgeon in the Confederate army. In 1850 his estate was valued at $1,939, and he owned no slaves. He died in Catonsville, Maryland.

SMITH, JAMES E. (1810–1864), King and Queen County, was born in Petersburg, the son of a prominent Baptist minister. He was an architect and building contractor who owned an estate valued at $3,500 and 37 slaves in 1850; he was married, with 6 children.

STANARD, ROBERT C. (1814–1851), city of Richmond, was the son of Robert Stanard (Convention of 1829–30). Born in Fredericksburg, he was educated in the Richmond city schools and studied law and practiced there in the Court of Appeals. He was a member of the state senate at the time of his death. He owned 5 properties valued at $28,000, $16,800, $8,800, $8,000, and $6,500 but no slaves in 1850.

STRAUGHAM, SAMUEL R., Northumberland County. No extant data.

TAYLOR, TAZEWELL (1810–1875), city of Norfolk, was educated at Georgetown College and the University of Virginia, studied law under St. George Tucker, and practiced at Norfolk. He was a vestryman. In 1850 his estate was valued at $2,400, and he owned 5 slaves; he was married, with 4 children. He died at Hampton.

TUNIS, JOHN, JR. (born 1806), city of Norfolk, was an "opulent merchant" listed as independently wealthy in the 1850 census. His estate was valued at $21,550, and he owned 1 slave; he was married, with 3 children. See Forrest, *Norfolk*.

WALLACE, THOMAS (1812–1868), Petersburg, was born in that city, was educated at William and Mary and the University of Virginia, and practiced law in Petersburg. He was the city's mayor, 1831–32, commonwealth's attorney, a Whig member in the House of Delegates, 1850–57, and a secessionist. His properties were valued at $1,500, $1,400, $1,100, $1,100, $650, and $530 in 1850. One of the houses served as the headquarters of General Grant during the seige of Richmond.

WATTS, SAMUEL, Norfolk County. No extant data.

WISE, HENRY A. (1806–1876), Accomack County, was born at Drummondtown and was educated at Margaret Academy, near Pungoteague, and at Washington and Jefferson College in Pennsylvania. He read law at Winchester under Henry St. George Tucker and in 1828 moved to Nashville, Tennessee, where he practiced his profession for the next two years. He returned to Virginia in 1830 and settled in Accomack County. He was a member of Congress, 1833–44. First elected as a Democrat, he left his party in 1837 to join the Whigs and during his last terms was a loyal supporter of President John Tyler, who in 1844 appointed him minister to Brazil, a post he held until 1847. He was active in Virginia politics after his return from Rio de Janeiro. Although an advocate of states' rights and a defender of slavery, Wise was sympathetic to the aspirations of the western counties of Virginia, and as a member of the Convention of 1850 he supported their demands for a more equitable distribution of seats in the General Assembly. In 1850 he owned land valued at $10,000 but no slaves. Wise, who meanwhile had returned to the Democratic party, campaigned in 1855 for the governorship of Virginia against Thomas S. Flournoy and was elected. During his term, 1856–60, the sectional crisis over slavery became more acute, and Wise sent troops to Harpers Ferry at the time of John Brown's raid. Soon after leaving the governorship, Wise settled in Princess Anne County and was elected as delegate from that constituency to the Secession Convention. He voted for secession on April 4 and again on April 17. He served throughout the war in the Confederate army and rose to the rank of major general. After the war he moved to Richmond and practiced law there in partnership with his son, John Sergeant Wise. See Simpson, *Henry A. Wise.*

Piedmont Delegates and Their Allies

ARTHUR, LEWIS C. (born 1805), Bedford County, was a farmer with 1,255 acres valued at $11,800 in 1850.

BANKS, ROBERT A. (1807–1878), Madison County, was a planter with an estate of 2,652 acres valued at $60,000 and 31 slaves in 1850. He was a Baptist. See Yorrell, *Madison County.*

BARBOUR, JAMES, JR. (1823–1895), Culpeper County, was a brother of Alfred M. Barbour who was elected to the Secession Convention from Jefferson County but resigned and was replaced by Richard H. Lee. James attended the University of Virginia and then practiced law in Culpeper County. He owned 203 acres valued at $3,663 and 17 slaves in 1850. Barbour was a member of the House of Delegates, 1852–53, 1857–63. He was a member of the board of visitors of the Virginia Military Institute. He attended the Secession Convention of 1861, voting for secession on April 4 and again on April 17. He served during the early part of the war with General Richard Ewell but resigned because of ill health. After the war, he resumed his political career and represented his county in the House of Delegates, 1877–79, 1885–88.

BOCOCK, WILLIS P. (1804–1887), Appomattox County, was born at Buckhorn. Educated at an elementary school established by his father and at the University of Virginia, he studied and practiced law. He was a Presbyterian who owned 1,137 acres valued at $8,000 and 20 slaves in 1850. He was a Democrat and attorney general of the state, 1848–57. He retired from public life in 1857 after a crippling accident.

BOWLES, DRURY (or DREWRY) W. K. (1802–1887), Fluvanna County, was raised on the family estate at Bowlesville. He was a Baptist who owned property worth $5,700 and 20 slaves in 1850; he was married, with 6 children. He was chosen a justice of the peace, 1824, and served as presiding judge of the county court until 1882.

CARTER, JOHN A. (1808–1865), Loudoun County, was born at Sabine Hall, Richmond County, and was a son of Landon Carter. He attended Andover Academy, the University of Virginia, and the law school of Judge Henry St. George Tucker in Winchester. Carter then settled in Leesburg and practiced law. He owned 925 acres valued at $32,000 and 22 slaves in 1850. He was a member of the House of Delegates, 1842–1844, and the state senate, 1859–61.

CHAMBERS, EDWARD R. (born 1795), Mecklenburg County, was educated at Chapel Hill College and admitted to the North Carolina bar in 1817. In 1850 he owned 450 acres valued at $3,083 but no slaves. He was commonwealth's attorney for Mecklenburg County, 1835–50.

CHILTON, SAMUEL (1804–1867), Fauquier County, was born at Warrenton and studied law in Winchester. He was a Whig in Congress, 1835–37, 1843–45. In 1850 his property was worth $4,000, and he had no slaves; he was married, with 5 children. In the early 1850s he moved to Washington, D.C., and became a prominent attorney there. He returned to Virginia at the outbreak of the Civil War and died at Warrenton.

CLAIBORNE, NATHANIEL C. (1820–1859), Franklin County, was educated at Washington and Lee College and practiced law. He served in the House of Delegates and the state senate in the 1840s. He owned property valued at $3,296 and 19 slaves in 1850.

COCKE, RICHARD IVANHOE (1820–1873), Fluvanna County, was the eldest son of John Hartwell Cocke of Bremo and was educated at the University of Virginia and William and Mary. He was a lawyer with property valued at $150 and 4 slaves in 1850. He served in the House of Delegates, 1849–50, and the state senate, 1865–70, and after 1845 was commonwealth's attorney. In 1870 he moved to Blandville, Boland County, Kentucky, where he died.

EDMONDS, JOHN R. (1812–1873), Halifax County, was a planter-lawyer educated at the University of Virginia. He was an Episcopalian with an estate, Redfield, worth $48,650 and 112 slaves in 1850. W. J. Carrington in *Halifax County*, 171–72, wrote: "He was a wealthy man before the Civil War, a staunch sympathizer with the South . . . he built for the Confederate government that section of the Southern Railway lying between Danville and Greensboro. He owned many slaves and other property and was also a large land-owner." He was a life member of the Virginia Agricultural Society. He died at Redfield in 1873.

EDWARDS, WILLIAM L. (1807–1877), Fairfax County, was born into a wealthy planter family of Northumberland County. William Wirt was for a time the family's tutor. He was a Methodist and a planter. He owned 10 acres of land valued at $50 in 1850.

FLOOD, THOMAS H. (1804–1873), Appomattox County, was educated at Washington and Lee College. He was a Presbyterian planter with an estate of 587 acres valued at $5,000 and 20 slaves in 1850. He served in the House of Delegates, 1831–45, from Buckingham County and again, 1861–62, from Appomattox. He was also in the state senate, 1852–53.

FUQUA, JOSEPH (born 1801), Buckingham County, was a lawyer and farmer whose estate was valued at $1,800 in 1850. He owned no slaves that year. He was married, with 3 children.

GARLAND, SAMUEL M. (1802–1880), Amherst County, was educated at William and Mary and was a lawyer. He was county clerk,

1837–64. He owned 393 acres valued at $7,000 in 1850 but no slaves. Garland also represented Amherst County in the Secession Convention, voting for secession on April 4 and again on April 17. Yancey, *Lynchburg,* 312–13.

GOODE, WILLIAM O. (1798–1860), Mecklenburg County: *see* Convention of 1829–30, Eastern Delegates. In 1850 he owned 2,534 acres valued at $6,012 and 18 slaves.

HILL, JOHN (1801–1880), Buckingham County, was born at New Canton, educated at Washington and Lee College, and practiced law. He was not listed in the tax records in 1850. He was a Whig in Congress, 1839–41, commonwealth's attorney, 1850–70, and county judge, 1870–79.

HOPKINS, HENRY L. (1800–1870), Powhatan County, was the son of Rev. Charles Hopkins. He studied law and practiced in the county until 1859 when he moved to Petersburg. He owned land worth $200 and 13 slaves in 1850; his three children were living with him that year, but no wife was listed in the census. He was commonwealth's attorney and member of the House of Delegates, 1862–63. He died near Warrenton, North Carolina.

JANNEY, JOHN (1798–1872), Loudoun County, was born in Alexandria. He was the son of Elisha Janney, a prosperous merchant and miller, and a cousin of Samuel McPherson Janney, a noted Quaker minister, author, and educator. He became a lawyer and practiced in Leesburg. Janney was a member of the Virginia House of Delegates, 1833–45. He was active in the affairs of the Colonization Society of Virginia. In 1850 he owned land valued at $1,500; he was married, with 2 children. Janney was elected as a moderate Unionist to the 1861 Secession Convention and was chosen president of that convention "as the candidate of the middle and . . . more conservative members of the body." He was described by Robert H. Turner of Warren County, one of his colleagues at that Convention, as "a venerable looking gentleman, far past the meridian of life, tall, spare and with a suit of white hair, of the purest and most unblemished character." Janney voted against secession on April 4 and again on April 17, but he later signed the ordinance of secession. After the war Janney resumed the practice of law in Leesburg. Williams, *Legends of Loudoun,* 226; Writers' Program, WPA, *Prince William,* 80–81; Robert Turner, "Recollections of the Virginia Convention of 1861," Virginia Historical Society.

JASPER, DANIEL, Stafford County, came from a Prince William County family. He was not listed in the Stafford County land and personal property tax records in 1850 nor in the census.

LEAKE, WALTER D. (1813–1873), Goochland County, was the son of Josiah and Eliza (or Elizabeth) Hatcher Leake. He was educated at the University of Virginia and William and Mary and became a lawyer. He lived at Rocky Spring and was married to Margaret Kean Leake, with 4 children. He owned property valued at $8,000 and 29 slaves in 1850. Leake was commonwealth's attorney in Goochland County and a member of the Virginia House of Delegates, 1842–47. He was also the county's delegate in the Secession Convention and voted for secession on April 4 and again on April 17. He served as a captain of artillery during the early months of the war.

LITTLEBERRY, N. LIGON, Nelson County. No extant data.

LYNCH, CHARLES H. (1800–1875), Campbell County, was related to John Lynch the founder of the town of Lynchburg. Colonel Charles Lynch was a farmer and a bachelor with land valued at $15,000 and 1 slave in 1850. He was in the state senate for eight years and a justice of the peace. Early, *Campbell Chronicles*, 456–58.

MARTIN, WILLIAM (born 1814), Henry County, was a son of Joseph Martin (Convention of 1829–30). He was educated at the University of Virginia and practiced law. He owned an estate valued at $8,000 but no slaves in 1850; he was married, with 3 children. He was commonwealth's attorney after the Civil War. Pedigo, *Patrick and Henry Counties.*

PERKINS, GEORGE W. (born 1820), Halifax County, was a small farmer (value of $100) and owned 5 slaves in 1850.

RANDOLPH, THOMAS JEFFERSON (1792–1875), Albemarle County, was Thomas Jefferson's son-in-law. In 1850 his estate was valued at $63,000, and he owned 46 slaves.

SAUNDERS, JAMES (1792–1864), Campbell County, was a tobacco manufacturer in Lynchburg with an estate worth $35,000 and 50 slaves in 1850. He was married, with 4 children.

SCOGGIN, JAMES (born 1820), Lunenburg County, was a small planter (value of $400) with 8 slaves in 1850. He was married, with two small children.

SCOTT, ROBERT E. (1808–1862), Fauquier County, was the son of Judge John Scott, Jr. (Convention of 1829–30). He was born in Warrenton, Fauquier County, and was educated at the University of Virginia. Scott was a lawyer and practiced in Fauquier County and surrounding counties. He owned 366 acres at Oakwood valued at $16,024 and 10 slaves in 1850. He was a member of the House of Delegates, 1835–42, 1845–52. He was also a member of the Secession Convention of 1861. He voted against the secession proposal of April 4 but for secession on April 17. He was a member of the Provisional Congress on the Confederacy from July 1861 until it adjourned in February 1862. He then "returned to Fauquier County, which was by this time overrun by the enemy. Deserters from the Union army had been terrorizing the neighborhood, and Scott and other citizens went in pursuit of these marauders. On May 3, 1862, they caught up with the deserters, and Scott was killed in the encounter that resulted." R. E. Scott, "Robert Eden Scott," in *Fauquier County Historical Society Bulletin*, no. 1 (n.d.): 78–82.

SHELL, JOHN E. (1800–1865), Brunswick County, was educated in the county schools, studied law, served in the House of Delegates, 1834–60, and was commonwealth's attorney the last year of his life. He was a Whig. In 1850 his estate was valued at $518, and he had no slaves. He was a bachelor.

SNOWDEN, EDGAR (1833–1892), Fairfax County, was born and raised in the town of Alexandria and was owner and editor of the *Alexandria Gazette*. He was in the state senate, 1869–75, and in 1875 was appointed the assistant postmaster of the U.S. House of Representatives. He had property valued at $5,000 but no slaves in 1850; he was married, with 9 children. He died in Washington, D.C.

SOUTHALL, VALENTINE W. (1804–1861), Albemarle County, was born at Westham, Goochland County. He was a lawyer and practiced in Albemarle County. He was appointed by Jefferson as the first secretary of the Board of Visitors of the University of Virginia. Southall was a member of the House of Delegates, 1833–46, serving as Speaker of the house, 1840–42, 1844–45. He was also a member of the Secession Convention of 1861. In 1850 he owned 62.5 acres adjacent to Charlottesville valued at $7,000 and 9 slaves; he was married, with 5 children. Southall, a Whig and moderate, voted against secession on April 4 but for it on April 17. Dodson, *Speakers and Clerks,* 63.

STROTHER, JAMES F. (1811–1868), Rappahannock County, was the grandson of French Strother (Convention of 1776). He was born in the town of Culpeper, educated at St. Louis University, and practiced law in Culpeper County. He was a member of the House of Delegates, 1840–50, and Speaker of that body, 1847–48. He was a Whig member of Congress, 1851–53. In 1850 his estate was valued at $12,700, and he owned 7 slaves; he was married, with 7 children.

STUART, ARCHIBALD, JR. (1795–1855), Patrick County: *see* Convention of 1829–30, Reform Delegates. In 1850 he owned 2,035 acres worth $4,394 and 27 slaves.

TREDWAY, WILLIAM M. (1807–1891), Pittsylvania County, was educated at Hampden-Sydney College. He was a lawyer and practiced in Danville. For a time he was commonwealth's attorney of Pittsylvania County. He was a member of Congress, 1845–47, and was also a member of the Secession Convention of 1861. There he voted against secession on April 4 but for it on April 17. In 1850 he owned 300 acres valued at $1,200 and 7 slaves; he was married, with 8 children. After the war, he was elected judge of the Fourth Judicial Circuit of Virginia and served from 1870 to 1879.

TURNBULL, ROBERT D., JR. (1817–1880), Brunswick County, son of Robert Turnbull (d. 1839) who was county clerk for twenty-three years, studied law and practiced at Lawrenceville. He was an Episcopalian and a Democrat. His estate was worth $3,534 in 1850, but he owned no slaves. He was married, with 2 children.

WHITE, ROBERT J. T. (born 1798), Loudoun County, was a planter with acreage valued at $8,000 and 8 slaves in 1850. He was married, but no children were listed as living with him in the census records.

WHITTLE, JAMES M. (1807–1863), Pittsylvania County, was the son of an Irish immigrant and a member of the Episcopalian church. He was a lawyer with property worth $4,720 and 14 slaves in 1850. He served in the state senate, 1861–63. See Clement, *Pittsylvania County.*

WILLIAMS, IRA (born 1806), Fairfax County, was a bachelor and a physician with property valued at $5,420 and 4 slaves in 1850.

WINGFIELD, GUSTAVUS A. (1808–1889), Bedford County, was born on the family estate Woodlands in Franklin County, attended an old-field school, and was deputy county clerk in 1824. He read law and was admitted to the bar in 1831. He served in the House of Delegates, 1842, 1857–58, 1859–60. He was elected judge of the Fourth Circuit Court in 1860 and served until his death. He owned 798 acres worth $15,000 in 1850 and no slaves.

WOOLFOLK, JOHN, Orange County. No extant data.

WORSHAM, BRANCH (1788–1872), Prince Edward County, was born in Amelia County, moved to Prince Edward County in 1802, and became deputy county clerk in 1808 and clerk of the circuit court, 1830–70. He was a Baptist and a lifetime member of the Virginia Bible Society. He owned 592 acres valued at $8,977 and 21 slaves in 1850. He was a trustee of Prince Edward Academy just before his death. See Bradshaw, *Prince Edward County.*

Valley Delegates and Their Allies

ANDERSON, JOHN T. (1804–1879), Botetourt County, was the grandson of a Scottish immigrant who came to the county via Delaware in 1769. He was a lawyer and a Whig who served in the House of Delegates and state senate, 1845–53. In 1850 his 4,481-acre plantation, Mount Joy, was valued at $10,843, and he owned 20 slaves.

BIRD, MARK (1810–1883), Shenandoah County (succeeded Green B. Samuels), of an old Valley family, was born at Bird's Nest. He was a lawyer with land valued at $1,000 and 5 slaves in 1850; he was married, with 7 children. He was a judge of the Eighteenth Judicial Circuit, 1876–83, and a trustee of Woodstock Female Seminary. See Wayland, *Shenandoah County.*

BLUE, CHARLES (born 1805), Hampshire County, was of one of the first families to settle the Valley from Pennsylvania (1725). He was a planter with an estate valued at $9,000 and 12 slaves in 1850; he was married, with 7 children. He was the brother-in-law of Adam See (Convention of 1829–30).

BYRD, RICHARD E. (c.1800–1872), Frederick County, was the grandfather of Thomas, Richard, and Harry Byrd. He was a lawyer. He was not listed in the 1850 Frederick County tax records.

DENEALE, GEORGE, Rockingham County. No extant data.

FAULKNER, CHARLES J. (1809–1884), Berkeley County, was educated at Georgetown University and studied law under Chancellor Tucker at Winchester. He was orphaned at the age of eight and was raised by Philip Pendleton (Convention of 1829–30) in Martinsburg. He married the daughter of Elisha Boyd (Convention of 1829–30). He was a member of the House of Delegates, 1833–36, where he pushed for the abolition of slavery in Virginia, and the state senate, 1841. He was a Whig until Clay's death and then became a Democrat. He was a minister to France, 1859–60. Faulkner was not listed in the 1850 tax records.

FLOYD, BENJAMIN R. (1811–1860), Wythe County. No extant data.

FULTZ, DAVID (born 1803), Augusta County, was born at Staunton of a family which came to the Valley from Pennsylvania in 1788. He studied law and in 1850 owned land valued at $10,000 and 10 slaves. He was a judge of the circuit court in the 1850s, a Democrat, and a member of Congress, 1865–67.

HOGE, DANIEL H. (1813–1867), Montgomery County, came from a prominent Giles County family line that went back to Dr. Moses Hoge of Frederick County, a noted theologian and teacher and president of Hampden-Sydney College. Daniel was also a preacher (Presbyterian) as well as a practicing lawyer. In 1850 he owned 226 acres and 26 slaves. In 1865 he was elected to the U.S. Congress as a Democrat.

HOPKINS, GEORGE W. (1802–1861), Washington County, was born in Goochland County, studied law, and practiced in the town of Lebanon. He was a congressman, 1835–47, 1857–58, serving as Speaker of the house, 1844. He also served in the House of Delegates, 1833–34, 1857–61, and was a judge of the circuit court. He owned land valued at $335 in 1850.

HUNTER, ANDREW (1804–1888), Jefferson County, was born at Martinsburg, the nephew of Philip Pendleton (Convention of 1829–30), with whom he studied law. He moved to Harpers Ferry, then to Charles Town, in 1831. He was an attorney for the Baltimore and Ohio Railroad, a Whig presidential elector, 1840, congressman, 1846–48, and member of the House of Delegates, 1848–50. He was a Unionist but sided with the South after Fort Sumter. He was appointed in 1859 by Governor Wise to assist Charles Harding in the prosecution of John Brown. His land was worth $10,750 and he owned 6 slaves in 1850. He was married, with 5 children, and was a Presbyterian. Evans, *Berkeley County*, 194.

KINNEY, JOHN (born 1802), Rockingham County, was a lawyer with an estate valued at $15,000 and no slaves in 1850.

LETCHER, JOHN (1813–1884), Rockbridge County, was governor of Virginia, 1860–64. In 1850 he owned land valued at $5,700. A full biography is F. N. Boney, *John Letcher of Virginia*.

LIONBERGER, JOHN (1803–1870), Page County, was a merchant whose estate was valued at $10,000 and who owned 6 slaves in 1850. He died in Booneville, Missouri. He was married, with 6 children.

LUCAS, WILLIAM (1800–1877), Jefferson County, was born in Charles Town and educated at Jefferson College, Gettysburg, Pennsylvania. He was a Democrat and a member of the House of Delegates, 1838, and Congress, 1839–43. A planter, in 1850 he owned acreage valued at $65,000 and 15 slaves. He was a widower, with 4 children.

McCAMANT, SAMUEL (born 1803), Grayson County, born in Pennsylvania, was a lawyer whose estate was valued at $2,000 in 1850 with no slaves. He was married, with 8 children.

MILLER, FLEMING BOWYER (1793–1874), Botetourt County: *see* Convention of 1829–30, Reform Delegates. He was not listed in the 1850 property tax records.

MOORE, SAMUEL McDOWELL (1796–1875), Rockbridge County: *see* Convention of 1829–30, Reform Delegates. In 1850 he owned land valued at $2,000 and 5 slaves.

MURPHY, DENNIS (born 1811), Berkeley County, was a physician who owned an estate worth $12,000 and 5 slaves in 1850. He was married, with 6 children.

NEWMAN, ANDERSON M. (born 1811), Pendleton County, was born in Shenandoah County and was related by marriage to Senator Isaac Pennypacker of Pennsylvania. He was a physician who served in the House of Delegates, 1846–47. He owned 3 slaves in 1850; he was married, with 3 children.

PENDLETON, ALBERT G. (1807–1875), Giles County, was born in Culpeper County, attended West Point Military Academy, and became a lawyer. He moved to Tazewell County in 1828 and then to Giles County in 1833. He was commonwealth's attorney in Tazewell County and a member of the House of Delegates from Giles County, 1842–67. He was a Democratic presidential elector in 1856. He was the son-in-law of Henley Chapman (Convention of 1829–30) and brother of John S. Pendleton, Virginia congressman, 1845–49, and minister to Chile. In 1850 his estate was worth $7,300 and he owned 9 slaves; he was married, with 1 child.

SAMUELS, GREEN B. (1794–1863), Shenandoah County, was born at Woodstock, the grandson of Samuel Pennypacker of Pennsylvania. He was a lawyer, a Lutheran, and a next-door neighbor of delegate Mark Bird. He owned 5 slaves in 1850; he was a widower, with 4 children. He was a Democratic congressman, 1839–41, and in 1850 became judge of the Supreme Court of Appeals succeeding Briscoe Baldwin (Convention of 1829–30).

SEYMOUR, WILLIAM (born 1805), Hardy County, was a bachelor lawyer whose land was worth $8,500, with no slaves, in 1850.

SHEFFEY, HUGH W. (1815–1889), Augusta County, was born in Wythe County and educated under the tutorship of his uncle at Staunton and at Yale University. He studied law and practiced in Staunton. His estate was worth $4,000 in 1850, and he had no slaves. He was the father of James W. Sheffey, a delegate to the Convention of 1861. He was a strong advocate of railroad construction, especially the Louisa Railroad, in the 1840s and a member of the House of Delegates, 1861–63.

STEPHENSON, ADAM, JR. (1811–1869), Highland County, was deputy sheriff of Bath County, 1840–47, and first clerk of Highland County, 1847–64. He was a farmer whose acreage was worth $4,000 in 1850, and he owned 3 slaves.

TATE, THOMAS M. (born 1801), Smyth County, a grandson of state Senator William Tate, was a physician and served as sheriff of Washington County and a member of the state senate, 1852–57. He was a Methodist who owned 18 slaves in 1850 and operated a gristmill in Rich Valley.

TRIGG, CONNALLY (1810–1880), Washington County (succeeded George Hopkins), born in Abingdon, was a lawyer and county clerk, 1838–52. In 1850 his estate, with no slaves, was valued at $4,000; he was married, with 4 children. In 1856 he moved to Knoxville, Tennessee, and in 1862 President Lincoln appointed him judge of the District Court of Western Tennessee. He died at his home near Bristol, Tennessee.

WATTS, WILLIAM (born 1817), Roanoke County, was born in Campbell County and received a law degree from the University of Virginia, 1842. He was a Methodist lawyer-planter who owned an estate at Big Lick valued at $715 and 27 slaves; he was married, with 7 children. He was a Clayite Whig and president of the Branch Exchange Bank of Virginia at Salem, 1850–60. He was a colonel in the Confederate army.

WILLIAMS, SAMUEL C. (1812–1862), Shenandoah County, was a lawyer. He was a member of the House of Delegates, 1836–37, 1840–43, and the Secession Convention of 1861, where he voted for secession on April 4 and again on April 17. He became clerk of Shenandoah County in 1845 and served in that position until his death. He was a director of the Valley Turnpike and of the Manassas Gap Railroad. He served as a captain in the Confederate army during the first year of the war. In 1850 he owned property valued at $5,200 but no slaves; he was married, with 8 children. Wayland, *Shenandoah County,* 660–61.

WYSOR, BENJAMIN F. (died 1863), Pulaski County, lived at Newbern, then in Montgomery County, and was educated at the University of Virginia. He was a lawyer and practiced in Pulaski County (formed from Montgomery and Wythe counties in 1839). He was commonwealth's attorney of Pulaski County and was also a member of the Secession Convention of 1861, where he voted for secession on April 4 and again on April 17. On May 14, 1863, he was killed at his house by Federal raiders. In 1850 he owned land valued at $4,500 and 6 slaves; he was married, with 2 small children.

Trans-Mountain Delegates

ARMSTRONG, EDWARD (1806–1877), Taylor County, was the son of an Irish immigrant and was born in Pennsylvania. He was a merchant with property valued at $4,000 and 7 slaves in 1850; he was married, with 5 children.

BLAND, THOMAS (1803–1861), Lewis County, was an innkeeper with a property worth $10,000 and 5 slaves in 1850; he was married, with 5 children. He was an Episcopalian.

BROWN, WILLIAM G. (1801–1884), Preston County, was born at Kingwood and read and practiced law. He had an estate worth

$8,000 and a female slave in 1850; he was married, with 1 son. He was a Democratic congressman from Virginia, 1845–49, and from West Virginia, 1861–65. He also served in the House of Delegates, 1832–34, 1840–43.

CAMDEN, GIDEON D. (1806–1866), Harrison County, was a Clarksburg lawyer and land speculator whose acreage in 1850 was worth $50,000; he was married, with 4 children. He represented Virginia in the Confederate Congress at Montgomery, Alabama, in 1861. He was partner in the land office firm of Camden, Bailey, and Camden, formed in 1841.

CAPERTON, ALLEN T. (1810–1877), Monroe County, was born near Union and was a son of Hugh Caperton. He was educated at the University of Virginia and Yale and became a lawyer. He was a member of the House of Delegates, 1841–42, 1857–61, and the state senate, 1844–48. He was a director of the James River and Kanawha Company. In 1850 he owned land valued at $28,366 and 9 slaves. Having been elected as a Unionist to the Secession Convention of 1861, he voted against secession on April 4 but for secession on April 17. Early in 1863 he was elected to the Confederate Senate to fill the vacancy caused by the death of William Ballard Preston, and he served in that body until it adjourned for the last time on March 18, 1865. After the war he returned to Monroe County and was active in promoting the region's coal, iron, and timber resources. In 1875 he was elected U.S. senator from West Virginia, and he served until his death in Washington, D.C.

CARLILE, JOHN S. (1817–1878), Barbour County, was born of Scotch-Irish parents in Winchester. His father died while he was still a small boy, and he was educated at home by his mother. He became a merchant but soon turned to the law and began his practice at Beverley, Randolph County. He was a member of the state senate, 1847–51. He moved to Clarksburg in Harrison County and in 1854 was elected to Congress, 1855–57. In 1850 he owned land valued at $1,500; he was married, with a three-year-old daughter. He was one of the most vigorous spokesmen for Virginia's continuance in the Union, and his efforts drew fierce criticism from such advocates of secession as the *Richmond Examiner*. At the Secession Convention he voted against secession on April 4 and again on April 17. He then returned to Clarksburg, and his pro-Unionist activities led to his expulsion from the Virginia Convention. On April 22, 1861, Carlile issued an address to the people of western

Virginia which led to the calling of the Wheeling (or Restored Government) Convention, and he was a member of that Convention. He was elected to the U.S. Congress from "loyal" Virginia, but before he could take his seat in the House of Representatives, the Wheeling Convention elected him to the U.S. Senate. Carlile became a member of the Senate Committee on Territories, and he helped guide the legislation that resulted in the establishment of the state of West Virginia. He served in the Senate until 1865, when he was defeated for reelection. Carlile died at Clarksburg.

CARTER, DALE (born 1805), Russell County, was born in Scott County and moved to Russell County in 1840. He was a planter-lawyer with land valued at $25,000 and 16 slaves in 1850. Pratt, *Russell County.*

CHAPMAN, AUGUSTUS A. (1807–1876), Monroe County, the son of Henley Chapman (Convention of 1829–30), was born at Mount Prospect in Giles County. He graduated from the University of Virginia and practiced law at the town of Union. He owned land worth $53,000 and 19 slaves in 1850. He was a Democrat who served in the House of Delegates, 1834–38, and Congress, 1843–48. Morton, *Monroe County.*

FERGUSON, JAMES (1817–1897), Logan County, was born of Scottish immigrant parents (his father was a poor itinerant cobbler), read law at Barboursville, and moved to Logan County in 1848. His property was worth $1,400 in 1850. He was a Whig and a supporter of the Wilmot Proviso. He served in the House of Delegates, 1848. He died in Kanawha County. Laidley, *Charleston and Kanawha County.*

FISCHER, HENRY J. (born 1805), Mason County, was a lawyer and a Methodist of a German family which came to the Kanawha Valley from Philadelphia between 1800 and 1815. His land was worth $5,000 in 1850; he was married, with 1 small son, age 4.

FULKERSON, SAMUEL V. C. (1822–1862), Scott County, was born in Washington County, moved with his family to Tennessee in 1835, and returned to Lee County, Virginia, in 1843 where he studied law. In 1846 he began practice in the town of Abingdon. In 1847 he returned to Tennessee and volunteered for service in the war with Mexico. In 1858 he was elected judge of the circuit court. He was killed while serving as a colonel in the Confederacy. He was not listed in the 1850 tax records.

GALLY, THOMAS M. (1822–1855), Ohio County, was the son of an Irish-born bricklayer. In 1850 his estate was worth $1,000.

HAYES, SAMUEL L. (1794–1871), Gilmer County, was born in Pennsylvania and was a farmer whose acreage was valued at $18,000 in 1850; he was married, with 5 children. He was a Democratic congressman, 1841–43, but a Whig in the House of Delegates, 1850. Writers Program, WPA, *Gilmer.*

JACOB, ZACHARIA (born 1829), Ohio County. No extant data.

JOHNSON, JOSEPH (1785–1877), Harrison County, defeated George W. Summers for governor in 1852. He was a captain in the War of 1812 and member of the House of Delegates, 1823–27. Johnson served one term in Congress, 1823–25. In 1850 he owned 6 slaves.

KILGORE, HIRAM (born 1823), Scott County, was a planter with acreage valued at $400 and 11 slaves in 1850.

KNOTE, JOHN (1799–1880), Ohio County, was born in Leesburg, graduated from Princeton Seminary, 1823, and was a Presbyterian minister at the town of Freeport. He was not listed in the tax rolls in 1850.

McCOMAS, ELISHA W. (born 1822), Cabell County, was the son of William Cabell McComas, a Methodist minister. Elisha was born at Barboursville and was a lawyer whose estate was worth $500 in 1850; he was married with 3 young children. He served in the Mexican War and was a justice of the peace in the Cabell County court. Wallace, *Cabell County.*

MARTIN, JEFFERSON T. (born 1803), Marshall County, was of a family which came to Monongalia County in the 1770s. He was a millwright whose property was worth $2,000 in 1850; he was married, with 9 children.

NEESON, JAMES (1822–1889), Marion County. No extant data.

PRICE, SAMUEL (1805–1877), Greenbrier County, was born in Fauquier County. His family moved to western Virginia and settled in what became Nicholas County. He was a lawyer and became commonwealth's attorney of Nicholas County in 1833. He was in the House of Delegates, 1834–36. In 1838 he moved to Greenbrier County and settled in Lewisburg. He was again a member of the House of Delegates as representative of Greenbrier County, 1847–

52. In 1850 he owned property valued at $6,000 and 11 slaves. A member of the Secession Convention, Price voted against secession on April 4 and again on April 17, but he subsequently signed the ordinance of secession. In 1864 he succeeded Robert L. Montague as lieutenant governor of Virginia, and he held that office until the end of the war. Price returned to Greenbrier County after the war and resumed the practice of law in Lewisburg. He was a member of the West Virginia Constitutional Convention of 1872 and served as president. In 1876 he was appointed to the U.S. Senate to fill the vacancy caused by the death of Senator Allen T. Caperton, and he served from August of that year until early in 1877.

SMITH, BENJAMIN H. (1797–1887), Kanawha County, was born in Rockingham County and moved in 1805 to Ohio. He attended Ohio University, read law, and returned to Virginia to practice in Kanawha County. He was a member of the House of Delegates, 1833–34, and the state senate, 1834–36. He was a Whig and a devout Methodist. In 1848 he received a M.A. from Ohio University. His property in 1850 was worth $23,000; he was married, with 2 children. He ran for the governorship of West Virginia in 1866 but was defeated.

SMITH, JOSEPH (1820–1887), Jackson County, was born in the state of Ohio and attended Salem Academy, Pennsylvania, and New Athens College, Ohio. He practiced law at the town of Ripley and was prosecuting attorney for the county early in 1852. He was not listed in the 1850 tax rolls, but the census records list him as married, with 2 small children, that year.

SMITH, WILLIAM (1774–1859), Greenbrier County: see Convention of 1829–30, Reform Delegates. In 1850 he owned 6 slaves and property worth $2,400; he was married, with 2 adult sons still living with him.

SNODEGRASS, JOHN F. (1808–1854), Wood County, was born in Berkeley County, studied law, and practiced in Parkersburg. He was a Democratic congressman, 1853–54. His estate, with no slaves, was worth $10,240 in 1850; he was married, with 5 children. He served one term in the U.S. Congress as a Democrat, 1853–55. Evans, *Berkeley County.*

STEWART, JAMES E. (1814–1890), Morgan County, was born in Berkeley County and was educated at Martinsburg Academy, Georgetown College, and Washington and Jefferson College,

Pennsylvania. He was not listed in the 1850 tax rolls for Berkeley or Morgan counties. He studied law at Baltimore and practiced in Berkeley County. He was a Presbyterian, member of the House of Delegates, 1844–45, clerk in the U.S. Treasury Department, 1854–61, and judge of the Page County court, 1873–79. For two years, 1850–52, he was editor of the *Martinsburg Gazette*.

SUMMERS, GEORGE W. (1804–1878), Kanawha County, was born in Fairfax County. His family moved to the Kanawha Valley about 1813 and settled at Charleston. Summers was educated at Washington and Lee College and Ohio University. In 1850 he owned property valued at $3,400 and 9 slaves; he was married, with 3 children. He was a lawyer and practiced in Charleston. Summers was a member of the House of Delegates, 1830–31, 1834–36, and a congressman, 1841–45. He was judge of the Eighteenth Judicial Circuit, 1852–58. He was a member of the Peace Conference that met at Washington early in 1861 in a vain attempt to find a basis for sectional reconciliation. As a delegate to the Secession Convention of 1861, he continued his efforts to keep Virginia in the Union and voted against secession on April 4 and April 17. He then resigned his seat in the Convention and withdrew from further political activity, taking no part in the war or in the movement that led to separate statehood for West Virginia. He continued to practice law in Charleston until his death.

VAN WINKLE, PETER G. (1807–1872), Wood County, was born in New York City and moved to Parkersburg in 1835. He was a lawyer and Whig politician and U.S. senator, 1863–67. He was not listed in the 1850 tax rolls.

WILLEY, WAITMAN T. (1811–1900), Monongalia County, was born in a log cabin near Farmington, Marion County. He was educated at Madison College in Uniontown, Pennsylvania. He was a lawyer and practiced at Morgantown. He married Elizabeth E. Ray. In 1850 he owned property valued at $5,000 and 5 slaves; he and his wife had 6 children. A member of the House of Delegates, 1832–37 and the state senate, 1839–47, he was an active Whig and was one of the leaders of the party. In 1859 he was a candidate for the lieutenant governorship, running on the same ticket with William L. Goggin, but he was defeated by Robert L. Montague. He was a strong Unionist and an opponent of secession. He was a member of the Wheeling (or Restored Government) Convention and of the first Constitutional Convention of West Virginia. In the meantime he had been elected from "loyal" Virginia to the U.S. Senate, serving 1861–63. In 1863 he was again elected to the U.S. Senate, this time from West Virginia, and served until 1871. He then resumed the practice of law and was a member of the West Virginia Constitutional Convention of 1872. His last public service was as clerk of Monongalia County, a position he held from 1882 until his death in Morgantownn.

Notes

PREFACE

1. *The Politics of Aristotle*, ed. Ernest Barker (New York, 1962), 101, 110–11; Thomas M. Cooley, *The General Principles of Constitutional Law in the United States of America* (Boston, 1880), chap. 2; Charles H. McIlwain, *Constitutionalism Ancient and Modern* (Ithaca, N.Y., 1940), 149; Alfred H. Kelly and Winfred A. Harbison, 4th ed., *The American Constitution: Its Origins and Development* (New York, 1970), 2.

2. Merrill D. Peterson, ed., *Democracy, Liberty, and Property: The State Constitutional Conventions of the 1820s* (Indianapolis, 1966); Fletcher M. Green, *Constitutional Development in the South Atlantic States, 1776–1860: A Study in the Evolution of Democracy* (Chapel Hill, N.C., 1930).

3. *The Mind and Faith of Justice Holmes: His Speeches, Essays, Letters, and Judicial Opinions*, ed. Max Lerner (New York, 1943), 51–52.

4. Harry N. Scheiber, "American Constitutional History and the New Legal History: Complimentary Themes in Two Modes," *Journal of American History* 68 (1981–82): 337–50.

I

1. See Jack P. Greene's essay on the Virginia gentry in *Society, Freedom, and Conscience: The American Revolution in Virginia, Massachusetts, and New York*, ed. Richard M. Jellison (New York, 1976), 191 n.1. See also Jackson T. Main, *The Upper House in Revolutionary America, 1763–1788* (Madison, Wis., 1967), and *The Social Structure of Revolutionary America* (Princeton, N.J., 1965); Charles S. Sydnor, *Gentlemen Freeholders: Political Practices in Washington's Virginia* (Chapel Hill, N.C., 1952); Hamilton J. Eckenrode, *The Revolution in Virginia* (New York, 1916); Albert O. Porter, *County Government*

in Virginia: A Legislative History, 1607–1904 (New York 1947); Herbert Sloan and Peter Onuf, "Politics, Culture, and the Revolution in Virginia: A Review of Recent Work," *Virginia Magazine of History and Biography,* 91 (1983): 259–84.

2. Jackson T. Main, *Political Parties before the Constitution* (Chapel Hill, N.C., 1973), 244.

3. P. W. Hirst, *Life and Letters of Thomas Jefferson* (New York, 1926), 63–64.

4. William S. Forrest, *Historical and Descriptive Sketches of Norfolk and Vicinity* (Philadelphia, 1853).

5. See Greene, in Jellison, *Society, Freedom, and Conscience,* 41.

6. A. E. Dick Howard, *Commentaries on the Constitution of Virginia,* 2 vols. (Charlottesville, Va., 1974), 2: 690.

7. Main, *Political Parties,* 245.

8. Jellison, *Society, Freedom, and Conscience,* 55. See also Marc Egnal, "The Origins of the Revolution in Virginia: A Reinterpretation," *William and Mary Quarterly,* 3d ser., 37 (1980): 401–428; Daniel P. Jordan, *Political Leadership in Jefferson's Virginia* (Charlottesville, Va., 1983), chaps. 1–2.

9. Here, for example, 10 percent of the adult men owned 70 percent of the land. See Main, *Social Structure,* 173–77.

10. Ibid., 46, 171–72.

11. Virginus Dabney, *Virginia, the New Dominion* (Garden City, N.Y., 1971), 121.

12. See Robert Hilldrup, "The Virginia Convention of 1776: A Study in Revolutionary Politics" (Ph.D. diss., University of Virginia, 1935).

13. Sylvia R. Frey, "Between Slavery and Freedom: Virginia Blacks in the American Revolution," *Journal of Southern History* 49 (1983): 375–98; Eckenrode, *Revolution in Virginia,* 54; *Revolutionary Virginia: The Road to Independence,* eds. Robert L. Scribner and Brent Tarter, 7 vols. (Charlottesville, Va., 1975–83), 3:229.

14. Robert Wormeley Carter to Landon Carter, Aug. 10, 1775, Sabine Hall Papers, University of Virginia Library; *The Statutes at Large; Being a Collection of All the Laws of Virginia from the First Session of the Legislature in the Year 1619,* ed. William W. Hening (Richmond, etc., 1809–23), 9:49; Eckenrode, *Revolution in Virginia,* 126–27.

15. Hening, *Statutes,* 9:52–60.

16. William Reynolds to Richard Lawrence, August 1775, William Reynolds Papers, Library of Congress; Edmund Pendle-

ton to Thomas Jefferson, Nov. 16, 1775, *The Papers of Thomas Jefferson,* ed. Julian P. Boyd (Princeton, N.J., 1950—), 1:260–61.

17. Quoted in Frank Moore, *Diary of the American Revolution* (New York, 1850), 204.

18. John Page to R. H. Lee, April 12, 1776, *Southern Literary Messenger* 6 (1840):255; Page to Jefferson, April 6, 26, 1776, Boyd, *Jefferson Papers,* 1:287–90; Richard Henry Lee to Patrick Henry, April 20, 1776, William Cabell Rives Papers, Lib. Cong.

19. Dabney, *Virginia,* 134.

20. Robert Howson, *History of Virginia* (Philadelphia, 1848), 2:87; Peter Force, ed., *American Archives,* 4th ser. (Washington, D.C., 1848–53), 1:1165; John E. Selby, "Richard Henry Lee, John Adams, and the Virginia Constitution of 1776," *VMHB* 84 (1976): 387–400.

21. "Concord Town Meeting Demands," in *Sources and Documents Illustrating the American Revolution, 1764–1788, and the Formation of the Federal Constitution,* ed. Samuel E. Morison (Oxford, Eng., 1961), 176–77.

22. Josiah Parker to Landon Carter, April 14, 1776, Sabine Hall Papers, UVa. Lib.; Force, *American Archives,* 4th ser. 6:1527; Hilldrup, "Convention of 1776," 134–35.

23. *The Proceedings of the Convention of Delegates Held at the Capitol in the City of Williamsburg in the Colony of Virginia on Monday the 6th of May* (Williamsburg, Va., 1776), 5–7; Hugh Blair Grigsby, *The Virginia Convention of 1776* (Richmond, 1855), 49–54; David J. Mays, *Edmund Pendleton, 1721–1803,* 2 vols. (Cambridge, Mass., 1952), 1:103–4; Scribner and Tarter, *Revolutionary Virginia,* 6:287–90, 7:1–15.

24. *Proceedings,* 21, 26–27, 30–33.

25. "Diary of Landon Carter," *WMQ,* 1st ser., 18 (1909): 38–39.

26. Irving Brant, *James Madison,* 6 vols. (New York, 1941–61), 1:217; Robert D. Meade, *Patrick Henry,* 2 vols. (New York, 1957–69), 2:102–11.

27. Edmund Randolph, "Edmund Randolph's Essays on the Revolutionary History of Virginia, 1774–1782," *VMHB* 44 (1936): 42, gives Randolph's impression of Henry's position. See Meade, *Henry,* 2:107, for the text of Henry's resolution.

28. *Proceedings,* 15; Scribner and Tarter, *Revolutionary Virginia,* 7:145–47.

29. *Proceedings,* 394–96.

30. Mays, *Pendleton,* 2:109; Grigsby, *Convention of 1776,* 17; Scribner and Tarter, *Revolutionary Virginia,* 7:3–5, 122–23, 143–43.

31. Scribner and Tarter, *Revolutionary Virginia,* 7:142–43.

32. Ibid.; Grigsby, *Convention of 1776,* 18.

33. Grigsby, *Convention of 1776,* 18.

II

1. Howard, *Commentaries,* 1:35; Scribner and Tarter, *Revolutionary Virginia,* 7:9–10, 143.

2. At first, on May 15, there were twenty-eight members of the committee listed. Between May 16 and 27 seven more members arrived in Williamsburg and sat on the committee from then on. These additions were Madison, Mason, Rutherford, Benjamin Watkins, Harvie, Curle, and Holt (*Proceedings,* 33).

3. Hilldrup, "Convention of 1776," 171–75; Scribner and Tarter, *Revolutionary Virginia,* 7:148 n.8.

4. Cabell paid taxes on ninety slaves. The Tuckahoes had only four practicing lawyers among their group.

5. In fact, when Mason arrived at the Convention on May 17, he was immediately appointed not only to the committee to draft a new government but also to the committees on privileges and elections and on the making of salt, saltpeter, and gunpowder (Kate Mason Rowland, *The Life of George Mason 1725–1792,* 2 vols. [New York, 1892], 1:chaps. 6–7).

6. *The Papers of George Mason, 1725–1792,* ed. Robert A. Rutland, 3 vols. (Chapel Hill, N.C., 1970), 1:201–9, 215–16.

7. Howard, *Commentaries,* 1:35.

8. Brant, *Madison,* 1:237–38.

9. Quoted in Hilldrup, "Convention of 1776," 183.

10. *Proceedings,* 100–101.

11. Rutland, *Papers of George Mason,* 1:275; Rowland, *Mason,* 1:240.

12. Hilldrup, "Convention of 1776," 192.

13. Rutland, *Papers of George Mason,* 1: 281, 289–90; Rowland, *Mason,* 1:241.

14. Rutland, *Papers of George Mason,* 1:277, 283, 285, 288, 290; Hilldrup, "Convention of 1776," 192.

15. Rutland, *Papers of George Mason,* 1:277–78, 280–81, 283–84.

16. Howard, *Commentaries,* 1:283.

17. Rowland, *Mason,* 1:241–42; Rutland, *Papers of George Ma-*

son, 1:274–82, 284, 286; Irving Brant, *The Bill of Rights: Its Origin and Meaning* (Indianapolis, 1965), 37.

18. Howard, *Commentaries*, 1:290.

19. It was this draft version of the declaration of rights, not the final declaration approved by the Convention, that was sent to the other states. This copy served as the model for their own bill of rights. The draft version was published on June 1 in the *Virginia Gazette*, on June 6 in the *Pennsylvania Evening Post*, and within a week in the *Pennsylvania Gazette* and *Maryland Gazette* (Rutland, *Papers of George Mason*, 1:286; Howard, *Commentaries*, 1:39).

20. Howard, *Commentaries*, 1:57; Boyd, *Jefferson Papers*, 1:290–91; Rutland, *Papers of George Mason*, 1: 287.

21. Howard, *Commentaries*, 1:61–62.

22. Rutland, *Papers of George Mason*, 1:277.

23. Ibid., 274–86; Howard, *Commentaries*, 1:74; Scribner and Tarter, *Revolutionary Virginia*, 7:277 n.9.

24. Howard, *Commentaries*, 1:81–94; Rutland, *Papers of George Mason*, 1:284–99.

25. Howard, *Commentaries*, 1:168. On the Phillips case, see Dumas Malone, *Jefferson and His Times*, 6 vols. (Boston, 1948–81), 1:292–93.

26. Rutland, *Papers of George Mason*, 1:270.

27. Leonard W. Levy, ed., *Essays on the Making of the Constitution* (New York, 1987), 268–69; Rutland, *Papers of George Mason*, 1:287–91.

28. Jellison, *Society, Freedom, and Conscience*, 46; A. E. Dick Howard, "State Constitutions and the Environment," *Virginia Law Review* 58 (1972): 196, 229.

29. Howard, *Commentaries*, x.

30. Malone, *Jefferson*, 1:235–36.

31. Thomas Jefferson to Thomas Nelson, May 16, 1776, Boyd, *Jefferson Papers*, 1:292–93; Malone, *Jefferson*, 1:235; Scribner and Tarter, *Revolutionary Virginia*, 7:5.

32. Green, *Constitutional Development*, 62–63.

33. Malone, *Jefferson*, 1: chap. 17.

34. Boyd, *Jefferson Papers*, 1:334; Malone, *Jefferson*, 1:218; Hilldrup, "Convention of 1776," 229–30.

35. Selby, "Richard Henry Lee," 387–400; Rutland, *Papers of George Mason*, 1:295–96.

36. Selby, "Richard Henry Lee," 391.

37. Page Smith, *John Adams*, 2 vols. (New York, 1962), 1:245–48, 279, 280, 439.

38. Selby, "Richard Henry Lee," 398.

39. Carter Braxton to Landon Carter, May 17, 1776, Lee Papers and Transcripts, 4, Virginia Historical Society, Richmond.

40. Eckenrode, *Revolution in Virginia*, 163; Force, *American Archives*, 4th ser., 6:748–54.

41. Meade, *Henry*, 2:118; Edmund Pendleton to Thomas Jefferson, May 24, 1776, Boyd, *Jefferson Papers*, 1:296–97.

42. *Proceedings*, 168–69.

43. Rutland, *Papers of George Mason*, 1:295–310.

44. Selby, "Richard Henry Lee," 392; Rutland, *Papers of George Mason*, 1:295–310.

45. Malone, *Jefferson*, 1:236.

46. Ibid., 238.

47. Ibid., 239.

48. Rutland, *Papers of George Mason*, 1:308–9; Boyd, *Jefferson Papers*, 1:384–86n.

49. Rutland, *Papers of George Mason*, 1:305.

50. Malone, *Jefferson*, 1:239; *Proceedings*, 168–69; Hilldrup, "Convention of 1776," 272–74; James E. Pate, "Constitutional Revision in Virginia Affecting the General Assembly," *WMQ*, 2d ser., 10 (April 1930): 108–9.

51. Malone, *Jefferson*, 1:239; Meade, *Henry*, 2:119–27.

52. Meade, *Henry*, 2:125–26; Hilldrup, "Convention of 1776," 203; Rowland, *Mason*, 1: lxxxiii, 241–42; Grigsby, *Convention of 1776*, 153; Scribner and Tarter, *Revolutionary Virginia*, 7:654, 659.

53. Malone, *Jefferson*, 1:239; Meade, *Henry*, 2:130, 142–43; Scribner and Tarter, *Revolutionary Virginia*, 7:706–9.

54. Malone, *Jefferson*, 1:235–97.

55. Hening, *Statutes*, 12:84–86; Boyd, *Jefferson Papers*, 2:550–77; Malone, *Jefferson*, 1:235–97; A. G. Roeber, *Faithful Magistrates and Republican Lawyers: Creators of Virginia Legal Culture, 1680–1810* (Chapel Hill, N.C., 1981), 206–8; Merrill D. Peterson, *Thomas Jefferson and the New Nation* (New York, 1970), 154–56.

56. Main, *Political Parties*, 251–56.

57. Boyd, *Jefferson Papers*, 1:564–71, 592–94, 605–7, 650–52, 2:578–87; see also Porter, *County Government*, 152–54.

III

1. Richard R. Beeman, *The Old Dominion and the New Nation, 1788–1801* (Lexington, Ky., 1972), 28.

2. Avery O. Craven, *Soil Exhaustion as a Factor in the Agricultural History of Virginia and Maryland, 1606–1860* (Urbana, Ill., 1926), 15–16; Joseph C. Robert, *Tobacco Kingdom: Plantation, Market, and Factory in Virginia and North Carolina, 1800–1860* (Durham, N.C., 1938), 15–75; Charles H. Ambler, *Sectionalism in Virginia, 1776–1861* (Chicago, 1910), 1:108–17; J. E. Norris, *History of the Lower Shenandoah Valley* (Chicago, 1890); John W. Wayland, *The German Element in the Shenandoah Valley of Virginia* (Charlottesville, 1907); Lewis P. Summers, *History of Southwest Virginia 1746–1786, Washington County 1870–1877* (Richmond, 1903), 420–70; James Morton Callahan and Bernard L. Butcher, eds., *Genealogical and Personal History of the Upper Monongahela Valley, West Virginia*, 3 vols. (New York, 1912), 1:3–71.

3. Robert P. Sutton, "Nostalgia, Pessimism, and Malaise: The Doomed Aristocrat in Late-Jeffersonian Virginia," *VMHB* 76 (1968): 51–55; Robert McColley, *Slavery and Jeffersonian Virginia* (Urbana, Ill., 1964); Early Lee Fox, *The American Colonization Society, 1817–1840* (Baltimore, 1919), 30–32. See also John H. Russell, *The Free Negro in Virginia, 1619–1865* (Baltimore, 1913), 61.

4. United States Census, Virginia, Population Schedules, 1840, Sussex, Lancaster, Halifax counties.

5. Ibid., Rockingham and Tazewell counties.

6. Land and Personal Property Tax Records, 1830, Sussex County, Virginia State Library and Archives.

7. Ibid., 1810 and 1830.

8. Ibid., Augusta County.

9. Ibid.

10. Ibid., 1830, Tazewell County.

11. Ibid., 1810, 1830; U.S. Census, Virginia, Population Schedules, 1810 and 1830.

12. See Malone, *Jefferson*, 1:235–36; Peterson, *Jefferson and the New Nation*, 101–4.

13. James Madison to Col. James Madison, April 15, 1783, James Madison Papers, Lib. Cong.; Mason to William Cabell, May 6, 1783, Rutland, *Papers of George Mason*, 2:768–69.

14. Madison to Jefferson, July 3, 1784, Boyd, *Jefferson Papers*, 7:359–62; Brant, *Madison*, 2:318.

15. Chapman Johnson to David Watson, Jan. 24, 1802, *VMHB* 29 (1921): 281–82; *Richmond Enquirer*, Dec. 24, 1804; Feb. 1, 1806.

16. *Journal of the House of Delegates, 1806–7*, 67–68; *Richmond Enquirer*, Jan. 1, 1807, Jan. 31, 1811; Julian A. C. Chandler, *Repre-

sentation in Virginia (Baltimore, 1896), 22. Accomack County delegates voted in favor of a convention, however.

17. *Journal of the House of Delegates, 1815–16,* 167.

18. *Alexandria Herald,* July 21, 1816.

19. *Richmond Enquirer,* June 19–Sept. 7, 1816, printed articles about agitation for the calling of a convention.

20. Ibid.

21. Ambler, *Sectionalism,* 95; Jefferson to Samuel Kercheval, July 16, 1816, Thomas Jefferson Papers, University of Virginia Library.

22. *Richmond Enquirer,* Aug. 6, Oct. 2, 1816, Feb. 8, 1817; Barbara J. Griffin, "Thomas Ritchie and the Founding of the Richmond Lancasterian School," *VMHB* 86 (1978): 447–60. See also Charles H. Ambler, *Thomas Ritchie: A Study in Virginia Politics* (Richmond, 1913).

23. *Journal of the House of Delegates, 1816–17,* 184–200; Ambler, *Ritchie,* 67–68; Harry Ammon, "The Richmond Junto," *VMHB* 61 (1953): 401–11. The reapportionment gave the West nine instead of four senators and decreased the East's number from twenty to fifteen.

24. Claude H. Hall, *Abel Parker Upshur, Conservative Virginian, 1790–1844* (Madison, Wis., 1964), 39–41; Ambler, *Sectionalism,* 138–42.

25. Abel P. Upshur to Francis Walker Gilmer, July 7, 1825, Francis Walker Gilmer Papers, UVa. Lib.; *Richmond Enquirer,* May 8, 21, 1824, Feb. 10, June 17, 21, 24, 28, July 8, 12, 19, 22, Aug. 2, 5, 9, 11, 1825, Jan. 28, 1826; Chandler, *Representation,* 29; Chilton S. Williamson, *American Suffrage: From Property to Democracy, 1760–1860* (Princeton, N.J., 1960), 223–34.

26. *Richmond Enquirer,* April 27, 1824; Thomas Jefferson to John Hampden Pleasants, April 19, 1824, Paul Leicester Ford, ed., *The Writings of Thomas Jefferson,* 10 vols. (New York, 1892–99), 10:302–4.

27. *Richmond Enquirer,* Aug. 2, 1825, said that thirty-five counties attended, but it appears that only thirty-one counties had representation at the meeting (Ambler, *Sectionalism,* 143; *Journal of the House of Delegates, 1825–26,* 12–15, 17, 20, 24–27–33, 37, 49, 93, 103–4). It was estimated that about 12,175 citizens had signed petitions.

28. Benjamin Watkins Leigh to Littleton Waller Tazewell, Aug. 22, 1825, Tazewell Papers, Va. State Lib. and Archives; *Richmond Enquirer,* Aug. 13, 16, 28, Sept. 13, 26, Oct. 4, 7, 11, 21, 1825.

29. Hall, *Upshur*, 43–44.

30. Ibid., 44; *Journal of the House of Delegates, 1826–27*, 103–6; *Richmond Enquirer*, Feb. 10, 13, 1827.

31. Hall, *Upshur*, 44; *Richmond Enquirer*, Jan. 23, 25, 27, Feb. 22, 1827; *Journal of the House of Delegates, 1826–27*, 112.

32. Chandler, *Representation*, 30.

33. *Journal of the House of Delegates, 1827–28*, 12, 33, 131; John Tazewell to Hugh Blair Grigsby, Feb. 9, 1829, Hugh Blair Grigsby Papers, Va. Hist. Soc.

34. *Journal of the House of Delegates, 1829–30*, Governor's Message with attached documents, no. 50.

35. Chandler, *Representation*, 61.

36. *Richmond Enquirer*, Jan. 22, Feb. 14, 1829.

37. *Journal of the House of Delegates, 1829–30*, 70, 143; *Richmond Enquirer*, Feb. 10, 12, 1829.

IV

1. Hugh Blair Grigsby and Thomas Green left eyewitness accounts of the first days of the Convention: Grigsby, *The Virginia Convention of 1829–30* (Richmond, 1856), and Joanne L. Gatewood, ed., "Richmond during the Virginia Constitutional Convention of 1829–30: An Extract from the Diary of Thomas Green," *VMHB* 84 (1976): 287–332.

2. In addition to those of Grigsby and Green, other accounts of the Convention in early October appeared in the *Richmond Enquirer*, Oct. 6, 1829; *Niles Weekly Register* 36 (1829–30):285, 300, 410; and *Southern Literary Messenger* 17 (1851):297–304. See also *Proceedings and Debates of the Virginia State Convention of 1829–30* (Richmond, 1830).

3. Peterson, *Democracy, Liberty, and Property*, 271.

4. Grigsby, Diary, no. 3, Grigsby Papers, Va. Hist. Soc.

5. U.S. Census, Virginia, Population Schedules, 1830 and 1840; Land Tax and Personal Property Tax Records, 1830, Va. State Lib. and Archives.

6. *Proceedings*, 290; Richard B. Davis, *Intellectual Life in Jefferson's Virginia, 1790–1830* (Chapel Hill, N.C., 1964), 22, 31–36, 38, 54, 327–48.

7. Davis, *Intellectual Life*, 15–17, 49, 53, 122, 128–36; U.S. Census, Virginia, Population Schedules, 1820, 1830, 1840; Edward Handy, *Genetic Study of Family Lines in Virginia* (Charlottesville, 1942); Jordan, *Political Leadership*, 46–48.

8. U.S. Census, Virginia, Population Schedules, 1810, 1820, 1830.

9. *Proceedings,* 6–11. See also the supporting *Journal, Acts, and Proceedings of a General Convention of the Commonwealth of Virginia in 1829* (Richmond, 1830), 21–22. A Committee of Twenty-four selected by Barbour actually made the assignments to the four standing committees.

10. *Proceedings,* 43–45, *Richmond Enquirer,* March 23, 1830. Doddridge and some reformers thought the questions of representation and suffrage would be left to the Committee on the Legislature where the reformers had a stronger position. Reformers on the Committee on the Declaration of Rights, therefore, retreated from their initial position in order to have the chance to push reform measures at a later and more opportune time.

11. Ammon, "Richmond Junto," 395–418; Hall, *Upshur,* 51; *Richmond Enquirer,* Oct. 17, 29, 1829.

12. *Proceedings,* 33; Albert J. Beveridge, *Life of John Marshall,* 4 vols. (Boston, 1916–19), 4:188–89.

3. *Proceedings,* 40, 43–50; Brant, *Madison,* 6:463.

14. *Proceedings,* 53.

15. Norma Lois Peterson, *Littleton Waller Tazewell* (Charlottesville, Va., 1983), 166–67.

16. Ibid., 169–70.

17. Green, "Diary," Oct. 27, 1829, ed. Gatewood, 303.

18. Grigsby, Diary, no. 3.

19. *Convention Journal,* 61–62.

20. Ibid., 76; Hall, *Upshur,* 53.

21. *Convention Journal,* 76–78; Hall, *Upshur,* 54.

22. Green, "Diary," Oct. 28, 1829, ed. Gatewood, 303; *Convention Journal,* 76–78.

23. Grigsby, Diary, no. 3; *Convention Journal,* 53.

24. *Convention Journal,* 126–27.

25. *Proceedings,* 85–88.

26. Ibid.; Hall, *Upshur,* 54–56.

27. *Proceedings,* 252–53.

28. Ibid., 153–54.

29. Ibid., 100, 125, 135–36, 155.

30. Ibid., 358.

31. Grigsby, Diary, no. 6; *Alexandria Gazette,* Nov. 3, 1829; *Proceedings,* 100.

32. Alden G. Bigelow, "Hugh Blair Grigsby, Historian and

Antiquarian" (Ph.D. diss., University of Virginia, 1957), 21–22, 29–30; John W. Murdaugh to Hugh Blair Grigsby, Nov. 3, 1829, Grigsby Papers, Va. Hist. Soc.

33. Hall, *Upshur,* 56; Brant, *Madison,* 6:463–64; Gordon Cloyd to David Cloyd, Oct. 6, 1829, Joseph Cloyd Papers, Va. Hist. Soc.; Grigsby, Diary, no. 6; Dice R. Anderson, *William Branch Giles: A Study in the Politics of Virginia and the Nation, 1790–1830* (Menasha, Wis., 1914), 231.

34. C. H. Harrison to J. C. Cabell, Nov. 16, 1829, J. C. Cabell to John H. Cocke, Dec. 8, 1829, Cabell Papers, UVa. Lib.; Charlottesville *Virginia Advocate,* Nov. 13, 1829; Brant, *Madison,* 6:466; *Proceedings,* 321.

35. *Proceedings,* 547. This plan would have given 13 western and 17 eastern men to a senate of 30, and 48 western and 72 eastern delegates to a lower house of 120.

36. Ibid., 453. Cabell was amazed at Gordon's attitude because, in Cabell's eyes, a compromise with the West on the representation issue meant that Gordon actually was stripping his own Piedmont of political power (William H. Cabell to J. C. Cabell, Nov. 8, 1829, Cabell Papers, UVa. Lib.).

37. *Proceedings,* 498; Beveridge, *Marshall,* 4:504–7.

38. Green, "Diary," Dec. 2, 1829, ed. Greenwood, 312, 492, 527, 571, 662–65.

39. Ibid., 574, 662–65, 668, 705; *Richmond Enquirer,* Dec. 31, 1829, Jan. 2, 1830.

40. *Proceedings,* 26–27, 31–32.

41. Ibid., 372.

42. Ibid., 363–67, 398–99.

43. Ibid., 141, 306, 312.

44. Ibid., 410–19, 425.

45. Ibid., 382, 900. The measure gave the vote to holders of a 25-acre freehold of improved land, holders of 50 acres of unimproved land, owners of a $25 freehold or a $25 joint tenantship, holders of a five-year lease with annual rent of $20 or more, and housekeepers who were both heads of families and taxpayers. The *Richmond Enquirer* estimated that this increased the number of voters from 44,325 to 52,253 out of an adult male population of 78,265. J. R. Pole, in "Representation and Authority in Virginia from the Revolution to Reform," *Journal of Southern History* 28 (1958): 49, shows the immediate result of the change was only a slight increase in voter participation in the state. Peterson esti-

mated that about one-third of the adult white male population was still disfranchised (*Democracy, Liberty, and Property,* 281).

46. *Proceedings,* 347; *Convention Journal,* no. 7; Julian A. C. Chandler, *History of Suffrage in Virginia* (Baltimore, 1901), 27–37; Williamson, *Suffrage,* 220; *Richmond Enquirer,* April-June 1829. See also Wilbur J. Cash, *The Mind of the South* (New York, 1941), 35–43, 91.

47. *Proceedings,* 468–69.

48. Ibid., 470–73, 485, 583, 717; *Convention Journal,* 150–51.

49. *Proceedings,* 526–30; Peterson, *Tazewell,* 312.

50. *Proceedings,* 532–35.

51. Roeber, *Faithful Magistrates,* 192–202.

52. *Proceedings,* 505, 880; *Convention Journal,* 173–74; Beveridge, *Marshall,* 4:481–501.

53. *Proceedings,* 789–91.

54. Green, "Diary," Jan. 15, ed. Gatewood, 328.

V

1. Peterson, *Democracy, Liberty, and Property,* 284.

2. Ibid., 285.

3. Doddridge stated that the serious division in reform ranks first occurred in an out-of-convention meeting on the Gordon plan. In this caucus, he said, it was evident that Cooke, Henderson, and Edwin Duncan were giving support to compromise even though most reformers still wanted to hold out for the white basis. Following this division Doddridge admitted there was little chance of reform success (*Richmond Enquirer,* Feb. 13, March 26, April 2, 1830).

4. *Staunton Spectator,* Feb. 12, 1830; *Richmond Enquirer,* March 30, April 6, 13, 23, May 11, 16, 1830.

5. *Lexington Intelligencer,* April 30, 1830.

6. *Richmond Enquirer,* Feb. 13, March 9, 26, April 2, 1830; Ambler, *Ritchie,* 139–40.

7. Green, "Diary," Jan. 13, 1830, ed. Gatewood, 328; William Wickham to L. W. Tazewell, May 1, 1830, Tazewell Papers, Va. State Lib. and Archives; *Richmond Enquirer,* Feb. 13, March 23, April 13, May 7, 1830.

8. Ambler, *Sectionalism,* 25–61; Chandler, *Representation,* 45–49; Green, *Constitutional Development,* 224.

9. *Documents Containing Statistics of Virginia Ordered to Be Printed by the State Convention Sitting in the City of Richmond, 1850–*

51 (Richmond, 1851), Appendix on Census; U.S. Census, Virginia, Population Schedules, 1840 and 1850, Sussex, Lancaster, Rockingham, Tazewell, and Marion counties.

10. J. Stephen Knight, Jr., "Discontent, Disunity, and Dissent in the Antebellum South: Virginia as a Test Case, 1844–1846," *VMHB* 81 (1973): 442; *Documents of Convention, 1850–51,* Appendix on Land and Property; Joseph Martin, *A New and Comprehensive Gazetteer of Virginia and the District of Columbia* (Charlottesville, 1836), 406; U.S. Census, Virginia, Population Schedules, 1840, 1850, Sussex and Marion counties.

11. Charles H. Ambler, *A History of Transportation in the Ohio Valley* (Glendale, Calif., 1932), 133–84; Craven, *Soil Exhaustion,* 133–34; I. F. Boughter, "Internal Improvements in Northwestern Virginia," (Ph.D. diss., University of Pittsburgh, 1930).

12. *Journal of the House of Delegates, 1841–42,* doc. no. 8; *Niles Weekly Register* 62 (1842): 80–87.

13. *Richmond Enquirer,* July 12, Aug. 19, 1842; *Lexington Valley Star,* July 17, 1845; *Lexington Gazette,* Nov. 13, 1845.

14. Ritchie, as head of the junto, dominated Virginia's Democratic party until he retired in 1851. Afterwards, the states'-rights wing of the party under Hunter and James M. Mason, among others, reorganized the direction of the party behind the Petersburg *Republican* and a strong defense of southern interests in the looming secession crisis. At about the same time Henry A. Wise emerged as the aggressive head of the other, less strident, states'-rights wing of the party with a power base in the western counties (Henry T. Shanks, *The Secession Movement in Virginia, 1847–1861* [Richmond, 1934], 15, 46–48).

15. *Richmond Enquirer,* May 8, 22, 1840, April 27, 1841, Dec. 4, 21, 1849; *Lynchburg Republican,* Dec. 3, 1849; Shanks, *Secession Movement,* 12–17; Henry H. Simms, *The Rise of the Whigs in Virginia, 1824–1840* (Richmond, 1929), 15, 32, 86–87.

16. Green, *Constitutional Development,* 288. Green makes the same claim about a party correlation in North Carolina and Maryland. On the sectional, as opposed to political party, alignment, see Francis P. Gaines, Jr., "The Virginia Constitutional Convention of 1850–51: A Study in Sectionalism" (Ph.D. diss., University of Virginia, 1950), 78–83.

17. *Richmond Enquirer,* Nov. 29, 1845. See also "Letter to Residents of the Wheeling District," ibid., Jan. 23, 1846.

18. *Journal of the House of Delegates, 1845–46,* 14–15.

19. *Richmond Enquirer,* June 6, Aug. 28, 29, Sept. 1, 1846; *Jour-*

nal of the House of Delegates, 1846–47, 114–15; ibid., *1847–48,* 378; ibid., *1848–49,* 115–17, 326.

20. Dabney, *Virginia,* 320–22.

21. *Richmond Enquirer,* Dec. 4, 14, 21, 28, 1849.

22. Quoted, ibid., Dec. 21, 1849.

23. *Documents of the House of Delegates of Virginia, 1849–50* (Richmond, 1850), doc. no. 1, 9–12.

24. *Richmond Enquirer,* Dec. 7, 1849.

25. Ibid., Feb. 12, 1850.

26. Ibid., Feb. 19, 22, March 5, 1851; William A. Cabell to J. C. Cabell, March 3, 1850, Cabell Papers, UVa. Lib.

27. The mixed basis formula provided that one delegate was to be elected for every 13,151 white citizens and one for each $7,000.24 paid in taxes. Chandler says the estimated white population in 1849 for the East was 402,630, for the West 485,087. That year the East paid taxes of $319,489.25, mainly on slaves, compared to $153,026.99 for the West (Chandler, *Representation,* 57–58; *House Documents, 1849–50,* nos. 31, 49). A breakdown of delegate strength shows the Tidewater with thirty-eight, the Piedmont thirty-eight, the Valley twenty-four, and the mountains thirty-five (*Acts of the General Assembly of Virginia, 1849–50* [Richmond, 1850], 9–11).

28. Returns are found in: *Richmond Enquirer,* April 25, March 29, 1850; Ambler, *Sectionalism,* 259–61; Virginia State Papers, Va. State Lib. and Archives; Chandler, *Representation,* 260–61; *Lexington Gazette,* Sept. 12, 19, 1850; *Richmond Enquirer,* March 21, 1850; *Richmond Whig,* March 16, 19, 1850. Louisa rejected the convention by 272 to 260 votes, and Amelia by 165 to 152. Warwick voted 20 to 0 against the convention.

29. *Richmond Whig,* May 31, 1850.

30. *Lexington Gazette,* Feb. 8, June 7, 1850; *Richmond Enquirer,* May 28, 1850.

31. *Richmond Enquirer,* May 21, 1850; *Richmond Whig,* July 12, 1850. Popular election of state judges was also advocated, and, in addition, it was suggested that they be given limited tenure of office. But this change was preeminently a western idea.

32. *Richmond Whig,* July 17, Aug. 2, 1850; *Lexington Valley Star,* July 25, 1850.

33. *Richmond Whig,* May 24, 1850; *Richmond Enquirer,* July 10, 17, 1850.

34. *Richmond Enquirer,* Aug. 29, 1850; *Lexington Valley Star,* Aug. 8, 1850; U.S. Census, Virginia, Population Schedules, 1850.

35. Alexander Rives to W. C. Rives, Nov. 15, 1850, W. C. Rives Papers, Lib. Cong.; William Radford to George M. Mumford, Aug. 10, 1850, Ellis-Mumford Papers, Duke University Library.

VI

1. *Journal, Acts, and Proceedings of a General Convention of the State of Virginia, Assembled at Richmond on Monday, the Fourteenth Day of October, Eighteen Hundred and Fifty* (Richmond, 1851), 5–6; Gaines, "Convention of 1850–51," 94–106.

2. *Journal*, 12–31.

3. See the auditor's report in *Documents of Convention, 1850–51*.

4. *Journal*, 71–75; *Richmond Enquirer*, Oct. 22, 1850.

5. *Journal*, 117–19, 125–28; Gaines, "Convention of 1850–51," 114–20.

6. *Journal*, 120, 252, 254–61; *Register of the Debates and Proceedings of the Virginia Reform Convention* (Richmond, 1851), 71, 90–100, 178.

7. *Richmond Whig*, Feb. 7, 11, 1851; *Convention Debates*, 90–100, 105–119, 178; see also *Richmond Enquirer*, Supplement, Feb. 18, 1851; *Norfolk and Portsmouth Herald*, Feb. 4, 1851.

8. *Journal*, 117, 283–85, and Appendix on the New Constitution, 24–28.

9. George W. Spicer, "Gubernatorial Leadership in Virginia," *Public Administration Review* 1 (1941): 442.

10. Howard, *Commentaries*, 2:577.

11. *Journal*, Appendix on the New Constitution, 27; Gaines, "Convention of 1850–51," 257–58.

12. Porter, *County Government*, 231–32; Lester J. Cappon, "Evolution of County Government in Virginia," *Inventory of County Archives of Virginia*, no. 21, *Chesterfield County* (Charlottesville, Va., 1938), 26; E. Lee Shepard, "Lawyers Look at Themselves: Professional Consciousness and the Virginia Bar, 1770–1850," *American Journal of Legal History* 25 (1981): 22.

13. *Journal*, Appendix on New Constitution, 28–34; Cappon, "Evolution of County Government," 26–27; *Richmond Whig*, June 20, 1851; *Richmond Enquirer*, Supplement, June 27, 1851.

14. Excluded from elections were the road surveyor, deputy clerk, deputy sheriff, and superintendent of schools (Howard, *Commentaries*, 1:83, 2:698 n.99; Gaines, "Convention of 1850–51," 269–76).

15. John Janney Papers, Southern Historical Collection, Library of the University of North Carolina at Chapel Hill; Whittle to Isaac Carrington, Jan. 18, 1851, Smith Papers, Duke University Library; *Journal,* Appendixes nos. 22 and 23.

16. *Documents of Convention, 1850–51,* Appendix on Debt and Resources; *Richmond Whig,* March 14, 1851; Pate, "Constitutional Revision," 113–14; *Journal,* Appendix on New Constitution, 15–19. See Howard, *Commentaries,* 2:1022–25, on reasons behind changes in the fiscal provisions of the legislative prerogative.

17. *Journal,* 252–53, 326–28; *Richmond Enquirer,* Supplement, July 22, 1851; *Richmond Whig,* Supplement, July 18, 22, 1851; *Norfolk and Portsmouth Herald,* July 14, 1851.

18. Howard, *Commentaries,* 2:1025; *Journal,* Appendix on New Constitution, 20–22, Article IV.

19. *Richmond Enquirer,* Jan. 7, 1851; *Journal,* 127. Two other schemes were mentioned, the all-white basis and the so-called federal numbers basis (the white population plus three-fifths of the slave population), neither of which was given serious consideration by the delegates.

20. James Whittle to Isaac Carrington, Smith Papers, Duke University Library.

21. *Richmond Enquirer,* May 23, 1851, commented upon the inordinate amount of time given to debate on the basis question.

22. *Convention Debates,* 293, 329, 344; *Richmond Enquirer,* Supplement, March 3, 7, 1851; Gaines, "Convention of 1850–51," 131. The only thing done to the Declaration of Rights in the 1850–51 Convention was to attach it to the new constitution (Howard, *Commentaries,* 1:45).

23. *Convention Debates,* 341–43, and Appendix, Speech of Robert Stanard, 5–6.

24. Clement Eaton, *Freedom of Thought in the South* (Durham, N.C., 1940), 180–81; *Richmond Enquirer,* Supplement, May 2, 1851; *Convention Debates,* 372, and Appendix, Speech of Robert Stanard, 18.

25. *Convention Debates,* 299, 333, 373; *Richmond Whig,* April 4, 1851.

26. *Richmond Enquirer,* Supplement, March 21, April 7, 1851; *Convention Debates,* 283, 285, 359–61, 473–74; *Documents of Convention, 1850–51,* Appendix on Census; Barton H. Wise, *The Life of Henry A. Wise of Virginia, 1806–1876* (New York, 1899), 483–94.

27. *Convention Debates,* 302, 316; Gaines, "Convention of 1850–51," 143–63.

28. Morgantown *Monongalia Mirror*, April 12, May 3, 1851. The West, led by Judge Summers, in late April had suggested a possible compromise to Plan B—that at the time of the ratification vote, a separate vote would be taken on the basis of representation; the people, not the delegates, would decide the question. Eastern men, led by Robert Scott, opposed the plan out of fear that the scheme would get adopted, and it was defeated by three votes with only two easterners, Wise and John Botts, voting in favor of compromise.

29. *Journal*, 206–8, and Committee of the Whole Appendix, 11–12. The plan apportioned the House according to the white population of the state but arbitrarily assigned representation in the Senate. See also *Norfolk and Portsmouth Herald*, May 16, 21, 1851; *Richmond Whig*, May 16, 1851; Gaines, "Convention of 1850–51," 197–203.

30. *Journal*, 13, 127–37, and Committee of the Whole Appendix, 11–20; *Richmond Whig*, May 16, 27, 1851; *Norfolk and Portsmouth Herald*, April 12, May 15, 1851.

31. *Journal*, 224–26, and Committee of the Whole Appendix, 19–20, 22. It is impossible from the extant evidence to evaluate the motives of the eastern mavericks. Two of the eight, Wise and Chilton, had supported compromise on principle. Six of them lived in Piedmont counties whose economic interests were closely tied in with Valley counties. Sheer physical exhaustion and the monotonous debate that often dragged on into late evening also might have played a part in the desire to get the business finished. Home reaction was hostile. Public meetings in Albemarle and Bedford counties and Williamsburg demanded the resignations of Arthur, Wingfield, and Borden. Although there were some who condemned the compromise (thirteen eastern counties sent resolutions condemning the surrender and some citizens of Buckingham, King and Queen, Mecklenburg, and Southampton counties threatened a division of the state), the major newspapers and both political parties in the East endorsed the plan. Western reaction was enthusiastic (*Richmond Enquirer*, May 27, 30, 31, June 10, 1851; *Richmond Whig*, May 30, June 6, 10, 1851; *Norfolk and Portsmouth Herald*, May 26, 27, June 5, 13, 16, 21, 1851).

32. Chandler, *Suffrage*, 41–43; *Journal*, 35, 46, 58, 126; *Norfolk and Portsmouth Herald*, Feb. 11, 1861; *Richmond Enquirer*, Supplement, Feb. 7, 1851. There were minority reports, though; one western committeeman, Charles Blue, wanted to minimize the residency requirement. Two eastern men, Hector Davis of Richmond

and William Edwards of Fairfax, thought some sort of minimum freehold requirement should be retained (*Journal,* Appendix on Suffrage Committee's Report; *Richmond Enquirer,* Supplement, Feb. 1, 1851).

33. *Richmond Whig,* Supplement, July 18, 1851; *Journal,* 310–12.

34. Eastern delegates voting against Garnett were Arthur, Banks, Barbour, Edwards, Jasper, Lyons, McCandlish, J. T. Martin, R. Scott, Wallace, White, and Wise. Westerners voting for the plan were Dale Carter, Kenney, Lucas, Moore, and Murphy; all but Murphy were Valley residents (*Journal,* 311, 317). Westerners voting no were Bird, Fischer, Floyd, Fulkerson, Fultz, Hoge, Lucas, Miller, Summers, Tate; all but Fischer were Valley residents (ibid., 312–16; Howard, *Commentaries,* 1:363).

35. *Richmond Enquirer,* Aug. 15, 1851.

36. Alexander Rives to W. C. Rives, July 10, 1851, W. C. Rives Papers, Lib. Cong.; *Journal,* 419–22.

37. *Journal,* Appendix on the Constitution, 37–40.

38. Morgantown *Monongalia Mirror,* Aug. 23, 1851; F. N. Boney, *John Letcher of Virginia: The Story of Virginia's Civil War Governor* (University, Ala., 1966), 50.

39. *Lexington Gazette,* Aug. 7, Oct. 16, 1851; *Lexington Valley Star,* Aug. 14, 1851; Morgantown *Monongalia Mirror,* Sept. 6, 1851; *Staunton Spectator,* Aug. 20, 1851; *Winchester Virginian,* Aug. 6, 1851. For a summary of the West's reaction, see Gaines, "Convention of 1850–51," 280–83.

40. *Norfolk and Portsmouth Herald,* Aug. 2, 15, 1851; *Lynchburg Virginian,* Aug. 14, 1851; *Richmond Enquirer,* Aug. 1, 15, 1851; *Richmond Whig,* Aug. 1, 1851; Gaines, "Convention of 1850–51," 283–85.

41. *Richmond Whig,* Nov. 24, 1851; Chandler, *Representation,* 70; *Journal,* Appendix on the Constitution, 37.

42. Shanks, *Secession Movement,* 46–52; Dabney, *Virginia,* 222–23.

43. *Richmond Whig,* Feb. 14, 27, March 12, 1852.

44. Ibid., Feb. 10, March 12, 1852.

45. Ambler, *Sectionalism,* 311–18; *Richmond Enquirer,* Aug. 10, 1855; Howard, *Commentaries,* 2:1024.

46. Convention of 1829–30, *Proceedings,* 476.

47. David L. Pulliman, *The Constitutional Conventions of Virginia* (Richmond, 1901), 140–41. Acting on this amendment procedure, the voters approved seven changes in the 1870

constitution. Two times, though, in 1888 and in 1897, they rejected the calling of a convention. In 1900, however, Virginians called their third convention, elected by the people, to rewrite their constitutional law.

EPILOGUE

1. *Richmond Enquirer,* Nov. 10, 18, 1861; Shanks, *Secession Movement,* 122; *Staunton Spectator,* Nov. 20, 1861.

2. Boney, *John Letcher,* 100–102; Shanks, *Secession Movement,* 142–50.

3. Shanks, *Secession Movement,* 153–54, 197–99; *Alexandria Gazette,* Feb. 8, 1861; *Journal of the Secret Convention* (Richmond, 1861), 3.

4. Shanks, *Secession Movement,* chap. 1. For sketches of delegates to the Secession Convention, see William H. Gaines, Jr., ed., *Biographical Register of the Members of the Virginia State Convention of 1861, First Session* (Richmond, 1969).

5. *Richmond Enquirer,* April 20, 1861; Shanks, *Secession Movement,* 210; H. Lewis, *How West Virginia Was Made* (Charleston, W.Va., 1909), 32–33.

6. See Charles H. Ambler and Festus P. Summers, *West Virginia, the Mountain State,* rev. ed. (Englewood Cliffs, N.J., 1958), 196–97.

7. Ibid., 197; Shanks, *Secession Movement,* 123–24, 211.

8. Lewis, *West Virginia,* 38–39.

9. Ibid., 41–42, 48, 50–51.

10. Ibid., 54–55, 58.

11. Ibid., 60, 64.

12. Ambler and Summers, *West Virginia,* 199 n.6.

13. Lewis, *West Virginia,* 78–79. These Piedmont counties were Loudoun and Fairfax.

14. Ibid., 84–86. The resolution was introduced by John Carlile.

15. Ibid., 86–87.

16. Ambler and Summers, *West Virginia,* 127, 200–220.

17. Ibid., 203; Wheeling *Daily Intelligencer,* July 20, 1861.

18. Lewis, *West Virginia,* 183; Ambler and Summers, *West Virginia,* 205.

19. *Debates and Proceedings of the First Constitutional Convention of West Virignia, 1861–63,* ed. Charles A. Ambler, 3 vols. (Huntington, 1939), 1:7–12.

20. Ibid., 1:43, 44, 49–65. Abolition was made a condition of admission to the Union, however. In 1863 the recalled session of the convention adopted the "Willey Amendment" outlawing slavery. On Feb. 17, with three delegates abstaining, the amendment was approved by a vote of 54 to 0. The referendum on the amended constitution showed that 27,749 voters approved and only 572 opposed it. Of the negative votes, 132 were cast by soldiers stationed outside the state.

21. Ambler and Summers, *West Virginia*, 229–38. For Jefferson's reform effort as a member of the House of Delegates, 1776–79, on matters of county government, see Malone, *Jefferson*, 1: chap. 18.

22. Thomas Jefferson, *Notes on the State of Virginia*, ed. William Peden (Chapel Hill, N.C., 1954), 239.

23. *Kamper* v. *Hawkins*, 3 Va. (1 Va. Cas.) 20 (1793).

24. Ibid.; 5 Grat. (46 Va.) 518; 9 Leigh (36 Va.) 109 (837).

25. Howard, *Commentaries*, 2:683–778, 832–41.

26. *Richmond Enquirer*, Feb. 25, 1846.

27. Ibid., Dec. 4, 1849.

28. *De Bow's Review* 30 (1861): 306.

Selected Bibliography

PRIMARY SOURCES
Manuscripts
Duke University Library, Durham, N.C.
  Ellis-Mumford Papers
  Smith Papers
Library of Congress, Washington, D.C.
  Robert Beverley Papers
  Patrick Henry Papers
  Thomas Jefferson Papers
  John Letcher Papers
  James Madison Papers
  John Randolph Papers
  William Reynolds Papers
  William Cabell Rives Papers
  John Taylor Papers
Southern Historical Collection, Library of the University of North
  Carolina at Chapel Hill
  John Janney Papers
University of Virginia Library, Charlottesville
  John J. Ambler Papers
  Barbour Family Papers
  Cabell Papers
  John H. Cooke Papers
  Edgehill-Randolph Papers
  William Branch Giles Papers
  Francis Walker Gilmer Papers
  Gooch Family Papers
  Thomas Jefferson Papers
  Richard Henry Lee Papers
  Benjamin Watkins Leigh Papers
  James McDowell Papers

Wilson Cary Nicholas Papers
John Randolph Papers
Rawlings Family Papers
William Cabell Rives Papers
Sabine Hall Papers
Stuart-Baldwin Papers
Creed Taylor Papers
United States Census. Virginia. Population Schedules, 1790,
    1800, 1810, 1820, 1830, 1840, 1850, 1860; Manufactur-
    ing Schedules, 1850
Virginia Historical Society, Richmond
John Strode Barbour Papers
Fleming Bates Papers
Samuel P. Branch Papers
William H. Broadax Papers
Elizabeth Coalter Bryant Diary
Joseph Cloyd Papers
John H. Cooke Papers
Philip Doddridge Papers
Thomas Green Diary
Hugh Blair Grigsby Papers
Lee Papers and Lee Transcripts
Benjamin Watkins Leigh Papers
Thomas Massie Papers
Abel Parker Upshur Papers
Virginia State Library and Archives, Richmond
Land Tax Records, 1800, 1820, 1830, 1840, 1850, 1860
Legislative Petitions, 1790–1861
Personal Property Tax Records, 1800, 1820, 1830, 1840,
    1850, 1860
Tazewell Papers
Virginia Convention Papers, Third Virginia Convention,
    1775
West Virginia, State of, State Auditor's Office, Charleston
Land Tax Records, 1800, 1820, 1830, 1840, 1850, 1860
Personal Property Tax Records, 1800, 1820, 1830, 1840,
    1850, 1860

Public Documents

Acts of the Privy Council, Colonial Levies, 1745–1776. London, 1912.
Calendar of the Virginia State Papers and Other Manuscripts. Ed. Wil-
    liam P. Palmer et al. 11 vols. Richmond, 1875–93.

Debates and Proceedings of the First Constitutional Convention of West Virginia, 1861–63. 3 vols. Ed. Charles A. Ambler. Huntington, 1939.

Documents Containing Statistics of Virginia Ordered to Be Printed by the State Convention Sitting in the City of Richmond, 1850–51. Richmond, 1851.

Executive Journals of the Council of Colonial Virginia. Ed. H. R. McIlwaine and W. L. Hall, 5 vols. Richmond, 1925–45.

Journal, Acts, and Proceedings of a General Convention of the Commonwealth of Virginia in 1829. Richmond, 1830.

Journal of the Acts and Proceedings of a General Convention of the State of Virginia Assembled at Richmond on February 13, 1861. Richmond, 1861.

Journal of the House of Delegates of the State of Virginia for the Extra Session. Richmond, 1861.

Journal of the Senate of the Commonwealth of Virginia . . . Extra Session. Richmond, 1861.

Journal, Acts, and Proceedings of a General Convention of the State of Virginia Assembled at Richmond on Monday, the Fourteenth Day of October, Eighteen Hundred and Fifty. Richmond, 1851.

Journals of the Convention of 1775–1776. Ed. A. Purdie. Williamsburg, 1776.

Journals of the Council of State of Virginia, 1776–1781. Ed. H. R. McIlwaine et al. 5 vols. Richmond, 1931–82.

Journals of the House of Burgesses, 1619–1776. Ed. H. R. McIlwaine and J. P. Kennedy. 13 vols. Richmond, 1905–15.

Journals of the House of Delegates of the Commonwealth of Virginia, 1770–1861. Richmond, 1827–61.

Journals of the Senate of the Commonwealth of Virginia, 1776–1861. Williamsburg and Richmond, 1776–1861.

Official Letters of the Governors of Virginia, 1776–1783. Ed. H. R. McIlwaine. 3 vols. Richmond, 1926–29.

Ordinances Passed at a General Convention of Delegates and Representatives from the Several Counties and Corporations of Virginia, 1775–1776. Richmond, 1816.

Preamble and Resolutions on the Subject of the Missouri Question Agreed To by the House of Delegates of the State of Virginia. Richmond, 1820.

Proceedings and Debates of the Virginia State Convention of 1829–1830. Richmond, 1830.

Proceedings of the Convention of Delegates for the Counties and Corporations in the Colony of Virginia, 1775–1776. Richmond, 1816.

Register of the Debates and Proceedings of the Virginia Reform Convention. Richmond, 1851.

Register of the General Assembly of Virginia. Ed. Earl C. Swem et al. Richmond, 1918.

The Statutes at Large; Being a Collection of All the Laws of Virginia from the First Session of the Legislature in the Year 1619. Ed. William Waller Hening. 13 vols. Richmond, etc., 1809–23.

The Statutes at Large of Virginia, 1792–1806. Ed. Samuel Shepherd. 3 vols. Richmond, 1835–36.

Writings of Contemporaries

Adams, John. *Works.* Ed. C. F. Adams. Boston, 1850–56.

Barbour, James. *Speech to the Virginia Reform Convention, Thursday, February 27, 1851.* Richmond, 1851.

Bland, Richard. *Papers.* Ed. Charles Campbell. Richmond, 1855.

Botts, John Minor. *The Past, the Present, and the Future of Our Country.* Washington, D.C., 1860.

Campbell, Alexander. *Memoirs.* 2 vols. Philadelphia, 1868–70.

Floyd, John. *Address at Roanoke College.* Wytheville, Va., 1859.

———. *Speech in Convention on Taxation.* Richmond, 1851.

Forrest, William S. *Historical and Descriptive Sketches of Norfolk and Vicinity.* Philadelphia, 1853.

Garnett, James Mercer. *A Reply to Freeholders of King and Queen, King William, Essex, Caroline, Middlesex.* Richmond, 1829.

———. *Substance of an Address Delivered by James M. Garnett to the People of Essex at Their Late Election for a Member of Congress.* Richmond, 1829.

Gateswood, Joanne L., ed. "Richmond during the Virginia Constitutional Convention of 1829–30: An Extract from the Diary of Thomas Green, October 1, 1829, to January 31, 1830," *Virginia Magazine of History and Biography* 84 (1976): 287–332.

Giles, William B. *Political Miscellanies.* Richmond, 1829.

Goggin, W. L. *Speech on Federal Relations in the Convention of Virginia, on the 26th and 27th February 1861.* Richmond, 1861.

Goode, William O. *Recollections of a Lifetime.* New York, 1906.

———. *Speech in the General Assembly of 1831–1832.* Richmond, 1882.

Grigsby, Hugh Blair. *Discourses on the Life and Character of Littleton W. Tazewell.* Norfolk, 1860.

———. "Sketches of Members of the Constitutional Convention of 1829–30." *Virginia Magazine of History and Biography* 61 (1953): 219–332.

——. *The Virginia Convention of 1776*. Richmond, 1855.

——. *The Virginia Convention of 1829–30*. Richmond, 1856.

Hunter, R. M. T. *Speech before the Democratic Mass Meeting at Pough-keepsie, on October 1, 1856*. New York, 1856.

Jefferson, Thomas. *Autobiography*. Capricorn Books ed. New York, 1959.

——. *Notes on the State of Virginia*. Ed. William Peden. Chapel Hill, N.C., 1954.

——. *The Papers of Thomas Jefferson*. Ed. Julian P. Boyd et al. 22 vols. to date. Princeton, N.J., 1950—.

——. *The Writings of Thomas Jefferson*. Ed. Paul Leicester Ford. 10 vols. New York, 1892–99.

——. *Writings*. Ed. Andrew A. Lipscomb and Albert E. Bergh. 20 vols. Washington, D.C., 1903–4.

Johnson, Chapman. *To the Freeholders of the District Composed of the Counties of Shenandoah, Rockingham, Pendleton, Bath, Rock-bridge, and Augusta*. N.p., 1810.

Jones, Thomas R. *Speech*. Richmond, 1829.

Kercheval, Samuel A. *A History of the Valley of Virginia*. Woodstock, 1850.

Lee, Arthur. *A Sword Appeal to the Justice and Interests of the People*. London, 1775.

Lee, Richard Henry. *The Letters of Richard Henry Lee*. Ed. James C. Ballagh. 2 vols. New York, 1911–14.

Leigh, Benjamin Watkins. *Substitute Intended to Be Offered to the Next Meeting of the Citizens of Richmond on the Subject of a Convention*. Richmond, 1824.

Letcher, John. *Speeches and Extracts from Speeches . . . Touching the Subject of Slavery*. Washington, D.C., 1856.

——. *Speech . . . on the Basis Question Delivered in Committee of the Whole Convention*, March 14, 1851.

McDowell, James. *Speech in the Legislature of Virginia in the Session of 1831–1832*. Richmond, 1832.

Madison, James. *The Writings of James Madison*. Ed. Gaillard Hunt. New York, 1900.

——. *The Papers of James Madison*. Ed. William T. Hutchinson and William M. E. Rachal. Vols. 1–3. Chicago, 1962–69.

Martin, Joseph. *A New and Comprehensive Gazetteer of Virginia and the District of Columbia*. Charlottesville, 1836.

Mason, George. *The Papers of George Mason, 1725–1792*. Ed. Robert A. Rutland. 3 vols. Chapel Hill, N.C., 1970.

Mazzei, Philip. *Researches sur les Etats-Unis.* Paris, 1788.

Meredith, John A. *Address to the Voters of New Kent, Charles City, Henrico, and the City of Richmond.* New Kent, Va., 1850.

Pendleton, Edmund. *The Letters and Papers of Edmund Pendleton, 1734–1803.* Ed. David J. Mays. Charlottesville, Va., 1967.

Purkins, George W. *Speech on the Basis Question Delivered in the Reform Convention, February 21, 1851.* Richmond, 1851.

Randolph, Edmund. *Essay on the Revolutionary History of Virginia (1744–1782).* Richmond, 1835.

Randolph, Thomas J. *Address of Thomas J. Randolph to the Voters of Albemarle, Nelson, and Amherst.* N.p., 1850.

Revolutionary Virginia: The Road to Independence. Ed. Robert L. Scribner and Brent Tarter. 7 vols. Charlottesville, 1973–83.

Rives, William C. *Speech on the Proceedings of the Peace Conference in the State of the Union, Delivered in Richmond, Virginia, March 8, 1861.* Richmond, 1861.

Robertson, Wyndham. *Speech on the State of the Country, Delivered in the House of Delegates on the 5th and 6th of March, 1860.* Richmond, 1860.

Robinson, Mason. *Views of the Constitution of Virginia, Contained in the Essay of the People.* Richmond, 1850.

Ruffner, Henry. *Address to the People of West Virginia, Delivered at Lexington, Virginia, Showing That Slavery Is Injurious to the Public Welfare, etc.* Wheeling, 1862.

Sheffey, Hugh. *Speech of A. W. Sheffey of Augusta in Committee of the Whole on the Basis Question, February 18, February 19, February 20, 1851.* Richmond, 1851.

Summers, George W. *Speech on Federal Relations in the Virginia Convention, Delivered March 11, 1861.* Richmond, 1861.

Taylor, John. *Construction Construed and Constitutions Vindicated.* Richmond, 1820.

——. *An Inquiry into the Principles and Policy of the Government of the United States.* Fredericksburg, Va., 1814.

——. *Tyranny Unmasked.* Washington, D.C., 1822.

Thompson, George W. *Secession Is Revolution; the Dangers of the South; the Barrier States, Their Position, Characters, and Duty; the Constitutional Democracy, in a Discourse Delivered at Wheeling, Virginia, December 1, 1860.* Wheeling, 1861.

Washington, George. *The Writings of George Washington.* Ed. W. C. Ford. New York, 1931–34.

Willey, Waitman T. *Speeches before the State Convention of Virginia on the Basis of Representation: on the County Courts and County Or-*

ganization and on the Election of Judges by the People. Richmond, 1851.

Wills and Administrations, Accomack County, Virginia, 1663–1800. Ed. Stratton Nottingham. Onancock, 1931.

Wirt, William. *Memoirs of the Life of William Wirt.* Ed. John P. Kennedy. Philadelphia, 1849.

——. *Sketches of the Life and Character of Patrick Henry.* Philadelphia, 1817.

Wise, Henry A. *Letters to Charles W. Russell.* Richmond, 1858.

——. *Letter to the People of Virginia.* Washington, D.C., 1855.

Woolfork, John. *Address to Citizens of Counties of Orange, Greene, Madison, and Culpeper, July 8, 1850.* Richmond, 1850.

Newspapers and Contemporary Periodicals

Alexandria Herald. 1816.
Alexandria Gazette. 1829, 1861.
Alexandria Gazette and Virginia Advertiser. 1860–61.
American Union. Morgantown, 1855–59.
Charleston Free Press. 1829.
Charleston Courier. 1860–61.
Daily Express. Petersburg, 1861.
Daily Intelligencer. Wheeling, 1859–61.
DeBow's Commercial Review of the Southern and Western States. 38 vols. New Orleans, 1846–70.
Democratic Banner. Fairmont, 1850.
Democratic Recorder. Fredericksburg, 1861.
Kanawha Valley Star. Charleston, 1855–61.
Lexington Gazette. 1845.
Lexington Intelligencer. 1830.
Lexington Valley Star. 1845, 1850.
Lynchburg Republican. 1849.
Lynchburg Virginian. 1830, 1851.
Monongalia Mirror. Morgantown, 1851.
Niles Weekly Register. 70 vols. Baltimore, 1811–49.
Norfolk and Portsmouth Herald. 1851.
Parkersburg Gazette and Western Virginian Courier. 1849–54.
Petersburg Intelligencer. 1827.
Richmond Christian Advocate. 1854–60.
Richmond Daily Dispatch. 1860–61.
Richmond Enquirer. 1804–61.
Richmond Whig. 1850–52.
Southern Quarterly Review. 26 vols. Charleston, S.C., 1842–56.

Staunton Spectator and General Advertiser. 1829–30, 1846–51, 1861.
Staunton Vindicator. 1846–61.
Virginia Advocate. Charlottesville, 1829–30.
Virginia Gazette. Williamsburg, 1725–76.

SECONDARY SOURCES

Books

Abernethy, Thomas P. *Western Lands and the American Revolution.* New York, 1937.

Adams, Willi Paul. *The First American Constitutions: Republican Ideology and the Making of the State Constitutions in the Revolutionary Era.* Chapel Hill, N.C., 1980.

Aler, F. Vernon. *Aler's History of Martinsburg and Berkeley County, West Virginia.* Hagerstown, Md., 1888.

Ambler, Charles H. *A History of Transportation in the Ohio Valley.* Glendale, Calif., 1932.

——. *A History of West Virginia.* New York, 1933.

——. *Life and Diary of John Floyd.* Richmond, 1918.

——. *Sectionalism in Virginia, 1776–1861.* Chicago, 1910.

——. *Thomas Ritchie: A Study in Virginia Politics.* Richmond, 1913.

—— and Festus P. Summers. *West Virginia, the Mountain State.* Rev. ed. Englewood Cliffs, N.J., 1958.

Anderson, Dice R. *William Branch Giles: A Study in the Politics of Virginia and the Nation, 1790–1830.* Menasha, Wis., 1914.

Aptheker, Herbert P. *American Negro Slave Revolts.* New York, 1943.

Armstrong, Zella, comp. *Notable Southern Families.* 2 vols. Chattanooga, 1918.

Atkinson, George W., et al. *Prominent Men of West Virginia.* Wheeling, 1890.

Bagby, Alfred. *King and Queen County, Virginia.* New York, 1908.

Bancroft, Frederic. *Slave-Trading in the Old South.* Baltimore, 1931.

Banning, Lance. *The Jeffersonian Persuasion: Evaluation of a Party Ideology.* Ithaca, N.Y., 1978.

Baritz, Loren. *City on a Hill: A History of Ideas and Myths in America.* New York, 1964.

Barnes, Isaac A. *The Methodist Protestant Church in West Virginia.* Baltimore, 1926.

Beeman, Richard R. *The Evolution of the Southern Backcountry: A Case Study of Lunenburg County, Virginia, 1746–1832.* Philadelphia, 1984.

――. *The Old Dominion and the New Nation, 1788–1801.* Lexington, Ky., 1972.

Bell, John W. *Memoirs of Governor William Smith of Virginia: His Political, Military, and Personal History.* New York, 1891.

Bennett, William W. *Memorials of Methodism in Virginia from Its Introduction into the State in the Year 1772 to the Year 1829.* Richmond, 1871.

Benson, Lee. *Turner and Beard: American Historical Writing Reconsidered.* Glencoe, Ill., 1960.

Berlin, Ira, and Ronald Hoffman, eds. *Slavery and Freedom in the Age of the American Revolution.* Charlottesville, Va., 1983.

Beveridge, Albert J. *Life of John Marshall.* 4 vols. Boston, 1916–19.

Bishop, William H. *History of Roane County, West Virginia, from the Time of Its Exploration to A.D. 1927.* Spencer, 1927.

Bodenhamer, David J., and James W. Ely, Jr., eds. *Ambivalent Legacy: A Legal History of the South.* Jackson, Miss., 1984.

Boney, F. N. *John Letcher of Virginia: The Story of Virginia's Civil War Governor.* University, Ala., 1966.

Bosworth, Albert S. *History of Randolph County, West Virginia, from Its Earliest Exploration and Settlement to the Present Time.* Elkins, 1916.

Bradshaw, Herbert C. *History of Prince Edward County, Virginia.* Richmond, 1955.

Brant, Irving. *The Bill of Rights: Its Origin and Meaning.* Indianapolis, 1965.

――. *James Madison.* 6 vols. Indianapolis, 1941–61.

Breen, T. H. *Tobacco Culture: The Mentality of the Great Tidewater Planters on the Eve of Revolution.* Princeton, N.J., 1985.

Brown, Robert E. *Virginia, 1705–1786: Democracy or Aristocracy.* East Lansing, Mich., 1964.

Brown, William G. *History of Nicholas County, West Virginia.* Richmond, 1954.

Bruce, Dickson D., Jr. *The Rhetoric of Conservativism: The Virginia Convention of 1829–30 and the Conservative Tradition in the South.* San Marino, Calif., 1982.

Bruce, Kathleen. *Virginia Iron Manufacturing in the Slave Era.* New York, London, 1930.

Bruce, William C. *John Randolph of Roanoke, 1773–1833.* 2d ed., rev. New York and London, 1939.

Brunk, Harry A. *History of the Menonnites in Virginia, 1727–1900.* Staunton, 1959.

Bushong, Millard K. *A History of Jefferson County, West Virginia.* Charleston, 1941.

Callahan, James M., and Bernard L. Butcher. *Genealogical and Personal History of the Upper Monongahela Valley, West Virginia.* 3 vols. New York, 1912.

Cappon, Lester J. *Virginia Newspapers, 1821–1935.* New York, 1936.

Carpenter, Jesse T. *The South as a Conscious Minority, 1789–1861.* New York, 1930.

Carrington, Wirt J. *A History of Halifax County, Virginia.* Richmond, 1924.

Carroll, Eber M. *Origins of the Whig Party.* Durham, N.C., 1925.

Cash, Wilbur J. *The Mind of the South.* New York, 1941.

Catterall, Helen H., ed. *Judicial Cases concerning Slavery and the Negro.* Vol. 1. *Cases from the Courts of England, Virginia, West Virginia, and Kentucky.* Washington, D.C., 1926–37.

Chambers, William N., and Walter Dean Burnham, eds. *The American Party System: Stages of Political Development.* New York, 1967.

Chandler, Julian A. C. *History of Suffrage in Virginia.* Baltimore, 1901.

———. *Representation in Virginia.* Baltimore, 1896.

Childs, James R. *Reliques of Rives.* Lynchburg, Va., 1929.

Chitwood, Oliver P. *John Tyler, Champion of the Old South.* New York and London, 1939.

———. *Justice in Colonial Virginia.* Baltimore, 1905.

Christian, William. *Lynchburg and Its People.* Lynchburg, Va., 1900.

Chumbley, George L. *Colonial Justice in Virginia: The Development of a Judicial System, Typical Laws, and Cases of the Period.* Richmond, 1938.

Clement, Maud C. *The History of Pittsylvania County, Virginia.* Lynchburg, 1929.

Cole, Arthur C. *The Whig Party in the South.* Washington, D.C., 1913.

Cooley, Thomas M. *The General Principles of Constitutional Law in the United States of America.* Boston, 1880.

Cooper, William J. *Liberty and Slavery: Southern Politics to 1860.* New York, 1983.

———. *The South and the Politics of Slavery.* Baton Rouge, La., 1978.

Couper, William. *History of the Shenandoah Valley.* 3 vols. New York, 1952.

Craven, Avery O. *Edmund Ruffin, Southerner: A Study in Secession.* New York and London, 1932.

———. *Soil Exhaustion as a Factor in the Agricultural History of Virginia and Maryland, 1606–1860.* Urbana, Ill., 1926.

Cresson, William P. *James Monroe.* Chapel Hill, N.C., 1946.

Dabney, Virginius. *Virginia, the New Dominion.* Garden City, N.Y., 1971.

Dangerfield, George. *The Awakening of American Nationalism, 1815–1828.* New York, 1965.

Davidson, Robert. *History of the Presbyterian Church in the State of Kentucky with a Preliminary Sketch of the Church in the Valley of Virginia.* Chapel Hill, N.C., 1947.

Davis, Richard B. *Francis Walker Gilmer: Life and Learning in Jefferson's Virginia.* Richmond, 1939.

——. *Intellectual Life in Jefferson's Virginia, 1790–1830.* Chapel Hill, N.C., 1964.

de Gruyter, Julius A. *A History of the Atlantic Coast Line Railroad.* Boston and New York, 1920.

Dewey, Frank L. *Thomas Jefferson, Lawyer.* Charlottesville, Va., 1986.

Dinkin, Robert J. *Voting in Revolutionary America: A Study of Elections in the Original Thirteen States, 1776–1789.* Westport, Conn., 1982.

Dodson, E. Griffith. *Speakers and Clerks of the Virginia House of Delegates.* Richmond, 1956.

du Bellett, Louise P. *Some Prominent Virginia Families.* 3 vols. Lynchburg, 1907.

Dumond, Dwight L. *The Secession Movement, 1860–61.* New York, 1931.

Dunaway, Wayland F. *History of the James River and Kanawha Company.* New York, 1922.

Early, Ruth H. *Campbell Chronicles and Family Sketches, Embracing the History of Campbell County, Virginia, 1782–1926.* Lynchburg, 1927.

Eckenrode, Hamilton J. *The Revolution in Virginia.* New York, 1916.

——. *Separation of Church and State in Virginia: A Study in the Development of the Revolution.* Richmond, 1910.

Ellis, Richard E. *The Jeffersonian Crisis: Courts and Politics in the Young Republic.* New York, 1971.

Evans, William F. *History of Berkeley County, West Virginia.* Martinsburg, 1928.

Fischer, David H. *The Revolution of American Conservatism: The Federalist Party in the Era of Jeffersonian Democracy.* New York, 1965.

Flaherty, David, ed. *Essays in the History of Early American Law.* Chapel Hill, N.C., 1969.

Fox, Early Lee. *The American Colonization Society, 1817–1840.* Baltimore, 1919.

Freehling, Alison Goodyear. *Drift toward Dissolution: The Virginia Slavery Debate of 1831–1832.* Baton Rouge, La., 1982.

Friedman, Lawrence. *A History of American Law.* New York, 1973.

Gaines, William H., Jr. *Biographical Register of the Members of the Virginia State Convention of 1861.* Richmond, 1969.

Garnett, James M. *Biographical Sketch of Hon. Charles Fenton Mercer, 1778–1858.* Richmond, 1911.

Gates, Paul W. *The Farmer's Age: Agriculture, 1815–1860.* New York, 1960.

Goode, G. B. *Virginia Cousins: A Study of the Ancestry and Posterity of John Goode of Whitby.* Richmond, 1887.

Goodrich, Carter. *Canals and American Economic Development.* New York, 1961.

Gordon, Armistead C. *The Gordons in Virginia, with Notes on Gordons of Scotland and Ireland.* Hackensack, N.J., 1918.

——. *Virginia Portraits.* Staunton, 1924.

——. *William Fitzhugh Gordon, A Virginian of the Old School: His Life, Times, and Contemporaries (1787–1858).* New York, 1909.

Gray, Lewis C. *History of Agriculture in the Southern United States to 1860.* 2 vols. Washington, D.C., 1933.

Green, Fletcher M. *Constitutional Development in the South Atlantic States, 1776–1860: A Study in the Evolution of Democracy.* Chapel Hill, N.C., 1930.

Hagans, John M. *Sketch of the Erection and Formation of the State of West Virginia from the Territory of Virginia.* Charleston, 1927.

Hall, Claude H. *Abel Parker Upshur, Conservative Virginian, 1790–1844.* Madison, Wis., 1964.

Hall, Kermit L., ed. *A Comprehensive Bibliography of American Constitutional and Legal Histories, 1896–1979.* 5 vols. New York, 1985.

Handy, Edward. *Genetic Study of Family Lines in Virginia.* Charlottesville, 1942.

Harman, John N. *Annals of Tazewell County, Virginia, from 1800 to 1922.* 2 vols. Richmond, 1922–25.

Harrell, Isaac S. *Loyalism in Virginia: Chapters in the Economic History of the Revolution.* Durham, N.C., 1926.

Harris, Malcom H. *History of Louisa County, Virginia.* Richmond, 1936.

Hart, Freeman H. *The Valley of Virginia in the American Revolution, 1763–1789.* Chapel Hill, N.C., 1942.

Head, James W. *History and Comprehensive Description of Loudoun County, Virginia.* Washington, D.C., 1909.

Heatwole, Cornelius J. *A History of Education in Virginia.* New York, 1916.

Hendrick, Burton J. *The Lees of Virginia.* Boston, 1935.

Henry, W. W., ed. *Patrick Henry: Life, Correspondence, and Speeches.* 3 vols. New York, 1891.

Hill, Helen D. *George Mason, Constitutionalist.* Cambridge, Mass., 1938.

Hilldrup, Robert L. *Life and Times of Edmund Pendleton.* Chapel Hill, N.C., 1939.

Hoadley, John F. *Origins of American Political Parties.* Lexington, Ky., 1986.

Hofstadter, Richard. *The Paranoid Style in American Politics and Other Essays.* New York, 1965.

Holladay, Elizabeth D. *Dinwiddie Family Records.* Charlottesville, Va., 1957.

Holladay, James M., comp. *A Partial History of Fincastle Presbyterian Church.* Richmond, 1902.

Howard, A. E. Dick. *Commentaries on the Constitution of Virginia.* 2 vols. Charlottesville, 1974.

Hungerford, Edward. *The Story of the Baltimore and Ohio Railroad, 1827–1927.* 2 vols. New York, London, 1928.

Hyneman, Charles S., and David S. Lutz. *American Political Writing during the Founding Era, 1760–1805.* Indianapolis, 1983.

Isaac, Rhys. *The Transformation of Virginia, 1740–1790.* Chapel Hill, N.C., 1982.

Jackson, Luther P. *Free Negro Labor and Property Holding in Virginia, 1830–1860.* New York, London, 1942.

Jellison, Richard M., ed. *Society, Freedom, and Conscience: The American Revolution in Virginia, Massachusetts, and New York.* New York, 1976.

Jenkins, William S. *Pro Slavery Thought in the Old South.* Chapel Hill, N.C., 1935.

Johnson, Guion G. *Ante Bellum North Carolina: A Social History.* Chapel Hill, N.C., 1937.

Johnston, David E. *A History of the Middle New River Settlements and Contiguous Territory.* Huntingdon, W.Va., 1906.

Johnston, Frederick. *Memorials of Old Virginia Courts.* Lynchburg, 1888.

Jordan, Daniel P. *Political Leadership in Jefferson's Virginia.* Charlottesville, 1983.

Kelly, Alfred H., and Winfred A. Harbison. *The American Constitution: Its Origins and Development.* 4th ed. New York, 1970.

Kercheval, Samuel. *A History of the Valley of Virginia.* 3d ed. Woodstock, 1902.

Ketcham, Ralph L. *James Madison, a Biography.* New York, 1971.

Kirk, Russell. *Randolph of Roanoke: A Study in Conservative Thought.* Chicago, 1951.

Kulikoff, Allan. *Tobacco and Slaves: The Development of Southern Cultures in the Chesapeake, 1680–1800.* Chapel Hill, N.C., 1986.

Kurland, Philip B., and Ralph Learner, eds. *The Founders' Constitution.* Chicago, 1907.

Laidley, William S. *History of Charleston and Kanawha County.* Chicago, 1911.

Lambert, Oscar D. *Pioneer Leaders of West Virginia.* Parkersburg, 1935.

Levy, Leonard W., Kenneth L. Karst, and Dennis J. Mahoney, eds. *The Encyclopedia of the American Constitution.* 5 vols. New York, 1986.

Lewis, Jan. *The Pursuit of Happiness: Family and Values in Jefferson's Virginia.* New York, 1983.

Leyburn, James G. *The Scotch-Irish: A Social History.* Chapel Hill, N.C., 1962.

Lindley, Denton R. *Apostle of Freedom.* St. Louis, 1957.

Lingley, Charles R. *The Transition in Virginia from Colony to Commonwealth.* New York, 1910.

Little, John P. *History of Richmond.* Richmond, 1933.

Lowery, Charles D. *James Barbour, the Biography of a Jeffersonian Republican.* University, Ala., 1984.

Lowther, Minnie K. *History of Ritchie County.* Wheeling, W.Va., 1911.

Lutz, Francis E. *Chesterfield, an Old Virginia County.* Richmond, 1954.

———. *The Prince George-Hopewell Story.* Richmond, 1957.

McClelland, Peter D., and Richard J. Zeckhauser. *Demographic Dimensions of the New Republic: American Interregional Migration, Vital Statistics, and Manumissions, 1800–1860.* New York, 1982.

McColley, Robert. *Slavery and Jeffersonian Virginia.* Urbana, Ill., 1964.

McCormick, Richard P. *The Second American Party System: Party Formation in the Jacksonian Era.* Chapel Hill, N.C., 1966.

McGregor, James C. *The Disruption of Virginia.* New York, 1922.

Main, Jackson T. *Political Parties before the Constitution.* Chapel Hill, N.C., 1973.

———. *The Social Structure of Revolutionary America.* Princeton, N.J., 1965.

———. *The Upper House in Revolutionary America, 1763–1788.* Madison, Wis., 1967.

Mason, Virginia. *The Public Life and Diplomatic Correspondence of James Murray Mason.* 2d ed. New York and Washington, D.C., 1906.

Maxwell, Hu. *History of Randolph County, West Virginia.* Morgantown, 1898.

———, and Harold Swischer. *History of Hampshire County.* Morgantown, W.Va., 1897.

Mays, David J. *Edmund Pendleton, 1721–1803: A Biography.* 2 vols. Cambridge, Mass., 1952.

Meade, Robert. *Patrick Henry.* 2 vols. Philadelphia, 1957–69.

Miller, James H. *History of Summers County from the Earliest Settlement to the Present Time.* Hinton, W.Va., 1908.

Miller, Thomas C., and Hu Maxwell. *West Virginia and Its People.* 3 vols. New York, 1913.

Morgan, Benjamin S. *Columbian History of Education in West Virginia.* Charleston, 1893.

Morgan, P. Robinson, *Virginia Counties: Those Resulting from Virginia Legislation.* Richmond, 1916.

Morison, Samuel Eliot, ed. *Sources and Documents Illustrating the American Revolution, 1764–1788, and the Formation of the Federal Constitution.* Oxford, Eng., 1961.

Morton, Owen F. *Annals of Bath County, Virginia.* Staunton, 1917.

———. *A Centennial History of Alleghany County, Virginia.* Dayton, 1923.

———. *History of Monroe County, West Virginia.* Dayton, Va., 1916.

———. *A History of Pendleton County, West Virginia.* Franklin, 1910.

———. *A History of Rockbridge County, Virginia.* Staunton, 1920.

———. *The Story of Winchester in Virginia, the Oldest Town in the Shenandoah Valley.* Strasburg, 1925.

Nelson, Margaret V. *A Study of Judicial Review in Virginia, 1789–1928.* New York, 1947.

Nelson, William E., and John Phillip Reid, eds. *The Literature of American Legal History.* New York, 1985.

Nevins, Allan. *The American States during and after the Revolution, 1775–1789.* New York, 1924.

Newsome, Albert R. *The Presidential Election of 1824 in North Carolina.* Chapel Hill, N.C., 1939.

Norris, J. E. *History of the Lower Shenandoah Valley.* Chicago, 1890.

Nuckolls, Benjamin F. *Pioneer Settlers of Grayson County, Virginia.* Bristol, Tenn., 1914.

Pedigo, Virginia and Lewis. *History of Patrick and Henry Counties, Virginia.* Roanoke, 1933.

Pemberton, Robert L. *A History of Pleasants County, West Virginia.* St. Mary's, 1929.

Peterson, Merrill D. *The Jefferson Image in the American Mind.* New York, 1960.

——, *Thomas Jefferson and the New Nation.* New York, 1970.

——, ed. *Democracy, Liberty, and Property: The State Constitutional Conventions of the 1820s.* Indianapolis, 1966.

——, ed. *Thomas Jefferson: A Reference Biography.* 1986.

Peterson, Norma Lois. *Littleton Waller Tazewell.* Charlottesville, Va., 1983.

Peyton, Lewis. *History of Augusta County.* Bridgewater, Va., 1953.

Porter, Albert O. *County Government in Virginia, A Legislative History, 1607–1904.* New York, 1947.

Potts, Louis W. *Arthur Lee: A Virtuous Revolutionary.* Baton Rouge, La., 1981.

Powell, Charles S. *History and Genealogies of the Powells in America.* N.p., 1935.

Pratt, Dorothy. *Russell County, Virginia.* Richmond, n.d.

Reardon, John J. *Peyton Randolph, 1721–1775: One Who Presided.* Durham, N.C., 1982.

Reid, John Philip. *Constitutional History of the American Revolution.* Madison, Wis., 1986.

Remini, Robert V. *The Election of Andrew Jackson.* New York, 1963.

Risjord, Norman K. *The Old Republicans: Southern Conservatism in the Age of Jefferson.* New York, 1965.

Robbins, Caroline. *The Eighteenth-Century Commonwealthman: Studies in the Transition, Development, and Circumstance of English Liberal Thought from the Restoration of Charles II until the War with the Thirteen Colonies.* New York, 1959.

Robert, Joseph C. *The Road from Monticello: A Study of the Virginia Slavery Debate of 1832.* Durham, N.C., 1941.

——. *The Story of Tobacco in America.* New York, 1949.

——. *Tobacco Kingdom: Plantation, Market, and Factory in Virginia and North Carolina, 1800–1860.* Durham, N.C., 1938.

Roeber, A. G. *Faithful Magistrates and Republican Lawyers: Creators of Virginia Legal Culture, 1680–1810.* Chapel Hill, N.C., 1981.

Rowland, Kate Mason. *The Life of George Mason, 1725–1792.* 2 vols. New York, 1892.

Royall, William L. *A History of Virginia Banks and Banking prior to the Civil War.* New York and Washington, D.C., 1907.

Russell, John H. *The Free Negro in Virginia, 1619–1865.* Baltimore, 1913.

Scott, James G., and Edward A. Wyatt. *Petersburg's Story, a History.* Petersburg, Va., 1960.

Scott, W. W. *History of Orange County, Virginia.* Richmond, 1907.

Shalhope, Robert E. *John Taylor of Caroline: Pastoral Republican.* Columbia, S.C., 1980.

Shanks, Henry T. *The Secession Movement in Virginia, 1847–1861.* Richmond, 1934.

Simms, Henry H. *Life of John Taylor: The Story of a Brilliant Leader in the Early Virginia State Rights School.* Richmond, 1932.

——. *Life of Robert M. T. Hunter: A Story in Sectionalism and Secession.* Richmond, 1935.

——. *The Rise of the Whigs in Virginia, 1824–1840.* Richmond, 1929.

Simpson, Craig M. *The Life of Henry A. Wise of Virginia.* Chapel Hill, N.C., 1985.

Smith, Joseph, ed. *The American Constitution: The First Two Hundred Years, 1787–1987.* Exeter, Mass., 1987.

Smith, Margaret V. *Virginia, 1492–1892: A History of the Executives.* Washington, D.C., 1893.

Starkey, Marion L. *The First Plantation: A History of Hampton and Elizabeth City County, Virginia, 1607–1887.* Hampton, 1936.

Starnes, George T. *Sixty Years of Branch Banking in Virginia.* New York, 1931.

Summers, Lewis P. *History of Southwest Virginia 1746–1786, Washington County 1777–1870.* Richmond, 1903.

Swem, Earl G. *A Register of the General Assembly of Virginia, 1776–1918, and the Constitutional Conventions.* Richmond, 1918.

Sydnor, Charles S. *The Development of Southern Sectionalism, 1819–1849.* Baton Rouge, La., 1948.

——. *Gentlemen Freeholders: Political Practices in Washington's Virginia.* Chapel Hill, N.C., 1952.

Taylor, William R. *Cavalier and Yankee: The Old South and American National Character.* New York, 1961.

Thorpe, Frances N. *The Federal and State Constitutions.* Washington, D.C., 1909.

Tushnet, Mark V. *Red, White, and Blue: A Critical Analysis of Constitutional Law.* Cambridge, Mass., 1988.

Tyler, Lyon G. *Letters and Times of the Tylers.* 2 vols. Richmond, 1884.

——., ed. *Encyclopedia of Virginia Biography.* 2 vols. New York, 1915.

Waddell, Joseph A. *Annals of Augusta County.* Bridgewater, Va., 1958.

Wagstaff, Henry M. *State Rights and Political Parties in North Carolina, 1776–1861.* Baltimore, 1906.

Wallace, George S. *Cabell County Annals and Families.* Richmond, 1935.

Warren, Charles. *A History of the American Bar.* New York, 1966.

Wayland, Francis F. *Andrew Stevenson, Democrat and Diplomat, 1785–1857.* Philadelphia, 1949.

Wayland, John W. *The German Element in the Shenandoah Valley of Virginia.* Charlottesville, 1907.

——.*A History of Rockingham County, Virginia.* Dayton, 1912.

——. *A History of Shenandoah County, Virginia.* Strasburg, 1927.

Wertenbaker, Thomas J. *Norfolk: Historic Southern Port.* Durham, N.C., 1931.

Whitelow, Ralph T. *Virginia's Eastern Shore.* 2 vols. Richmond, 1951.

Whitfield, Theodore M. *Slavery Agitation in Virginia, 1829–1832.* Baltimore, 1930.

Willey, Waitman T. *A Sketch of the Life of Philip Doddridge.* Morgantown, W.Va., 1875.

Williams, Harrison. *Legends of Loudoun.* Richmond, 1938.

Williamson, Chilton S. *American Suffrage: From Property to Democracy, 1760–1860.* Princeton, N.J., 1960.

Wingfield, Marshall. *A History of Caroline County, Virginia, from Its Formation in 1727 to 1924.* Richmond, 1924.

Wise, Barton H. *The Life of Henry A. Wise of West Virginia, 1806–1876.* New York, 1899.

Wood, Gordon. *The Creation of the American Republic, 1774–1787.* New York, 1969.

Woods, Edgar. *Albemarle County in Virginia: Giving Some Account of What It Was by Nature, of What It Was Made by Man, and of the Men Who Made It.* Bridgewater, 1932.

Woodson, Carter G. *Free Negro Heads of Families in the United States in 1830, Together with a Brief Treatment of the Free Negro.* Washington, D.C., 1925.

Writer's Program, WPA, Virginia. *Dinwiddie County.* Richmond, 1942.

———. *Gilmer: The Birth of a County.* Charleston, W.Va., 1940.
———. *Prince William: The Story of Its People and Its Places.* Richmond, 1941.
Yancey, Rosa F. *Lynchburg and Its Neighbors.* Richmond, 1935.
Yorrell, Claude L. *A History of Madison County, Virginia.* Strasburg, 1926.

Articles

Ammon, Harry, "Republican Party in Virginia," *Virginia Magazine of History and Biography* 71 (1963): 53–67.
———, "The Richmond Junto," *Virginia Magazine of History and Biography* 61 (1953): 395–418.
Anderson, Dice R., "Jefferson and the Virginia Constitution," *American Historical Review* 21 (1916): 750–54.
Bailor, Keith M., "John Taylor of Caroline: Continuity, Change, and Discontinuity in Virginia's Sentiments toward Slavery, 1790–1820," *Virginia Magazine of History and Biography* 75 (1967): 290–304.
Beach, Rex, "Judge Spencer Roane," *William and Mary Quarterly* 2d ser., 21 (1942): 1–17.
Bean, William G., "The Ruffner Pamphlet of 1847: An Antislavery Aspect of Virginia Sectionalism," *Virginia Magazine of History and Biography* 61 (1953): 395–418.
Brackett, Jeffery R., "Democracy and Aristocracy in Virginia in the 1830s," *Sewanee Review* 4 (1896): 257–67.
Bradford, S. Sydney, "Negro Iron Workers in Antebellum Virginia," *Journal of Southern History* 25 (1959): 194–206.
Braverman, Howard, "Economic and Political Background of the Conservative Revolt in Virginia 1836–40," *Virginia Magazine of History and Biography* 60 (1952): 266–87.
Butterfield, L. H., "The Jubilee of Independence July 4, 1826," *Virginia Magazine of History and Biography* 61 (1953): 119–40.
Chandler, Julian A. C., "Constitutional Revision in Virginia," *Proceedings of the American Political Science Association, Fifth Annual Meeting* (Baltimore, 1909): 192–202.
Dill, Alonzo Thomas, "Sectional Conflict in Colonial Virginia," *Virginia Magazine of History and Biography* 87 (1979): 300–315.
Eaton, Clement, "A Dangerous Pamphlet in the Old South," *Journal of Southern History* 2 (1939): 323–34.
———, "Henry Wise, a Liberal of the Old South," *Journal of Southern History* 7 (1941): 482–94.

Egnal, Marc, "The Origins of the Revolution in Virginia: A Reinterpretation," *William and Mary Quarterly*, 3d ser., 37 (1980): 401–28.

Ellis, Henry G., "Edmund Ruffin, His Life and Times," *John P. Branch Historical Papers of Randolph-Macon College* 3 (1901): 99–123.

Frey, Sylvia R., "Between Slavery and Freedom: Virginia Blacks in the American Revolution," *Journal of Southern History* 49 (1983): 375–98.

Goodrich, Carter, "Virginia System of Mixed Enterprise," *Political Science Quarterly* 22 (1907): 355–87.

Green, Fletcher M., "Democracy in the Old South," *Journal of Southern History* 22 (1946): 3–23.

Griffin, Barbara J., "Thomas Ritchie and the Founding of the Richmond Lancasterian School," *Virginia Magazine of History and Biography* 86 (1978): 447–60.

Harrison, Joseph Hobson, Jr. "Oligarchs and Democrats—The Richmond Junto." *Virginia Magazine of History and Biography* 78 (1970): 184–98.

Hay, Robert P., "The Glorious Departure of the American Patriarchs: Contemporary Reactions to the Deaths of Jefferson and Adams," *Journal of Southern History* 35 (1969): 543–56.

Hemphill, W. Edwin, ed., "Petitions of Western Virginians to Their General Assembly in Richmond," *West Virginia History* 18 (1956): 105–15.

Howard, A. E. Dick, "State Constitutions and the Environment," *Virginia Law Review* 58 (1972): 193–229.

Jackson, Luther P., "The Virginia Free Negro Farmer and Property Owner, 1830–1860," *Journal of Negro History* 24 (1939): 390–439.

Johnston, Ross A., "Methodism in West Virginia, 1800–1825," *West Virginia History* 3 (1941): 18–59.

Keim, Clarence R., "Influence of Primogeniture and Entail in the Development of Virginia," *University of Chicago Abstracts of Theses, Humanistic Series* (1938): 287–92.

Lippincott, Isaac, "Early Salt Trade in the Ohio Valley," *Journal of Political Economy* 20 (1912): 1029–52.

Moore, George E., "Slavery as a Factor in the Formation of West Virginia," *West Virginia History* 18 (1956): 5–90.

Morton, Richard L., "The Virginia State Debt and Internal Improvements, 1820–38," *Journal of Political Economy* 25 (1919): 339–73.

Pate, James E., "Constitutional Revision in Virginia Affecting the General Assembly," *William and Mary Quarterly,* 2d ser., 10 *(April 1930): 105–22.*

Pleasants, Hugh R., *"Sketches of the Virginia Convention of 1829–30," Southern Literary Messenger* 17 (1851): 147–54, 297–304.

Pole, J. R., "Representation and Authority in Virginia from the Revolution to Reform," *Journal of Southern History* 28 (1958): 16–50.

Prettyman, E. B., "John Letcher," *John P. Branch Historical Papers of Randolph-Macon College* 3 (June 1912): 314–19.

Preyer, Kathryn, "Crime, the Criminal Law, and Reform in Post-Revolutionary Virginia," *Law and History Review* 1 (1983): 53–85.

Prufer, Julius F., "The Franchise in Virginia from Jefferson through the Convention of 1829," *William and Mary Quarterly,* 2d ser., 7 (1928): 17–32.

Scheiber, Harry, "American Constitutional History and the New Legal History: Contemporary Themes in Two Modes," *Journal of American History* 68 (1981): 337–50.

——, "Introduction: The Bicentennial and the Rediscovery of Constitutional History," *Journal of Southern History* 74 (1988): 668–74.

Selby, John E., "Richard Henry Lee, John Adams, and the Virginia Constitution of 1776," *Virginia Magazine of History and Biography* 84 (1976): 387–400.

Shepard, E. Lee, "Courts in Conflict: Town-County Relations in Post-Revolutionary Virginia," *Virginia Magazine of History and Biography* 85 (1977): 184–99.

——, "Lawyers Look at Themselves: Professional Consciousness and the Virginia Bar, 1770–1850," *American Journal of Legal History* 25 (1981): 1–23.

Sloan, Herbert, and Peter Onuf, "Politics, Culture, and the Revolution in Virginia: A Review of Recent Work," *Virginia Magazine of History and Biography* 91 (1983): 259–84.

Spicer, George W., "Gubernatorial Leadership in Virginia," *Public Administration Review* 1 (1941): 441–57.

Steele, Ester C., "Chapman Johnson," *Virginia Magazine of History and Biography* 25 (1917): 116–74, 246–53.

Sutton, Robert P., "Nostalgia, Pessimism, and Malaise: the Doomed Aristocrat in Late-Jeffersonian Virginia," *Virginia Magazine of History and Biography* 76 (1968): 41–55.

——, "Sectionalism and Social Structure: A Case Study of Jeffersonian Democracy," *Virginia Magazine of History and Biography* 80 (1972): 70–84.

Swem, Earl G., "Bibliography of Conventions and Constitutions of Virginia," *Virginia State Library Bulletin* 3 (1910): 355–441.

Trent, William P., "The Case of Josiah Philips," *American Historical Review* 1 (1896): 444–54.

Turner, Charles W., "The Early Railroad Movement in Virginia," *Virginia Magazine of History and Biography* 55 (1947): 350–71.

Upton, Anthony, "The Road to Power in Virginia in the Early Nineteenth Century," *Virginia Magazine of History and Biography* 62 (1954): 259–81.

Vail, R. W., "The Last Meeting of the Giants," *New York Historical Society Quarterly* 22 (1948): 69–76.

Wren, J. Thomas, "The Ideology of Court and County in the Virginia Ratifying Convention of 1788," *Virginia Magazine of History and Biography* 93 (1985): 309–408.

——, "A Two-Fold Character: The Slave as Person and Property in Virginia Court Cases, 1800–1860," *Southern Studies* 24 (1985): 417–31.

Theses and Dissertations

Ammon, Harry. "The Republican Party in Virginia, 1798–1824." Ph.D. diss., University of Virginia, 1948.

Beach, Rex. "Judge Spencer Roane, a Champion of States Rights." M.A. thesis, University of Virginia, 1957.

Boughter, I. F. "Internal Improvements in Northwestern Virginia." Ph.D. diss., University of Pittsburgh, 1930.

Coleman, Elizabeth C. "The Story of the Virginia Central Railroad, 1850–60." Ph.D. diss., University of Virginia, 1957.

Coyner, Martin B., Jr. "John Hartwell Cocke of Bremo: Agriculture and Slavery in the Ante-Bellum South." Ph.D. diss., University of Virginia, 1961.

Dingledine, Raymond C. "The Political Career of William Cabell Rives." Ph.D. diss., University of Virginia, 1947.

Gaines, Francis P., Jr. "The Virginia Constitutional Convention of 1850–51: A Study in Sectionalism." Ph.D. diss., University of Virginia, 1950.

Harrison, Joseph H. "The Internal Improvement Issue in the Politics of the Union, 1793–1825." Ph.D. diss., University of Virginia, 1954.

Hickin, Patricia E. P. "Antislavery in Virginia, 1831–1861." 3 vols. Ph.D. diss., University of Virginia, 1968.

Hilldrup, Robert L. "The Virginia Convention of 1776: A Study in Revolutionary Politics." Ph.D diss., University of Virginia, 1935.ep Lowe, Richard G. "Republicans, Rebellion, and Reconstruction: The Republican Party in Virginia, 1856–1870." Ph.D. diss., University of Virginia, 1968.

Meade, Richard A. "A History of the Constitutional Provisions for Education in Virginia." Ph.D. diss., University of Virginia, 1941. Neely, Frank T. "The Development of Virginia Taxation, 1775–1860." Ph.D. diss., University of Virginia, 1953.

Oliver, George B. "Constitutional History of Virginia, 1776–1860." Ph.D. diss., Duke University, 1959.

Paterson, Robert W. "The Population, Industry, and Income of Virginia." Ph.D. diss., University of Virginia, 1953.

Poteet, H. H. "The Virginia Convention of 1850–51." Ph.D. diss., Johns Hopkins University, 1929.

Rich, Philip M. "Internal Improvements in Virginia." Ph.D. diss., University of North Carolina, 1948.

Steiner, Bruce. "The Prelude of Conservatism, 1781–1822: An Account of the Early Life, First Ventures, and Legal Career of Benjamin Watkins Leigh." M.A. thesis, University of Virginia, 1959.

Tanner, Carol M. "Joseph C. Cabell, 1778–1856." Ph.D. diss., University of Virginia, 1958.

Toombs, Kenneth E. "Early Life of Littleton Waller Tazewell, 1774–1815." M.A. thesis, University of Virginia, 1955.

Turner, Charles W. "The Virginia Railroads 1528–1860." Ph.D. diss., University of Minnesota, 1946.

Index